Learning Test-Driven Development

A Polyglot Guide to Writing Uncluttered Code

Saleem Siddiqui

Beijing · Boston · Farnham · Sebastopol · Tokyo

Learning Test-Driven Development

by Saleem Siddiqui

Published by O'Reilly Media, Inc., 1005 Gravenstein Highway North, Sebastopol, CA 95472.

O'Reilly books may be purchased for educational, business, or sales promotional use. Online editions are also available for most titles (*http://oreilly.com*). For more information, contact our corporate/institutional sales department: 800-998-9938 or *corporate@oreilly.com*.

Acquisitions Editor: Melissa Duffield	**Indexer:** Ellen Troutman-Zaig
Development Editor: Michele Cronin	**Interior Designer:** David Futato
Production Editor: Kristen Brown	**Cover Designer:** Karen Montgomery
Copyeditor: Piper Editorial Consultants, LLC	**Illustrator:** Kate Dullea
Proofreader: Paula L. Fleming	

October 2021:   First Edition

Revision History for the Early Release

2021-10-12:   First Release

See *http://oreilly.com/catalog/errata.csp?isbn=9781098106478* for release details.

978-1-098-10647-8

[LSI]

For

اُمّی Ammi,

آپا Apa,

Janelle, and

Safa.

Without your love and support, neither this book nor its author would be complete.

Table of Contents

Foreword

Throughout my 30-year career as a computer science and software engineering educator, especially since my brief stint in industry in 2001, few other techniques have shaped and pervaded my teaching (and research) as much as automated unit testing, the general approach that test-driven development (TDD) operationalizes into a specific, yet widely applicable technique.

I still remember catching on to TDD in a concrete sense, almost as a side effect, after adopting Martin Fowler's 2003 text, *UML Distilled* (3rd edition), as a UML reference for my object-oriented development course. There, Martin discusses three key practices that are usually found in successful iterative development processes: automated regression tests, refactoring, and continuous integration. This concise description strongly resonated with me, and I've always enjoyed convincing my students to have more fun by writing additional code to test the rest of their code and receiving instant feedback in the form of colorful test results.

My other aha moment came almost a decade later, around 2012, when I started to listen to some *Software Engineering Radio* podcasts about software architecture. I was reading up on some of the references mentioned in the podcasts and came across a brief subsection entitled "Serendipitous Architecture" in "Uncle Bob" Robert C. Martin's book *Agile Software Development: Principles, Patterns, and Practices*, which discussed how focusing on making one's code testable almost automatically leads to good, maintainable architecture.

Taken together, these two points highlight the way automated testing ties together process and architecture, as well as functional and nonfunctional requirements: by giving us more confidence in the extent to which our code satisfies the functional requirements, testability arguably becomes the most important nonfunctional requirement.

This summer, almost another decade later, Saleem Siddiqui contacted me regarding his book. Incidentally, next year will be the 25th anniversary of Saleem having taken three graduate-level courses with me! It has been highly rewarding to see him become a successful technology professional—a ThoughtWorker like Martin Fowler—and author. I felt honored that he asked me to write this foreword for his book and was eager to learn more about his perspective on TDD.

What excites me most about Saleem's book is that it engages the reader in the TDD process in a hands-on yet methodical way, using a highly familiar running example from everyday life. The red-green-refactor cycle sets the tone for the process regardless of programming language. The successive features from the financial currency domain are concrete and easy to relate to but lead the reader through progressively more complex challenges, thereby building confidence, exposing nuanced tradeoffs, and awakening curiosity to explore further. The final code review along the three dimensions of profile, purpose, and process integrates the insights gathered along the way.

By using three highly visible languages with rather complementary designs—of which JavaScript and Python already occupy top positions in the market and Go is quickly on the rise—Saleem makes a strong case for the broad applicability of the TDD approach. In addition, he provides the reader with additional touchpoints and awareness of the relationship between language design and the "three Ps" just mentioned.

My great hope is for Saleem's book to have a multiplier effect by resonating with new generations of software developers drawn to impactful languages, such as Go, JavaScript, and Python, and pulling them onto the virtuous path of test-driven development. To borrow the words of the great jazz saxophonist Cannonball Adderley when describing hipness to his live audience in New York, it's not a state of mind, it's a fact of life.

— Konstantin Läufer
Professor of Computer Science,
Loyola University Chicago
Chicago, Illinois, September 2021

Preface

Test-driven development is a way of managing fear during programming.

—Kent Beck

We are so ineffably lucky! We've had test-driven development for years.

Several decades have passed since the developers who wrote the code for the Mercury Space Program practiced Punch Card TDD (test-driven development) (*https://oreil.ly/pKpSZ*). XUnit libraries that facilitate the adoption of test-driven development date back to the turn of the century. In fact, Kent Beck, who wrote *Test-Driven Development: By Example* (Addison-Wesley Professional, 2002) *and* developed the JUnit framework, refers to himself as having "rediscovered" (and not invented) the practice of TDD (*https://oreil.ly/zDyBr*). That statement is evidence of his humility, yet it is also the truth. TDD is as old as software development itself.

Then why is it that test-driven development is still far from the standard way to write code? Why is it often the first practice that gets sacrificed when there is schedule pressure, or when IT budgets need to be trimmed, or (my personal favorite) when there is a desire to "increase the velocity of the software-delivery team"? All these reasons are proffered despite the ready availability of empirical *and* experimental evidence (*https://oreil.ly/2Xxyb*) that TDD reduces defect count, creates simpler design, and improves developers' confidence in their own code.

Why is TDD adopted grudgingly and abandoned readily? The following arguments, heard often from those who are reluctant to practice it, may explain why:

I don't know where and how to start.
> Perhaps the most common reason is lack of awareness and exposure. Like any other skill, writing code in a test-driven style is something that needs to be learned. Many developers either haven't had the external inducement (time, resources, guidance, encouragement) or internal motivation (overcoming one's own reluctance and fear) to learn this skill.

TDD works in toy programs or during coding interviews, but not when writing "real-world" code.

This is untrue yet understandable. Most test-driven development tutorials and books—including this one—are constrained to pick relatively simple examples from an obvious domain. It's difficult to write a TDD article or book with actual code from a piece of software plucked from a commercially deployed application (say, from a financial institution, a healthcare management system, or a self-driving automobile). For one thing, much of such real-world code is proprietary and is not open source. For another, it's the job of the author to show code from a domain that has the widest appeal to the largest audience. It would be illogical, bordering on obscurantism, to show TDD in the context of a highly specialized domain. Doing so would require, before anything else, a lengthy explanation of the arcane jargon and cant of that domain. That would defeat the very purpose of the author: making TDD understandable, approachable, even lovable.

These obstacles to using real-world code in TDD literature notwithstanding, developers regularly write production software using test-driven development. Perhaps the best and most convincing example is the suite of unit tests for the JUnit framework (*https://oreil.ly/UCPcg*) itself. The Linux Kernel—possibly the most strenuously used piece of software in the world—is being improved with unit tests (*https://oreil.ly/hBbq0*).

Writing tests after the fact is sufficient; TDD is too restrictive and/or pedantic.

This is more refreshing to hear than the occasional rant that "unit testing is over-rated" (*https://oreil.ly/Y7S5M*)! Writing tests *after* writing production code is an improvement over writing no tests at all. Anything that raises the developers' confidence in their code, reduces accidental complexity, and provides authentic documentation is a good thing. However, writing unit tests *before* writing the production code provides a forcing function against creating arbitrary complexity.

TDD guides us to simpler design because it provides these two practical rules as guardrails:

1. Only write production code to fix a failing test.
2. Refactor energetically when, and only when, tests are green.

Does test-driven development guarantee that all the code we ever write will automatically and inevitably be the simplest code that works? No, it does not. No practice, rule, book, or manifesto can do that. It's up to the *people* who bring these practices to life to ensure that simplicity is achieved and retained.

This book's *content* explains and instructs how test-driven development works in three different programming languages. Its *purpose* is to instill in developers the habit and self-belief to use TDD as a regular practice. That purpose may be ambitious, but I'm hopeful it isn't elusive.

What Is Test-Driven Development?

Test-driven development is a technique for designing and structuring code that encourages simplicity and increases one's confidence in code, even as its size increases.

Let's take a look at the various parts of this definition.

A Technique

Test-driven development is a technique. It's true that this technique is borne of a set of beliefs about code, namely:

- That simplicity—the art of maximizing the amount of work *not* done, is essential[1]
- That obviousness and clarity are more virtuous than cleverness
- That writing uncluttered code is a key component of being successful

Despite being rooted in these beliefs, as a practical matter, TDD is a technique. Like riding a bike, kneading dough, or solving differential equations, it's a skill that no one is born with and that everyone has to learn.

Other than this section, this book does not dwell on the belief system behind test-driven development. It's assumed that you either subscribe to it already or that you're willing to give TDD a try as a new (or forgotten) skill.

The mechanics of that technique—writing a failing unit test first, then briskly writing just enough code to make it pass, and then taking the time to clean up—occupy the bulk of this book. There will be ample opportunity to try this technique for yourself.

In the final analysis, it is more satisfying to learn a skill *and* imbue oneself with the beliefs that support it—just like riding a bike is more enjoyable if you remind yourself that it's good for your health and the environment!

---

1 This definition of simplicity is enshrined in one of the 12 principles of the Agile Manifesto (*https://agilemanifesto.org/principles.html*).

Designing and Structuring Code

Notice that TDD is not fundamentally about testing code. It is true that we use unit tests to drive the code, but the purpose of TDD is to improve the design and structure of the code.

This focus is vital. If TDD were only about testing, we couldn't really mount an effective case for writing tests *before* rather than *after* the business code is written. It's the goal of designing better software that spurs us on; the tests are simply a vehicle for this progress. The unit tests that we end up with via TDD are an added bonus; the primary benefit is the simplicity of design we get.

How do we achieve this simplicity? It is through the mechanism of *red-green-refactor*, which is described in detail at the beginning of Chapter 1.

A Bias Toward Simplicity

Simplicity isn't a mere esoteric notion. In software, we can measure it. Fewer lines of code per feature, lower cyclomatic complexity (*https://oreil.ly/5Gj2b*), fewer side effects, smaller runtime or memory requirements—any subset of these (or other) requirements can be taken as an objective measure of simplicity.

Test-driven development, by forcing us to craft "the simplest thing that works" (i.e., that which gets all tests to pass), constantly nudges us toward these metrics of simplicity. We aren't allowed to add superfluous code "in case we need it" or because "we can see it coming." We must first write a failing test to justify writing such code. The act of writing the test first acts as a forcing function—compelling us to deal with arbitrary complexity *early*. If the feature we're about to develop is ill-defined, or our understanding of it flawed, we'll find it hard to write a good test up front. This will force us to address these issues *before* we write a line of production code. This is the virtue of TDD: by exercising the discipline of driving our code through tests, we weed out arbitrary complexity at every juncture.

This virtue isn't mystical: using test-driven development won't cut your development time, the lines of code, or defect count by half. What it *will* allow you to do is to arrest the temptation to introduce artificial and contrived complexity. The resultant code—driven by the discipline of writing failing tests first—will emerge as the most straightforward way to gets the job done, i.e., the simplest code that meets the needs of the tests.

Increased Confidence

Code should inspire confidence, especially code we have authored ourselves. This confidence, while itself a nebulous feeling, is grounded in an expectation of predictability. We are confident in things whose behavior we can presage. If the corner coffee shop undercharges me one day and overcharges me by the same amount the next day, I'm likely to lose confidence in the staff even though I break even over the two days. It's human nature that we value *regularity* and *predictability* even more than *net value*. The world's luckiest gambler, who may have just won 10 times in a row at a roulette table, wouldn't say that they "trust" or have "confidence" in the wheel. Our affinity for predictability survives even dumb luck.

Test-driven development increases our confidence in our code because each new test flexes the system in new and previously untested ways—literally! Over time, the suite of tests we create guards us against regression failures.

This steadily increasing battery of tests is the reason that as the size of the code grows, so does its quality and our confidence in it.

Who Is This Book For?

This is a book for developers—people who write software.

There are many professional titles that go with this vocation: "software engineer," "application architect," "devops engineer," "test automation engineer," "programmer," "hacker," "code whisperer," and countless others. Titles may be impressive or humble, trendy or solemn, traditional or modern. However, the one thing that's held in common by the people professing these titles is this: they spend at least a part of their week—if not each day—in front of a computer, reading and/or writing source code.

I have chosen the term *developers* to represent this community of which I'm both a humble and grateful member.

Writing code is one of the most liberating and egalitarian activities one may imagine. In theory, all one needs by way of physical prowess is the possession of a brain. Age, gender, sex, nationality, national origin—none of these should be a barrier. Having physical disabilities shouldn't be a barrier.

However, it would be naive to assume that reality is as neat or fair as that. Access to computing resources isn't equitable. A certain level of wealth, freedom from want, and security are necessary. Access is thwarted even further by badly written software, badly designed hardware, and myriad other usability limitations that prevent all people from learning to program based solely on their interest and effort.

I have tried to make this book accessible to as many people as possible. In particular, I've tried to make it approachable to people with physical disabilities. The images have alt-text to facilitate e-reading. The code is available via GitHub. And the prose is straightforward.

In terms of experience, this book is intended both for people who are still learning how to program and for those who already know how to program. If you are ramping up on one (or more) of the three languages in this book, you are well within the target audience.

However, this book does not teach the *basics* of programming in any language, including Go, JavaScript, or Python. The ability to read and write code in at least one of the programming languages is a requirement. If you are absolutely new to programming, it'd be wise to solidify the foundations of writing code in one of the three languages before you proceed with this book.

The sweet spot for this book spans developers who are beyond their early forays into programming, all the way to seasoned architects, as shown in Figure P-1. (Kent Beck is an outlier.)

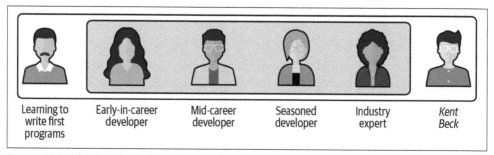

| Learning to write first programs | Early-in-career developer | Mid-career developer | Seasoned developer | Industry expert | Kent Beck |

Figure P-1. This is a book for software developers

Writing code can be, by turns, exhilarating and exasperating. However, even at its most frustrating, there should *always* be more than a glimmer of optimism and a bushel of confidence that we can make code do our bidding. With perseverance, you'll find that your journey through this book is fruitful and that the joy of writing code in a test-driven manner is one you want to savor long after you're done reading Chapter 14.

What Are the Prerequisites for Reading This Book?

By way of equipment and technical prowess, you should:

- Have access to a computer with internet connectivity.

- Be able to install and delete software on that computer. That is, your access on that computer should not be restricted; in most cases this would require having "Administrator" or "Superuser" access on that computer.

- Be able to launch and use a shell program, a web browser, a text editor, and optionally an integrated development environment (IDE) on that computer.

- Have installed (or be able to install) the runtime tools for one of the languages used in this book.

- Be able to write and run a simple program—"Hello World"—in one of the languages used in this book.

"Setting Up Your Development Environment" on page 1 in Chapter 0 has more installation details.

How to Read This Book

The subject matter of this book is "how to do test-driven development in Go, JavaScript, and Python." While the concepts discussed are applicable to all three languages, the treatment of each language necessitates some separation of the material in each chapter. The best way to learn test-driven development (like any other acquired skill) is through practice. I encourage you to both read the text and write the code on your own. I call this style *"following the book"*—because it includes active reading and active coding.

To get the most out of this book, write the code for the Money example in all three languages.

Most of the chapters have general-purpose sections that are applicable to all three languages. These are followed by language-specific sections, where the code for one of the three languages is described and developed. These language-specific sections are *always* clearly marked by their headings: *Go, JavaScript,* or *Python.* At the end of each chapter is one or two sections that summarize what we have accomplished thus far and what comes next.

Chapters 5 through 7 are unique insofar as they each deal exclusively with one of the three languages: Go, JavaScript, and Python, respectively.

Figure P-2 shows a flowchart describing the layout of this book and the different ways to follow it.

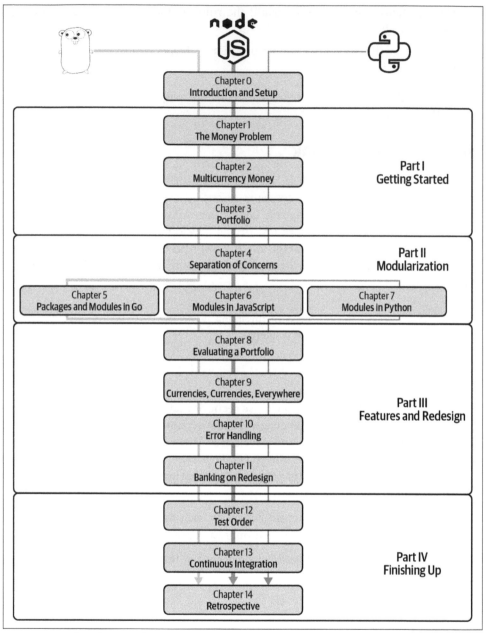

Figure P-2. Flowchart on how to read this book

Here are some "reading pathways" for how to best follow this book.

Follow the Book One Language at a Time

I recommend this pathway if one or more of these conditions apply to you:

1. I am aching to dive into one of these languages before tackling the other two.
2. I'm particularly curious (or skeptical!) about how TDD works in one of the three languages.
3. I learn best by working in one language at a time, rather than multiple languages simultaneously.

Follow the flowchart shown in Figure P-2 one line at a time. For example, if you are eager to learn TDD in Go first, skip the sections marked JavaScript and Python in the first reading. Then do a second pass through the book for JavaScript, and a third to finish things off in Python. Or you may do the languages in a different order. The second and third pass *should* be quicker than the first; however, be prepared for the unique quirks of each language!

If you follow the book this way, you will find that writing the code successively in each language gives you greater insight into TDD *as a principle*—beyond the details of testing *as a language feature*. Getting into the habit of writing tests is necessary; however, understanding the reasons for why test-driven development works across languages is even more important.

Follow the Book in Two Languages First and Then in the Third Language

I recommend this pathway if you identify with any of the following statements:

1. I want to build and compare the solutions to the same problem in two languages.
2. I am less comfortable with one of the languages and want to tackle it after the other two.
3. I can code in two languages at a time but would find it difficult to juggle all three at once.

Follow the flowchart shown in Figure P-2 two lines at a time. After you're done with following the Money problem for two languages, do a second pass through the book to follow the third language.

It can happen that you want to follow two languages in the first pass, yet cannot decide which language to defer to a second reading. Here are some suggestions on how to pick two out of the three languages:

1. Do you want to contrast a dynamically typed language with a statically typed one and keep the language tech stack simple? Follow Go and Python first, and JavaScript next.

2. Are you ready to learn contrasting ways to build code in two different languages and ready to tackle tech stack variations? Follow Go and JavaScript first, and Python later.

3. Do you want to compare and contrast two dynamically typed languages? Follow JavaScript and Python first, and Go next.

If you read the book this way, you'll quickly discover the similarities and differences of doing TDD in multiple languages. While the syntactical and design variations in the languages create obvious differences, you may be surprised by how deeply the discipline of TDD permeates into *how* you write code, regardless of *the language* in which you write code.

Follow the Book in All Three Languages Simultaneously

I recommend this pathway if any of these statements apply to you:

1. You want to gain the best value by learning the contrasts and similarities of the three languages.

2. You find it easier to read a book from start to finish instead of doing multiple passes through it.

3. You have some experience in all three languages but haven't practiced TDD in any of them.

If you can write code in three languages simultaneously without getting overwhelmed, I recommend this pathway.

Regardless of the pathway you choose, be mindful that when you're writing code, you will likely face challenges that have to do with your specific development environment. While the code in this book has been tested for correctness (and its continuous integration build is green (*https://github.com/saleem/tdd-book-code/actions*)), that does not mean it will work on *your* computer at first go. (On the contrary, I can *almost* guarantee that you will find interestingly steep portions on the learning curve.) One of the key benefits of TDD is that *you* control the speed at which you proceed. When you get stuck, slow down. If you make progress in smaller increments, it is easier to find where the code went astray. Writing software means dealing with errant dependencies, unreliable network connections, quirky tools, and the thousand natural shocks that code is heir to. Slow down when you feel overwhelmed: make your changes smaller and discrete. Remember: TDD is a way of managing the fear of writing code!

Conventions Used in This Book

There are two categories of conventions used in this book that require explanation:
typographical and contextual.

Typographical Conventions

The prose in this book is in the font-type used in this sentence. It is meant to be read
and not entered verbatim as code. When there are words used in prose that are *also*
used in code—such as `class`, `interface`, or `Exception`—a fixed-width font is used.
This alerts you that the term is or will be used—spelled exactly the same way—in
code.

Longer segments of code are separated into their own blocks, as shown below.

```
package main

import "fmt"

... ❶

func main() {
    fmt.Println("hello world")
}
```

❶ Ellipses mean irrelevant code or output has been omitted.

Everything in a code block is either something you type in verbatim *or* something the
program produces as the literal output, with two exceptions.

1. Within code blocks, *ellipses* (...) are used to indicate either omitted code or
   omitted output. In both cases, whatever is omitted is irrelevant to the current
   topic. You should *not* type these ellipses in code or expect to see them in the output. An example is shown in the code block above.

2. Within code blocks that show output, there can be *ephemeral values*—memory
   addresses, timestamps, elapsed time, line numbers, autogenerated filenames,
   etc.—that will almost certainly be different for you. When reading such output,
   you may safely ignore the *specific* ephemeral values, such as the memory
   addresses in the following block:

```
AssertionError: <money.Money object at 0x10417b2e0> !=
                <money.Money object at 0x10417b400>
```

Tips are suggestions that can be helpful to you while you write code. They are separated from the main text for easy reference.

 Important information that is vital to the topic is identified like this. Often there are hyperlinks or footnotes to resources that provide more information on the subject.

In most chapters, there is extended development and discussion of code in each of the three languages. (The exceptions are Chapters 5, 6, and 7, which deal exclusively with Go, JavaScript, and Python respectively.) To separate the discussion of each language, a heading and an icon in the margin indicate the language that's the exclusive purview of that section. Keep your eyes peeled for these three headings and icons:

- *Go*

- *JavaScript*

- *Python*

Lexical Conventions

This book discusses core software concepts and backs up those discussions with code in three different languages. The languages are sufficiently different in their individual terminology so as to present challenges when discussing common concepts.

For example, Go does not have classes or class-based inheritance. JavaScript's type system has prototype-based objects—which means that everything is really an object, including things typically thought of as classes. Python, as used in this book, has the more "traditional" class-based objects.[2] A sentence like "We will create a new class named Money" isn't merely confusing, but is downright incorrect when interpreted in the context of Go.

---

2 Python is very fluid in its support for object-oriented programming (OOP). For example, see prototype.py (*https://oreil.ly/ZKivt*), which implements prototype-based objects in Python.

To reduce the potential for confusion, I've adopted the general terminology shown in Table P-1 to refer to key concepts.

Table P-1. General terminology used in this book

Term	Meaning	Equivalent in Go	Equivalent in JavaScript	Equivalent in Python
Entity	A singular, independently meaningful domain concept; a key noun	Struct type	Class	Class
Object	An instance of an Entity; a reified noun	Struct instance	Object	Object
Sequence	A sequential list of Objects of dynamic length	Slice	Array	Array
Hashmap	A set of (key-value) pairs, where both keys and values can be arbitrary Objects and no two keys can be the same	Map	Map	Dictionary
Function	A set of operations with a given name; Functions may (or may not) have entities with both inputs and outputs, but they're not associated directly with any one Entity	Function	Function	Function
Method	A Function that is associated with an Entity. A method is said to be "called on" an instance of that Entity (i.e., an Object)	Method	Method	Method
Signal an error	Mechanism by which a Function or Method indicates failure	Error return value (conventionally, the last return value of a function/method)	Throw an exception	Raise an exception

The goal is to use terms that explain the concepts without favoring one programming language's terminology over others. After all, the biggest takeaway from this book ought to be that test-driven development is a discipline that can be practiced in *any* programming language.

In sections of the book that deal with one of the three languages (which are clearly marked in the heading), the text uses language-specific terms. For example, in a Go section, there will be instructions to "define a new struct named Money." The context makes it clear that this instruction is specific to a particular language.

Using Code Examples

The source code for this book is available at *https://github.com/saleem/tdd-book-code*.

If you have a technical question or a problem using the code examples, please send an email to *bookquestions@oreilly.com*.

This book is here to help you learn and practice the art of test-driven development. In general, you may use any code provided in this book in your programs and documentation. You do not need to contact us for permission unless you're reproducing a significant portion of the code. For example, writing a program that uses several chunks of code from this book does not require permission. Selling or distributing examples from O'Reilly books does require permission. Answering a question by citing this book and quoting example code does not require permission. Incorporating a significant amount of example code from this book into your product's documentation does require permission.

We appreciate, but generally do not require, attribution. An attribution usually includes the title, author, publisher, and ISBN. For example: "*Learning Test-Driven Development* by Saleem Siddiqui (O'Reilly). Copyright 2022 Saleem Siddiqui, 978-1-098-10647-8."

If you feel your use of code examples falls outside fair use or the permission given above, feel free to contact us at *permissions@oreilly.com*.

How to Contact Us

We have a web page for this book, where we list errata, examples, and any additional information. You can access this page at *https://oreil.ly/learningTDDbook*.

Email *bookquestions@oreilly.com* to comment or ask technical questions about this book.

For news and information about our books and courses, visit *http://oreilly.com*.

TDD—The Whys

Critiques of TDD—and by implication, this book—can come in various forms. Some of them are creatively humorous, such as the refreshing cartoon by Jim Kersey shown in Figure P-3.

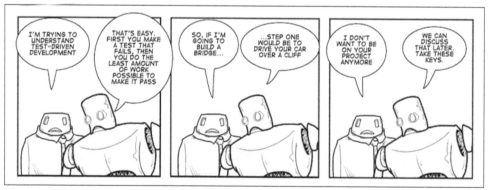

Figure P-3. TDD humor: don't cross a bridge you haven't built yet! (Source: https://robot kersey.com)

Less facetiously, it's natural to have questions about the content and structure of the book. What follows are answers to a few such questions.

Why Does This Book Use Go, JavaScript, and Python?

This book uses Go, JavaScript, and Python as the three languages with which to demonstrate the practice of test-driven development. It's a fair question: why these three languages?

Here are some reasons.

1. Variety

The three languages in this book represent a diversity of design options, as shown in Table P-2.

Table P-2. Comparison of Go, JavaScript, and Python

Feature	Go	JavaScript	Python
Object-oriented	"Yes and no" (*https://oreil.ly/M3u1P*)	Yes (as an ES.next compliant language)	Yes
Static vs. Dynamic types	Statically typed	Dynamically typed	Dynamically typed
Explicit vs. Implicit types	Mostly explicit, variable types can be implicit	Implicitly typed	Implicitly typed
Automatic type coercion	No type coercion	Partial type coercion (for Boolean, Number, String, Object). No coercion for arbitrary `class` types	Some implicit type coercion (e.g., `0` and `""` are falsey)
Exception mechanism	By convention, second return type of methods is `error`, caller must explicitly check if this is `nil` or not	The keyword `throw` is used to signal an Exception and `try ... catch` is used to respond to it	The keyword `raise` is used to signal an Exception and `try ... except` is used to respond to it
Generics	Not yet! (*https://oreil.ly/ORveC*)	Not needed due to dynamic typing	Not needed due to dynamic typing
Testing support	Part of language (i.e., the `test ing` package and the `go test` command); libraries available (e.g., stretchr/testify)	Not part of language, many libraries available (e.g., Jasmine, Mocha, Jest)	Part of language (i.e., the `unittest` library); libraries available (e.g., PyTest)

2. Popularity

Python, JavaScript, and Go are the top three new languages that developers want to learn, as found in several annual surveys by Stack Overflow in 2017 (*https://oreil.ly/CbnCx*), 2018 (*https://oreil.ly/uhhLx*), 2019 (*https://oreil.ly/BdAQJ*), and 2020 (*https://oreil.ly/mHqNs*). Figure P-4 shows the result of the 2020 survey.

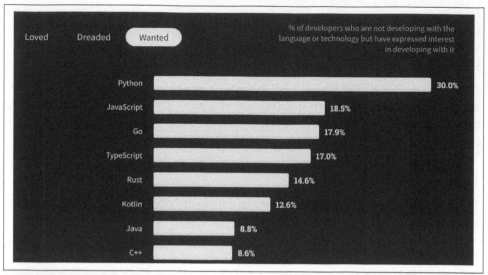

Figure P-4. Most desirable new languages to learn, as noted in a survey of developers by Stack Overflow

In the 2021 Stack Overflow survey (*https://oreil.ly/hzMVk*), TypeScript climbs into second place, relegating JavaScript and Go to third and fourth places, respectively. Python retains its top spot.

Syntactically, TypeScript is a strict superset of JavaScript (*https://oreil.ly/aATAD*). Therefore, it could be argued that every developer wishing to learn TypeScript has to know JavaScript. I harbor the hope that TypeScript developers will also find this book valuable.

3. A personal reason

Over the last five years or so, I had the opportunity to work on several projects where the tech stack featured one of these three as the primary programming language. While working with other developers I found that, in general, their eagerness to learn and practice TDD was evenly matched by their inability to find resources (or muster the discipline) to do so. They wanted to practice TDD, but didn't know how or couldn't find the time for it. Tellingly, this was as true for seasoned developers as it was for "noobs."

I hope this book serves as both a practical guide and a source of inspiration to those who want to learn and practice TDD in *any* language—not just in Go, JavaScript, or Python.

Why Not This Other Language?

For starters, there is a *vast* number of programming languages. One could conceivably write half a dozen books like this and still cover only a small fraction of the languages that developers over the world use on a daily basis to write code for academic, business, and recreation purposes.[3]

Besides, there is an excellent book already available for test-driven development in Java. Kent Beck's seminal work is what inspired me, as it did countless other developers, to fall in love with the art and science of TDD. It also begot the "money problem" that's a major theme in this book.

I am sure there are many other languages for which a practical TDD guide would be beneficial. How about R? Or SQL? Or even COBOL?

Let me assure you: the reference to COBOL was neither a straw man argument nor a cheap shot. In the mid 2000s, I worked on a project where I demonstrated the ability to do TDD in COBOL using COBOLUnit. It was the most fun I've had in a language that's more than a decade older than I am!

I'm hoping that *you* will pick up the mantle. That *you* will learn, teach, and espouse the skills and discipline necessary to practice test-driven development in other languages. That *you* will write a blog, an open source project, or the next book in this series.

Why Does This Book Have a "Chapter 0"?

The vast majority of programming languages use 0-based indexing for arrays and other countable sequences.[4] This is certainly true for the three programming languages that form the basis of this book. In one sense, this book honors the rich history of programming culture by numbering the chapters starting at 0.

I also want to pay homage to the number zero itself, which is a radical idea. Charles Seife has written a whole book on this lonely number. In tracing the history of zero, Seife notes the reservations that the Greeks had about a number that represents nothing:

---

3 Although one book about TDD on a certain language is unlikely to get approval from publishers. Its name starts with "Brain" and ends with an expletive!

4 Lua is a notable exception. My friend Kent Spillner once gave a fascinating talk on this subject, which I summarized here (*https://oreil.ly/E9M41*).

> In that [i.e., the Greek] universe there is no such thing as nothing. There is no zero. Because of this, the West could not accept zero for nearly two millennia. The consequences were dire. Zero's absence would stunt the growth of mathematics, stifle innovation in science, and, incidentally, make a mess of the calendar. Before they could accept zero, philosophers in the West would have to destroy their universe.
>
> —Charles Seife, *Zero: The Biography of a Dangerous Idea*

At the risk of getting too sublime: test-driven development occupies a similar place in programming culture today as zero did in Western philosophy a few millennia ago. There is a resistance to adopting it, born of a strange combination of dismissiveness, unease, and a belief that it's just too much fussiness about nothing. *"Why should I be fastidious about writing tests first—I already know how I'm going to code the feature!" "Test-driven development is pedantic: it only works in theory and never in practice." "Writing tests after you're done writing production code is at least as effective as, if not more than, writing tests first."* These and other objections to TDD make it resemble the number zero in how radical it is!

The practice of a book having a Chapter 0 isn't entirely radical, anyway. Carol Schumacher has written *an entire book* titled *Chapter Zero: Fundamental Notions of Abstract Mathematics (https://oreil.ly/nXJdV)*, which is a standard textbook for advanced mathematics in many college-level curricula. No prizes for guessing what numbered chapter *that* book begins with!

Dr. Schumacher, in the Instructor's Manual for her book, says something that I have found illuminating:

> Your task as a writer is to give the right cues to your readers, cues that will make it as easy as possible for them to understand what you are trying to say.
>
> —Carol Schumacher, Instructor's Resource Manual for use with *Chapter Zero*

I have taken this advice to heart. Pragmatically, a title containing "0" helps to set Chapter 0 apart from the treatise that follows it. Chapter 1 of this book puts us on a TDD journey which carries on through the next dozen chapters. Chapter 0 is about describing what that journey is, what we need to know and have before we embark on it, and what to expect when we are on it.

With the clarifications out of the way, let's move right on to Chapter 0!

Chapter 0: Introduction and Setup

Squeaky clean code is critical to success.

—Ron Jeffries, "Clean Code: A Learning," Aug 23, 2017, *ronjeffries.com*

Before we start our journey into the demanding and rewarding world of test-driven development, we need to ensure we have a working development environment. This chapter is all about preparing and setting things up.

Setting Up Your Development Environment

Regardless of which reading pathway you follow (see Figure P-2), you need a clean development environment to follow this book. The rest of the book assumes that you have set up the development environment as described in this section.

 Regardless of which of Go, JavaScript, or Python you start with, set up your development environment as described in this section.

Common Setup

Folder structure

Create a folder that will be the root for *all* the source code we'll write in this book. Name it something that will be clear and unambiguous to you weeks from now, e.g., *tdd-project*.

Under this folder, create a set of folders as follows:

```
tdd-project
├─ go
├─ js
└─ py
```

Create all these folders before you write the first line of code, even if you're planning to follow this book in multiple passes, one language at a time. Creating this folder structure provides the following benefits:

1. It keeps code in the three languages separate yet in close proximity to each other.

2. It ensures that *most* commands in this book will work without changes.

   • Commands that deal with fully qualified file/folder names are an exception—and such commands are rare. One of them is in this section.

3. It allows easy adoption of advanced features, such as continuous integration, across all three languages.

4. It matches the folder structure in the accompanying code repository (*https://github.com/saleem/tdd-book-code*). This can be useful for comparing and contrasting your code as it evolves.

Throughout the rest of this book, the term *TDD Project Root* is used to refer to the root folder containing all the source code—named `tdd-project` above. The folders named `go`, `js`, and `py` are referred to by these very names—the meaning is clear from the context.

 TDD Project Root is the name used to refer to the folder containing all the source code developed in this book. It's the parent of three folders named `go`, `js`, and `py`.

Declare an environment variable named `TDD_PROJECT_ROOT` and set its value to the fully qualified name of the *TDD Project Root* folder. Doing this once in each shell (or better yet, once in your shell initialization script such as the `.bashrc` file) ensures that all subsequent commands work seamlessly.

```
export TDD_PROJECT_ROOT=/fully/qualified/path/to/tdd-project
```

For example, on my macOS system, the fully qualified path for the TDD_PROJECT_ROOT is `/Users/saleemsiddiqui/code/github/saleem/tdd-project`.

Removing Tedium

You will need to define the environment variable TDD_PROJECT_ROOT in every new shell you launch. If you find this cumbersome, you may set it once in the appropriate configuration file. *How* you set it varies from one operating system to another and from one shell to another. For Bash-like shells that we will use in this book, environment variables can be defined in a configuration file; although the details still vary. For example, on most Linuxes (and on macOS), you can add the export TDD_PROJECT_ROOT=... statement in a file named .bashrc in your home folder (*https://oreil.ly/SMmFc*). If you're using Git BASH on Windows—as described later in this chapter—you may need to use the .bash_profile file instead (*https://oreil.ly/pkgxg*).

In short: removing tedium in your work is a good thing. Use an appropriate mechanism to define the environment variables reliably and consistently in all shells you use throughout this book.

Text editor or IDE

We'll need a text editor to edit source files. An *integrated development environment* (*IDE*) can help by providing a single tool within which we can edit, compile, and test code in multiple languages. However, this is a matter of choice and personal preference; choose what works best for *you*.

Appendix A describes IDEs in more detail.

Shell

We'll need a shell—a command-line interpreter—to run our tests, examine the output, and carry out other tasks. Like IDEs, shell choices are many and often the subject of exuberant opinion sharing among developers. This book assumes a *Bash-like shell* for the commands that need to be typed. On most—if not all—Unix-like operating systems (and on macOS), a Bash shell is readily available.

For Windows, shells like Git BASH (*https://gitforwindows.org*) are available. On Windows 10, the Windows Subsystem for Linux (*https://oreil.ly/UZ0KU*) provides native support for the Bash shell, among many other "Linux goodies." Either of these options, or something similar, is sufficient (and necessary) to follow the code examples in this book.

Figure 0-1 shows a Bash-like shell with the results of a command typed in it.

```
tdd-project> python3
Python 3.9.6 (default, Jun 29 2021, 05:25:02)
[Clang 12.0.5 (clang-1205.0.22.9)] on darwin
Type "help", "copyright", "credits" or "license" for more information.
>>> _
```

Figure 0-1. A Bash-like shell, like the one shown here, is needed to follow the coding examples in this book

Git

Chapter 13 introduces the practice of continuous integration (CI) using GitHub Actions. To follow the content of that chapter, we need to create a GitHub project of our own and push code to it.

Git is an open source distributed version control system. GitHub is a collaborative internet hosting platform that allows people to preserve and share the source code of their projects with each other.

 Git (*https://git-scm.com*) is a free, open source, distributed version control system. GitHub (*https://www.github.com*) is a code-sharing platform that uses Git.

To ensure we can adopt continuous integration, we'll do some preparation now and defer some work until Chapter 13. Specifically, we'll set up the Git version control system on our development environment. We'll postpone the creation of a GitHub project until Chapter 13.

First, download and install the Git version control system (*https://git-scm.com/down loads*). It is available for macOS, Windows, and Linux/Unix. After you install it, verify that it works by typing git --version on a terminal window and hitting Enter. You should see the installed version of Git in response, as shown in Figure 0-2.

```
tdd-project> git --version
git version 2.32.0
tdd-project> _
```

Figure 0-2. Verify that Git is installed by typing git --version and hitting Enter on a shell

Next, we'll create a new Git project in our TDD_PROJECT_ROOT. In a shell window, type the following commands:

```
cd $TDD_PROJECT_ROOT
git init .
```

This should produce an output saying Initialized empty Git repository in */your/fully/qualified/project/path/*.git/. This creates a shiny new (and currently empty) Git repository in our TDD_PROJECT_ROOT. We should have these folders under our TDD-PROJECT-ROOT folder now:

```
tdd-project
├── .git
├── go
├── js
└── py
```

The .git folder is used by Git for bookkeeping. There is no need to make any changes to its contents.

As we write source code in the following chapters, we will periodically commit our changes to this Git repository. We'll use the Git CLI (command line interface) to do this.

 We'll frequently commit our code changes to the Git repository in the rest of this book. To highlight this, we'll use the git Git icon.

Go

We need to install Go version 1.17 to follow this book. This version is available to download (*https://golang.org/dl*) for different operating systems.

To verify that Go is correctly installed, type go version on a shell and hit Enter. This should print the version number of your Go installation. See Figure 0-3.

```
tdd-project> go version
go version go1.17 darwin/amd64
tdd-project> _
```

Figure 0-3. Verify that Go is working by typing go version and hitting Enter on a shell

We also need to set a couple of Go-specific environment variables:

1. The `GO111MODULE` environment variable should be set to on.

2. The `GOPATH` environment variable *should not* include the `TDD_PROJECT_ROOT` or any folder under in, such as the go folder.

Execute these two lines of code in the shell:

```
export GO111MODULE="on"
export GOPATH=""
```

We need to create a bare-bones `go.mod` file to get ready to write code. These are the commands to do it:

```
cd $TDD_PROJECT_ROOT/go
go mod init tdd
```

This will create a file named `go.mod` whose contents should be:

```
module tdd

go 1.17
```

For all Go development from this point on, make sure that the shell is in the go folder under `TDD_PROJECT_ROOT`.

 For the Go code in this book, make sure to first enter `cd $TDD_PROJECT_ROOT/go` before running any Go commands.

A quick word on Go package management

Go's package management is in the midst of a seismic shift. The old style—which used the `GOPATH` environment variable—is being phased out in favor of the newer style using a `go.mod` file. The two styles are largely incompatible with each other.

The two environment variables we defined above, and the bare-bones `go.mod` file we generated, ensure that the Go tools can work correctly with our source code, especially when we create packages. We'll create Go packages in Chapter 5.

JavaScript

We need Node.js v14 ("Fermium") or v16 to follow this book. Both these versions are available from the Node.js website (*https://nodejs.org/en/download*) for different operating systems.

To verify that Node.js is correctly installed, type `node -v` on a shell and hit Enter. The command should print a one-line message, listing the version of Node.js. See Figure 0-4.

```
tdd-project> node -v
v16.6.2
tdd-project> _
```

Figure 0-4. Verify that Node.js is working by typing `node -v` *and hitting Enter on a shell*

A quick word on testing libraries

There are several unit-testing frameworks in the Node.js ecosystem. By and large, they are excellent for writing tests and doing TDD. However, this book eschews *all* of them. Its code uses the `assert` NPM package for assertions, and a simple class with methods to organize the tests. The simplicity is to keep our focus on the *practice and semantics* of TDD instead of the *syntax* of any one library. Chapter 6 describes the organization of tests in more detail. Appendix B enumerates the testing frameworks and the detailed reasons for not using any of them.

Another quick word, on JavaScript package management

Similar to testing frameworks, JavaScript has many ways to define packages and dependencies. This book uses the CommonJS style. In Chapter 6, there is a discussion of the other styles: the ES6 and UMD styles are shown in detail with source code, and the AMD style more briefly, without source code.

Python

We need Python 3.10 to follow this book, which is available from the Python website (*https://oreil.ly/xNLPa*) for different operating systems.

The Python language underwent significant changes between "Python 2" and "Python 3." While an older version of Python 3 (e.g., 3.6) may work, *any* version of Python 2 will be inadequate for the purpose of following this book.

It is possible that you have Python 2 already installed on your computer. For example, many macOS operating systems (including Big Sur) come bundled with Python 2. It is not necessary (or recommended) to *uninstall* Python 2 to follow this book; however, it *is* necessary to ensure that Python 3 is the version that's used.

To prevent ambiguity, this book uses `python3` explicitly as the name of the executable in commands. It is possible—although also unnecessary—to "alias" the `python` command to refer to Python 3.

Here's a simple way to find out which command you need to type to ensure that Python 3 is used. Type `python --version` on a shell and hit Enter. If you get something starting with `Python 3`, you're in good shape. If you get something like `Python 2`, you may need to explicitly type in `python3` for all the commands in this book.

Figure 0-5 shows a development environment with *both* Python 2 and Python 3.

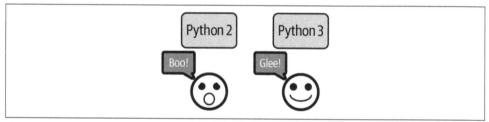

```
tdd-project> python3 --version
Python 3.9.6
tdd-project> python --version
Python 2.7.16
tdd-project> _
```

Figure 0-5. Verify that Python 3 is installed and the command you need to type to use it (python3 as shown here)

Use Python 3 to follow the code in this book. Do *not* use Python 2 —it won't work.

Figure 0-6 shows a mnemonic to simplify the preceding Python version rigmarole!

Figure 0-6. Simple mnemonic to clarify which version of Python is needed for this book!

Where We Are

In this preliminary chapter, we got acquainted with the toolchain we'll need to start writing our code in a test-driven fashion. We also learned how to prepare our development environment and to verify that it is in working condition.

Now that we know what this book is about, what's in it, how to read it, and most importantly how to set up our working environment to follow it, we are ready to solve our problem, chiseling one feature at time, driven forward by tests. We'll commence that journey in Chapter 1. Let's roll!

PART I

Getting Started

The Money Problem

I would not give a fig for the simplicity this side of complexity, but I would give my life for the simplicity on the other side of complexity.

—Oliver Wendell Holmes Jr.

Our development environment is ready. In this chapter, we'll learn the three phases that support test-driven development. We'll then write our first code feature using test-driven development.

Red-Green-Refactor: The Building Blocks of TDD

Test-driven development follows a three-phase process:

1. *Red*. We write a failing test (including possible compilation failures). We run the test suite to verify the failing tests.

2. *Green*. We write just enough production code to make the test green. We run the test suite to verify this.

3. *Refactor*. We remove any code smells. These may be due to duplication, hardcoded values, or improper use of language idioms (e.g., using a verbose loop instead of a built-in iterator). If we break any tests during refactoring, we prioritize getting them back to green before exiting this phase.

This is the red-green-refactor (RGR) cycle, shown in Figure 1-1. The three phases of this cycle are the essential building blocks of test-driven development. All the code we'll develop in this book will follow this cycle.

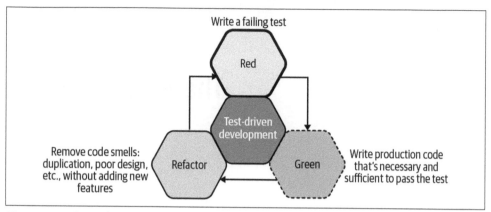

Figure 1-1. The red-green-refactor cycle is the foundation on which test-driven development rests

The three phases of the *red-green-refactor* cycle are the essential building blocks of TDD.

RGR in Action

Throughout this book, we'll use the three phases of the RGR cycle. We'll stick to this regimen rather meticulously, so it's important to start slowly and then speed up. In this chapter, the three phases are clearly marked in the relevant sections. In subsequent chapters, we'll move briskly, and often seamlessly, from the red to the green phase. We'll then redirect our attention to identify what to refactor. The transitions will get smoother as the pace of our development gets quicker. However, the three phases will always be there, and in that order.

What's the Problem?

We have a money problem. No, not the kind that almost *everyone* has: not having enough of it! It's more of a "we want to keep track of our money" problem.

Say we have to build a spreadsheet to manage money in more than one currency, perhaps to manage a stock portfolio.

Stock	Stock exchange	Shares	Share price	Total
IBM	NASDAQ	100	124 USD	12400 USD
BMW	DAX	400	75 EUR	30000 EUR
Samsung	KSE	300	68000 KRW	20400000 KRW

To build this spreadsheet, we'd need to do simple arithmetic operations on numbers in any one currency:

$$5\ USD \times 2 = 10\ USD$$
$$10\ EUR \times 2 - 20\ EUR$$
$$4002\ KRW\ /\ 4 = 1000.5\ KRW$$

We'd also like to convert between currencies. For example, if exchanging 1 EUR gets us 1.2 USD, and exchanging 1 USD gets us 1100 KRW:

$$5\ USD + 10\ EUR = 17\ USD$$
$$1\ USD + 1100\ KRW = 2200\ KRW$$

Each of the aforementioned line items will be one (teeny tiny) feature that we'll implement using TDD. We already have several features to implement. In order to help us focus on one thing at a time, we'll highlight the feature we're working on **in bold**. When we're done with a feature, we'll signal our satisfaction by ~~crossing it out~~.

So where should we start? In case the title of this book isn't an obvious giveaway, we'll start by writing a test.

Our First Failing Test

Let's start by implementing the very first feature in our list:

$$\textbf{5 USD} \times \textbf{2} = \textbf{10 USD}$$
$$10\ EUR \times 2 = 20\ EUR$$
$$4002\ KRW\ /\ 4 = 1000.5\ KRW$$
$$5\ USD + 10\ EUR = 17\ USD$$
$$1\ USD + 1100\ KRW = 2200\ KRW$$

We'll start by writing a failing test, corresponding to the *red* phase of the RGR cycle.

Go

In a new file called `money_test.go` in the go folder, let's write our first test:

```go
package main ❶

import (
    "testing" ❷
)

func TestMultiplication(t *testing.T) { ❸
    fiver := Dollar{ ❹
        amount: 5,
    }
    tenner := fiver.Times(2) ❺
    if tenner.amount != 10 { ❻
        t.Errorf("Expected 10, got: [%d]", tenner.amount) ❼
    }
}
```

❶ Package declaration

❷ Imported "testing" package, used in `t.Errorf` later

❸ Our test method, which must start with `Test` and have one `*testing.T` argument

❹ Struct representing "USD 5." `Dollar` does not exist yet

❺ Method under test: `Times`—which also does not exist yet

❻ Comparing actual value with expected value

❼ Ensuring test fails if expected value is not equal to actual value

This test function includes a bit of boilerplate code.

The `package main` declares that all ensuing code is part of the `main` package. This is a requirement for standalone executable Go programs. Package management (*https:// oreil.ly/yvh3S*) is a sophisticated feature in Go. It's discussed in more detail in Chapter 5.

Next, we import the `testing` package using the `import` statement. This package will be used in the unit test.

The unit test `function` is the bulk of the code. We declare an entity representing "5 USD." This is the variable named `fiver`, which we initialize to a struct holding 5 in its `amount` field. Then, we multiply `fiver` by 2. And we expect the result to be 10 dollars, i.e., a variable `tenner` whose `amount` field must equal 10. If this isn't the case, we print a nicely formatted error message with the actual value (whatever that may be).

When we run this test using "`go test -v .`" from the TDD Project Root folder, we should get an error:

```
... undefined: Dollar
FAIL    tdd [build failed]
FAIL
```

We get the message loud and clear: that's our first failing test!

"`go test -v .`" runs the tests in the current folder, and "`go test -v ./...`"[1] runs tests in the current folder and any subfolders. The `-v` switch produces verbose output.

JavaScript

In a new file called `test_money.js` in the `js` folder, let's write our first test:

```
const assert = require('assert'); ❶

let fiver = new Dollar(5); ❷
let tenner = fiver.times(2); ❸
assert.strictEqual(tenner.amount, 10); ❹
```

❶ Importing the `assert` package, needed for the assertion later

❷ Object representing "USD 5." `Dollar` does not exist yet

❸ Method under test: `times`—which also does not exist yet

❹ Comparing actual value with expected value in a `strictEqual` assert statement

JavaScript has minimal boilerplate code—the only line in addition to the test code is the `require` statement. This gives us access to the `assert` NPM package.

After that line are the three lines of code that form our test. We create an object representing 5 USD, we multiply it by 2, and we expect the result to be 10.

---

1 The three dots in "`go test -v ./...`" and "`go fmt ./...`" are to be typed literally; these are the only instances in this book where they do *not* stand for omitted code!

ES2015 introduced the `let` (*https://oreil.ly/jBMPk*) keyword for declaring variables and the `const` (*https://oreil.ly/GfYQ5*) keyword to declare constants.

When we run this code from the TDD Project Root folder using `node js/ test_money.js`, we should get an error that starts like this:

```
ReferenceError: Dollar is not defined
```

That's our first failing test. Hooray!

`node file.js` runs the JavaScript code in `file.js` and produces output. We use this command to run our tests.

Python

In a new file called `test_money.py` in the py folder, let's write our first test:

```python
import unittest ❶

class TestMoney(unittest.TestCase): ❷
  def testMultiplication(self): ❸
    fiver = Dollar(5) ❹
    tenner = fiver.times(2) ❺
    self.assertEqual(10, tenner.amount) ❻

if __name__ == '__main__': ❼
    unittest.main()
```

❶ Importing the `unittest` package, needed for the `TestCase` superclass.

❷ Our test class, which must subclass the `unittest.TestCase` class.

❸ Our method name must start with `test` to qualify as a test method.

❹ Object representing "USD 5." `Dollar` does not exist yet.

❺ Method under test: `times`—which also does not exist yet.

❻ Comparing actual value with expected value in an `assertEqual` statement.

❼ The `main` idiom ensures this class can be run as a script.

Python requires importing the `unittest` package, creating a class that subclasses `TestCase`, and defining a function whose name starts with `test`. To be able to run the class as a standalone program, we need the common Python idiom (*https://docs.python.org/3/library/__main__.html*) that runs the `unittest.main()` function when `test_money.py` is run directly.

The test function describes how we expect our code to work. We define a variable named `fiver` and initialize it to a desired (but yet-to-be-created) class `Dollar` with 5 as a constructor argument. We then multiply `fiver` by 2 and store the result in a variable `tenner`. Finally, we expect the `amount` in `tenner` to be `10`.

When we run this code from the `TDD_PROJECT_ROOT` folder using `python3 py/test_money.py -v`, we get an error:

```
NameError: name 'Dollar' is not defined
```

That's our first failing test. Hooray!

 `python3 file.py -v` runs the Python code in `file.py` and produces verbose output. We use this command to run our tests.

Going for Green

We wrote our tests as we would expect them to work, blithely ignoring all syntax errors for the moment. Is this smart?

In the *very* beginning—which is where we are—it is smart to start with the smallest bit of code that sets us on the path to progress. Of course our tests fail because we haven't defined what `Dollar` is. This *may* seem the perfect time to say "Duh!" However, a wee bit of patience is warranted for these two reasons:

1. We have just finished the *first* step—getting to *red*—of our *first* test. Not only is this the beginning, it's the very beginning of the beginning.

2. We can (and will) speed up the increments as we go along. However, it's important to know that we can slow down when we need to.

The next phase in the RGR cycle is to get to *green*.

It's clear we need to introduce an abstraction `Dollar`. This section defines how to introduce this, and other abstractions, to get our test to pass.

Go

Add an empty `Dollar` struct to the end of `money_test.go`.

```go
type Dollar struct {
}
```

When we run the test now, we get a new error:

```
... unknown field 'amount' in struct literal of type Dollar
```

Progress!

The error message is directing us to introduce a field named `amount` in our `Dollar` struct. So let's do this, using an `int` data type for now (which is sufficient for our goal):

```go
type Dollar struct {
    amount int
}
```

Adding the `Dollar` struct, rather predictably, gets us to the next error:

```
... fiver.Times undefined (type Dollar has no field or method Times)
```

We see a pattern here: when there is something (a field or method) that's undefined, we get this `undefined` error from the Go runtime. We will use this information to speed up our TDD cycles in the future. For now, let's add a function named `Times`. We know, from how we wrote our test, that this function needs to take a number (the multiplier) and return another number (the result).

But how should we calculate the result? We know basic arithmetic: how to multiply two numbers. But if we were to write the simplest code that works, we'd be justified in *always* returning the result that our test expects, that is, a struct representing 10 dollars:

```go
func (d Dollar) Times(multiplier int) Dollar {
    return Dollar{10}
}
```

When we run our code now, we should get a short and sweet response on our terminal:

```
=== RUN   TestMultiplication
--- PASS: TestMultiplication (0.00s)
PASS
```

That's the magic word: we made our test PASS!

JavaScript

In `test_money.js`, right after the `const assert = require('as sert');` line, define an empty class named `Dollar`:

```
class Dollar {
}
```

When we run the `test_money.js` file now, we get an error:

```
TypeError: fiver.times is not a function
```

Progress! The error clearly states that there is no function named `times` defined for the object named `fiver`. So let's introduce it inside the `Dollar` class:

```
class Dollar {
    times(multiplier) {
    }
}
```

Running the test now produces a new error:

```
TypeError: Cannot read properties of undefined (reading 'amount') ❶
```

❶ This message is from Node.js v16; v14 produces a slightly different error message

Our test expects an object with a property `amount`. Since we're not returning anything from our `times` method, the return value is `undefined`, which does not have an `amount` property (or any other property, for that matter).

> In the JavaScript language, functions and methods do not explicitly declare any return types. If we examine the result of a function that returns nothing, we'll find the return value is `undefined`.

So how should we make our test go green? What's the simplest thing that could work? How about if we *always* create an object representing 10 USD and return it?

Let's try it out. We add a `constructor` that initializes objects to a given amount and a `times` method that obstinately creates and returns "10 USD" objects:

```
class Dollar {
    constructor(amount) { ❶
        this.amount = amount; ❷
    }

    times(multiplier) { ❸
        return new Dollar(10); ❹
    }
}
```

❶ The constructor function is called whenever a Dollar object is created.

❷ Initialize the this.amount variable to the given parameter.

❸ The times method takes a parameter.

❹ Simple implementation: always return 10 dollars.

When we run our code now, we should get no errors. This is our first green test!

Because strictEqual and other methods in the assert package only produce output when the assertions *fail*, a successful test run will be quite silent with no output. We'll improve this behavior in Chapter 6.

Python

Since 'Dollar' is not defined, let's define it in test_money.py before our TestMoney class:

```python
class Dollar:
  pass
```

When we run our code now, we get an error:

```
TypeError: Dollar() takes no arguments
```

Progress! The error is clearly telling us that there is currently no way to initialize Dollar objects with any arguments, such as the 5 and 10 we have in our code. So let's fix this by providing the briefest possible initializer:

```python
class Dollar:
  def __init__(self, amount):
    pass
```

Now the error message from our test changes:

```
AttributeError: 'Dollar' object has no attribute 'times'
```

We see a pattern here: our test is still failing, but for *slightly different* reasons each time. As we define our abstractions—first Dollar and then an amount field—the error messages "improve" to the next stage. This is a hallmark of TDD: steady progress at a pace we control.

Let's speed things up a bit by defining a times function *and* giving it the minimum behavior to get to green. What's the minimum behavior necessary? Always returning a "ten dollar" object that's required by our test, of course!

```
class Dollar:
  def __init__(self, amount): ❶
    self.amount = amount ❷

  def times(self, multiplier): ❸
    return Dollar(10) ❹
```

❶ The __init__ function is called whenever a Dollar object is created.

❷ Initialize the self.amount variable to the given parameter.

❸ The times method takes a parameter.

❹ Simple implementation entails always returning 10 dollars.

When we run our test now, we get a short and sweet response:

```
Ran 1 test in 0.000s

OK
```

It's possible that the test may not run in 0.000s, but let's not lose sight of the magic word OK. This is our first green test!

Cleaning Up

Do you feel bemused that we got to green by hardcoding "10 USD" in our tests? Fret not: the refactoring stage allows us to address this discomfort by teasing out *how* we can remove the hardcoded and duplicated value of "10 USD."

Refactor is the third and final stage of the RGR cycle. We may not have many lines of code at this point; however, it's still important to keep things tidy and compact. If we have any formatting clutter or commented-out lines of code, now is the time to clean it up.

More significant is the need to remove duplication and make code readable. At first blush, it may seem that in the 20 or so lines of code we've written, there can't be any duplication. However, there is already a subtle yet significant bit of duplication.

We can find this duplication by noticing a couple of quirks within our code:

1. We have written just enough code to verify that "doubling 5 dollars should give us 10 dollars." If we decide to change our existing test to say "doubling 10 dollars should give us 20 dollars"—an equally sensible statement—we will have to change *both* our test and our Dollar code. There is a dependency, a *logical coupling*, between the two segments of code. In general, coupling of this kind should be avoided.

2. In both our test and our code, we had the magic number 10. Where did we come up with that? We obviously did the math in our heads. We realize that doubling 5 dollars should give us 10 dollars. So we wrote 10 in both our test and in our Dollar code. We should realize that the 10 in the Dollar entity is really 5 * 2. This realization would allow us to remove this duplication.

Duplicated code is often the symptom of some underlying problem: a missing code abstraction or bad coupling between different parts of the code.[2]

Let's remove the duplication and thereby get rid of the coupling as well.

Go

Replace the 10 in the Times function by its equivalent 5 * 2:

```
func (d Dollar) Times(multiplier int) Dollar {
    return Dollar{5 * 2}
}
```

The test should still be green.

Writing it this way makes us realize the missing abstraction. The hardcoded 5 is really d.amount, and the 2 is the multiplier. Replacing these hardcoded numbers with the correct variables gives us the non-trivial implementation:

```
func (d Dollar) Times(multiplier int) Dollar {
    return Dollar{d.amount * multiplier}
}
```

Yay! The test still passes, and we have removed the duplication and the coupling.

There is one final bit of cleanup.

In our test, we explicitly used the field name amount when initializing a Dollar struct. It's also possible to omit field names when initializing a struct, as we did in our Times method.[3] Either style—using explicit names or not using them—works. However, it's important to be consistent. Let's change the Times function to specify the field name:

```
func (d Dollar) Times(multiplier int) Dollar {
    return Dollar{amount: d.amount * multiplier}
}
```

---

2 Kent Beck's opinion is worth quoting here: "If dependency is the problem, duplication is the symptom."

3 If there are multiple fields in the struct—which currently there are not—then *either* the order of the fields must be the same in both struct definition and initialization *or* field names must be specified during struct initialization. See *https://gobyexample.com/structs*.

Remember to run go fmt ./... periodically to fix any formatting issues in code.

JavaScript

Let's replace the 10 in the times method by its equivalent 5 * 2:

```
times(multiplier) {
    return new Dollar(5 * 2);
}
```

The test should still be green.

The missing abstraction is now clear. We can replace 5 with this.amount and 2 with multiplier:

```
times(multiplier) {
    return new Dollar(this.amount * multiplier);
}
```

Yay! The test is still green, and we have eliminated both the duplicated 10 and the coupling.

Python

Let's replace the 10 in the times method by its equivalent 5 * 2:

```
def times(self, multiplier):
    return Dollar(5 * 2)
```

The test stays green, as expected.

This reveals the underlying abstraction. The 5 is really self.amount and the 2 is the multiplier:

```
def times(self, multiplier):
    return Dollar(self.amount * multiplier)
```

Hooray! The test remains green, and the duplication and the coupling are gone.

Committing Our Changes

We have finished our first feature using TDD. Lest we forget, it's important to commit our code to our version control repository at frequent intervals.

A green test is an excellent place to commit code.

In a shell window, let's type these two commands:

```
git add . ❶
git commit -m "feat: first green test" ❷
```

❶ Add all files, including all changes in them, to the Git index.

❷ Commit the Git index to the repository with the given message.

Assuming code for all three languages exists in the correct folders, we should get a message like this.

```
[main (root-commit) bb31b94] feat: first green test ❶
 4 files changed, 56 insertions(+)
 create mode 100644 go/go.mod
 create mode 100644 go/money_test.go
 create mode 100644 js/test_money.js
 create mode 100644 py/test_money.py
```

❶ The hex number, bb31b94, represents the first several digits of the unique "SHA hash" associated with the commit. It will be different for every person (and every commit).

This indicates that all our files are safely in our Git version control repository. We can verify this by executing the `git log` command on our shell, which should produce output similar to the following:

```
commit bb31b94e90029ddeeee89f3ca0fe099ea7556603 (HEAD -> main) ❶
Author: Saleem Siddiqui ...
Date:   Sun Mar 7 12:26:06 2021 -0600

    feat: first green test ❷
```

❶ This is the first commit, with its full SHA hash.

❷ This is the message we typed for our first commit.

It's important to realize that the Git repository to which we have committed our code also resides on our local filesystem. (It's inside the .git folder under our TDD_PROJECT_ROOT). While this doesn't save us from accidental coffee spills on our computer (always use lids), it does provide assurance that we can go back to a previous known good version if we get tangled up somewhere. In Chapter 13, we'll push all our code to a GitHub repository.

We'll use this strategy of committing our code to our local Git repository in each chapter, using the same set of commands.

We'll use the two commands `git add .` and `git commit -m _com mit message_` to frequently commit our code in each chapter.

The only thing that'll vary is the commit message, which will follow the semantic commit style and include a short, one-line description of the changes.

The `git commit` messages in this book follow the semantic commit style (*https://oreil.ly/MhE1b*).

Where We Are

This chapter introduced test-driven development by showing the *very first* red-green-refactor cycle. With our first tiny feature successfully implemented, let's cross it off. Here's where we are in our feature list:

~~5 USD × 2 = 10 USD~~
10 EUR × 2 = 20 EUR
4002 KRW / 4 = 1000.5 KRW
5 USD + 10 EUR = 17 USD
1 USD + 1100 KRW = 2200 KRW

Let's take a moment to review and savor our code before we move on to the next challenge. The source code for all three languages is reproduced below. It's also accessible in the GitHub repository. For the sake of brevity, future chapters will list the corresponding branch name only.

Go

Here's how the file `money_test.go` looks right now:

```go
package main

import (
    "testing"
)

func TestMultiplication(t *testing.T) {
    fiver := Dollar{amount: 5}
    tenner := fiver.Times(2)
    if tenner.amount != 10 {
```

```
        t.Errorf("Expected 10, got: [%d]", tenner.amount)
    }
}

type Dollar struct {
    amount int
}

func (d Dollar) Times(multiplier int) Dollar {
    return Dollar{amount: d.amount * multiplier}
}
```

JavaScript

Here's how the test_money.js file looks at this point:

```
const assert = require('assert');

class Dollar {
    constructor(amount) {
      this.amount = amount;
    }

    times(multiplier) {
        return new Dollar(this.amount * multiplier);
    }
}

let fiver = new Dollar(5);
let tenner = fiver.times(2);
assert.strictEqual(tenner.amount, 10);
```

Python

Here's how the test_money.py file looks right now:

```
import unittest

class Dollar:
  def __init__(self, amount):
    self.amount = amount

  def times(self, multiplier):
    return Dollar(self.amount * multiplier)

class TestMoney(unittest.TestCase):
  def testMultiplication(self):
    fiver = Dollar(5)
    tenner = fiver.times(2)
    self.assertEqual(10, tenner.amount)
```

```
if __name__ == '__main__':
    unittest.main()
```

 The code for this chapter is in a branch named "chap01" in the
GitHub repository (*https://github.com/saleem/tdd-book-code/tree/
chap01*). There is a branch for each chapter in which code is
developed.

In Chapter 2, we'll speed things up by building out a couple more features.

Multicurrency Money

Followed fast and followed faster

   —Edgar Allen Poe, The Raven

Did the *red-green-refactor* cycle we followed in Chapter 1 seem a tad too slow?

A response of "Heck yes!" (or some rhyming phrase) is understandable!

The goal of test-driven development isn't to *force* us to go slow—or fast, for that matter. Its goal is to *allow* us to go at a pace we're comfortable with: speeding up when we can, slowing down when we should.

In this chapter, we'll introduce additional currencies and the ability to multiply and divide money in any currency. Let's see if we can kick up the pace a bit.

Enter the Euro

The second item on our list of features introduces a new currency:

~~5 USD × 2 = 10 USD~~
10 EUR × 2 = 20 EUR
4002 KRW / 4 = 1000.5 KRW
5 USD + 10 EUR = 17 USD
1 USD + 1100 KRW = 2200 KRW

This indicates that we need a more general entity than the `Dollar` we created in the previous chapter: something like `Money`, which encapsulates an `amount` (which we already have) and a `currency` (which we do not yet have). Let's write tests to flesh out this new feature.

Go

Let's write a new test in `money_test.go`. This test requires that when a struct representing "10 EUR" is multiplied by 2, we get "20 EUR":

```go
func TestMultiplicationInEuros(t *testing.T) {
    tenEuros := Money{amount: 10, currency: "EUR"}
    twentyEuros := tenEuros.Times(2)
    if twentyEuros.amount != 20 {
        t.Errorf("Expected 20, got: [%d]", twentyEuros.amount)
    }
    if twentyEuros.currency != "EUR" {
        t.Errorf("Expected EUR, got: [%s]", twentyEuros.currency)
    }
}
```

The test expresses the concepts of "10 EUR" and "20 EUR" with `struct` instances containing a `currency` as well as an `amount`.

By now, we know that when we run this test, we'll get an error notifying us of `undefined: Money`. We can eliminate this by introducing a new struct:

```go
type Money struct {
    amount   int
    currency string
}
```

We now get the error `type Money has no field or method Times`, which we know how to get around. We define a `Times` method for `Money`:

```go
func (m Money) Times(multiplier int) Money {
    return Money{amount: m.amount * multiplier, currency: m.currency}
}
```

Yay! Green tests again.

JavaScript

Let's write a test for representing a `Money` object with `amount` and `currency`. We verify that when an object representing "10 EUR" is multiplied by 2, we get "20 EUR." We define this test at the very end of `test_money.js`:

```javascript
let tenEuros = new Money(10, "EUR");
let twentyEuros = tenEuros.times(2);
assert.strictEqual(twentyEuros.amount, 20);
assert.strictEqual(twentyEuros.currency, "EUR");
```

By now, we anticipate the `ReferenceError: Money is not defined` error we get when running the tests. We can eliminate this by introducing a new class named `Money` with the minimally desired behavior; that is, a `constructor` that initializes both amount and currency, and a times method that multiplies the amount with a given multiplier, returning a new Money object.

```
class Money {
    constructor(amount, currency) {
        this.amount = amount;
        this.currency = currency;
    }

    times(multiplier) {
        return new Money(this.amount * multiplier, this.currency);
    }
}
```

Yay! Both our tests are now green.

Python

Let's add a new test in the TestMoney class. This test would verify that multiplying an object representing "10 EUR" by 2 gives us an object representing "20 EUR":

```
def testMultiplicationInEuros(self):
    tenEuros = Money(10, "EUR")
    twentyEuros = tenEuros.times(2)
    self.assertEqual(20, twentyEuros.amount)
    self.assertEqual("EUR", twentyEuros.currency)
```

By now, we anticipate the NameError: name 'Money' is not defined error we get when we run the tests. We know that we need a new Money class. What's the least behavior in this Money class to make the test green? We need an __init__ method that initializes both amount and currency, and a times method that returns a new Money object whose amount is a product of the multiplier and the amount of the original Money object:

```
class Money:
    def __init__(self, amount, currency):
        self.amount = amount
        self.currency = currency

    def times(self, multiplier):
        return Money(self.amount * multiplier, self.currency)
```

Yay! Both our tests are now green.

Keeping Code DRY

Wait a minute: didn't we just create a horrendous duplication in our code? The new entity we created to represent Money subsumes what we wrote earlier for Dollar. This can't possibly be good. A oft-quoted rule in writing code is the DRY principle: Don't Repeat Yourself.

Recall the red-green-refactor cycle. What we did in the previous section got us to green, but we haven't done the necessary refactoring yet. Let's remove the duplication in the code while keeping our tests green.

Go

We realize that the Money struct can do everything that the Dollar struct can, and more. Money has currency, which Dollar does not.

Let's delete the Dollar struct and its Times method.

When we do this, the TestMultiplication test predictably breaks with an undefined: Dollar error. Let's refactor that test to use Money instead:

```go
func TestMultiplicationInDollars(t *testing.T) {
    fiver := Money{amount: 5, currency: "USD"}
    tenner := fiver.Times(2)
    if tenner.amount != 10 {
        t.Errorf("Expected 10, got: [%d]", tenner.amount)
    }
    if tenner.currency != "USD" {
        t.Errorf("Expected USD, got: [%s]", tenner.currency)
    }
}
```

Both tests now pass. Notice that we renamed the test to be more descriptive: Test MultiplicationInDollars.

JavaScript

The Money class can do everything that Dollar does, and more. This means that we can delete the Dollar class in its entirety.

When we do this and run the tests, we get our old friendly error: Ref erenceError: Dollar is not defined. Let's refactor the first test to use Money instead:

```javascript
let fiver = new Money(5, "USD");
let tenner = fiver.times(2);
assert.strictEqual(tenner.amount, 10);
assert.strictEqual(tenner.currency, "USD");
```

Both tests now pass.

Python

The `Money` class's functionality is a superset of that of the `Dollar` class. Which means we don't need the latter. Let's delete the `Dollar` class in its entirety.

Having done this, we get the familiar `NameError: name 'Dollar' is not defined` message when we run the tests. Let's refactor the first test to use `Money` instead of the erstwhile `Dollar`:

```python
def testMultiplicationInDollars(self):
    fiver = Money(5, "USD")
    tenner = fiver.times(2)
    self.assertEqual(10, tenner.amount)
    self.assertEqual("USD", tenner.currency)
```

Both tests now pass. Notice that we renamed the test to be more descriptive: `Test MultiplicationInDollars`.

Didn't We Just Say "Don't Repeat Yourself"?!

Hmm. The two tests—the one for dollars and the one for euros—are *very* similar. The currencies and amounts vary, but they test pretty much the same feature.

Repetition in code comes in varied forms. Sometimes we have identical lines of code (perhaps caused by "copy pasta" programming). In these cases, we need to extract the common lines to a function or method. At other times, we have parts of code that are not identical but are conceptually similar. This is the case with our two tests.

We *could* delete one of the tests and still feel confident about our code. However, we also want to safeguard against accidental regression in our code. Recall that our very first implementation used hardcoded numbers (10 or 5 * 2). Having two distinct tests with different values ensures that we won't accidentally go back to that naive implementation.

Regression—"a return to a primitive or less developed state"—is a common theme in writing software. Having a battery of tests is a reliable way to ensure that we don't break existing features as we build new ones.

Let's keep both test cases for now. We'll add an item to the end of our checklist noting our desire to remove redundancy in tests. We'll revisit this item later, after we address division.

Here's our feature list:

~~5 USD × 2 = 10 USD~~
~~10 EUR × 2 = 20 EUR~~
4002 KRW / 4 = 1000.5 KRW
5 USD + 10 EUR = 17 USD
1 USD + 1100 KRW = 2200 KRW
Remove redundant Money multiplication tests

Divide and Conquer

The next requirement is to allow division. On the surface, it looks very similar to multiplication. We know from elementary mathematics that dividing by x is the same as multiplying by $1/x$.[1]

Let's test-drive this new feature and see how our code evolves. By now, we are getting into the groove of starting with a failing test. As an indicator of our growing confidence, we'll introduce two new things in our test:

1. A new currency: Korean won (KRW)

2. Numbers with fractional parts (e.g., 1000.5)

Go

Let's write our new test for division.

```
func TestDivision(t *testing.T) {
    originalMoney := Money{amount: 4002, currency: "KRW"}
    actualMoneyAfterDivision := originalMoney.Divide(4)
    expectedMoneyAfterDivision := Money{amount: 1000.5, currency: "KRW"}
    if expectedMoneyAfterDivision != actualMoneyAfterDivision {
        t.Errorf("Expected %+v Got %+v",
            expectedMoneyAfterDivision, actualMoneyAfterDivision)
    }
}
```

Notice that we write this test a bit differently. We define variables for the two structs: `actualMoneyAfterDivision` and `expectedMoneyAfterDivision`. And instead of comparing `amount` and `currency` separately, we compare the two structs as a whole. If the structs don't match, we print them both.

---

1 $\forall x \neq 0$, i.e., as long as x isn't zero…thank you to all math teachers for what you do!

In Go, printing a struct with the %+v format "verb" prints the struct's field names as well as values.

We anticipate the `type Money has no field or method Divide` error we get when we run this test. Let's define this missing method, taking our cue from the existing `Times` method:

```
func (m Money) Divide(divisor int) Money {
    return Money{amount: m.amount / divisor, currency: m.currency}
}
```

Ah! The test fails with a new error: `constant 1000.5 truncated to integer`.

It's clear that we need to change the `amount` field in the `Money` struct so that it can hold fractional values. The `float64` data type is appropriate for this purpose:

```
type Money struct {
    amount    float64
    currency string
}
```

This gives us new errors when we run our test:

```
... invalid operation: m.amount * multiplier (mismatched types float64 and int)
... invalid operation: m.amount / divisor (mismatched types float64 and int)
```

Using an IDE can be useful because it flags syntax errors and type errors without any need to run the tests.

We need to modify our arithmetic operations (multiplication and division) to use the same data type for all operands. We know from our domain that the multipliers and divisors are likely to be integers (number of shares of a stock) whereas the amount can be a fractional number (trading price of a particular stock). Let's use this knowledge to convert the `multiplier` and `divisor` to `float64` before using them in our arithmetic operations. We can do this by calling the `float64()` function:

```
func (m Money) Times(multiplier int) Money {
    return Money{amount: m.amount * float64(multiplier), currency: m.currency}
}

func (m Money) Divide(divisor int) Money {
    return Money{amount: m.amount / float64(divisor), currency: m.currency}
}
```

Now we get different wrong type failures:

```
... Errorf format %d has arg tenner.amount of wrong type float64
... Errorf format %d has arg twentyEuros.amount of wrong type float64
```

A careful reading of the error messages reveals that we are using the wrong format "verb" in our earlier tests to print the amount field. Since our newest test—TestDivision—successfully compares entire structs, we can refactor our earlier two multiplication tests to do something similar. This way, we'll sidestep the whole issue of having used the incorrect formatting "verb" for float64 type.

Here's how TestMultiplicationInDollars looks after changing its assertion statement. (The other test, TestMultiplicationInEuros, needs similar changes.)

```
func TestMultiplicationInDollars(t *testing.T) {
    fiver := Money{amount: 5, currency: "USD"}
    actualResult := fiver.Times(2)
    expectedResult := Money{amount: 10, currency: "USD"}
    if expectedResult != actualResult {
        t.Errorf("Expected [%+v], got: [%+v]", expectedResult, actualResult)
    }
}
```

 If compilation or assertion failures crop up during a test run, pay attention to the error messages.

After these changes, all our tests are green.

JavaScript

Let's write our new test for division at the end of test_money.js.

```
let originalMoney = new Money(4002, "KRW")
let actualMoneyAfterDivision = originalMoney.divide(4)
let expectedMoneyAfterDivision = new Money(1000.5, "KRW")
assert.deepStrictEqual(actualMoneyAfterDivision, expectedMoneyAfterDivision)
```

Notice that we wrote this test a bit differently. We define variables for the two objects: actualMoneyAfterDivision and expectedMoneyAfterDivision. And instead of comparing amount and currency separately, we compare the two objects at once using the deepStrictEqual method in assert.

In Node.js's `assert` module, the `deepStrictEqual` method compares two objects and their child objects for equality using the JavaScript === operator.[2]

We anticipate the `TypeError: originalMoney.divide is not a function` error we get when we run this test. So let's define this missing method, taking inspiration from the existing `times` method:[3]

```
class Money {

    ...

    divide(divisor) {
        return new Money(this.amount / divisor, this.currency);
    }
}
```

Yay! The tests are all green. JavaScript's dynamic types make implementing this feature easier than languages with static typing (*https://oreil.ly/3bkGT*).

Python

Let's write our new test for division in class `TestMoney`:

```
def testDivision(self):
    originalMoney = Money(4002, "KRW")
    actualMoneyAfterDivision = originalMoney.divide(4)
    expectedMoneyAfterDivision = Money(1000.5, "KRW")
    self.assertEqual(expectedMoneyAfterDivision.amount,
                     actualMoneyAfterDivision.amount)
    self.assertEqual(expectedMoneyAfterDivision.currency,
                     actualMoneyAfterDivision.currency)
```

Notice that we wrote this test a bit differently. We define variables for the two objects: `actualMoneyAfterDivision` and `expectedMoneyAfterDivision`.

---

2 The === operator tests whether both the values and the types of the two objects being compared are equal. See this W3Schools documentation (*https://oreil.ly/6fTHI*).

3 The ECMAScript standard (*https://oreil.ly/1wLGp*) defines a method as a "function that is the value of a property [of an object]."

We anticipate the `AttributeError: 'Money' object has no attribute 'divide'` message we get when we run this test. So let's define this missing method, taking our cue from the existing `times` method:[4]

```python
def divide(self, divisor):
    return Money(self.amount / divisor, self.currency)
```

Yay! The tests are green. Python is a dynamically (and strongly) typed language. This makes implementing this feature easier than in languages with static typing (*https://oreil.ly/72qm9*).

Cleaning Up

Let's finish off this chapter with a bit of housecleaning, while keeping the tests green.

Go

We now have three tests with three assertion blocks, each of which is a three-line `if` block. Except for the variable names in each test, the `if` blocks are identical. This duplication is ripe for removal by extracting it into a helper function, which we can call `assertEqual`.

"Extract method" or "Extract function" (*https://oreil.ly/UWNWf*) is a common refactoring. It involves replacing common blocks of code with a call to a new function/method that encapsulates the block of code *once*.

```go
func assertEqual(t *testing.T, expected Money, actual Money) {
    if expected != actual {
        t.Errorf("Expected %+v Got %+v", expected, actual)
    }
}
```

The function's body is identical to any of the three existing `if` blocks. We can now call this function from each of the three tests. The `TestDivision` function is shown below:

```go
func TestDivision(t *testing.T) {
    originalMoney := Money{amount: 4002, currency: "KRW"}
    actualResult := originalMoney.Divide(4)
    expectedResult := Money{amount: 1000.5, currency: "KRW"}
    assertEqual(t, expectedResult, actualResult)
}
```

---

4 The Python standard (*https://oreil.ly/mGhKJ*) defines a method as "bound function objects." That is, methods are always associated with objects, whereas functions are not.

We can modify the `TestMultiplicationInEuros` and `TestMultiplicationInDollars` tests similarly.

JavaScript

The assertion using `deepStrictEqual` that we used for our last test is elegant: it compares the two objects (`actual` and `expected` values) at once. We can use it for our two other tests.

While we're doing it, we can also address a subtle assumption in these two lines of code in our tests:

```
let tenner = fiver.times(2);
...
let twentyEuros = tenEuros.times(2);
```

From the perspective of the test, it is a bit presumptuous to assume that multiplying 5 dollars or 10 euros by 2 will yield 10 dollars or 20 euros, respectively. Indeed, that's the *very* thing the tests purport to verify. We can improve our tests by inlining the call to the `times` method, thereby saving ourselves the trouble of naming the variable:

```
let fiveDollars = new Money(5, "USD");
let tenDollars = new Money(10, "USD");
assert.deepStrictEqual(fiveDollars.times(2), tenDollars);
```

"Inline variable" (*https://oreil.ly/pGbUG*) is a refactoring that replaces a named variable with an directly evaluated (usually anonymous) variable.

We can refactor the test for multiplying euros similarly.

Python

Comparing two `Money` objects piecemeal is verbose and tedious. In our tests, we verify that the `amount` and `currency` fields of `Money` objects are equal, over and over. Wouldn't it be nice to be able to compare two `Money` objects directly in a single line of code?

In Python, object equality is ultimately resolved by an invocation of the `__eq__` method. By default, this method returns true if the two object references being compared point to the same object. This is a very strict definition of equality: it means that an object is only equal to itself, not any other object, even of the two objects have the same state.

The default implementation of **__eq__** method means that in Python, two object references are equal if and only if they point to the same object. That is: equality is determined by reference, not by value (*https://oreil.ly/zLUCO*).

Fortunately, it is not only possible but recommended to override the **__eq__** method when needed. Let us explicitly override this method within the definition of our Money class:

```
class Money:

    ...

    def __eq__(self, other):
        return self.amount == other.amount and self.currency == other.currency
```

After defining the **__eq__** method, we can compare Money objects in a single line.

While we're refactoring, we can also address a subtle assumption implicit in how we named a couple of variables in our tests:

```
tenner = fiver.times(2)
...
twentyEuros = tenEuros.times(2)
```

From the test's perspective, it isn't a given that multiplying 5 dollars or 10 euros by 2 will yield 10 dollars or 20 euros, respectively. Indeed, that's the *very* thing the test exists to validate. We can improve our tests by doing an inline-variable refactoring, along with the single-line assertion that we can now write.

Here's the complete testMultiplicationInDollars:

```
def testMultiplicationInDollars(self):
    fiveDollars = Money(5, "USD")
    tenDollars = Money(10, "USD")
    self.assertEqual(tenDollars, fiveDollars.times(2))
```

We initialize fiveDollars and tenDollars explicitly. We then verify that multiplying the former by 2 yields an object that's equal to the latter. We also do it in one line, keeping our code readable and succinct.

The other two tests can be refactored similarly.

Committing Our Changes

We have written a couple more tests and the associated code to make them green. Time to commit these changes to our local Git repository:

```
git add . ❶
git commit -m "feat: division and multiplication features done" ❷
```

❶ Add all files, including all changes in them, to the Git index.

❷ Commit the Git index to the repository with the given message.

At this point, we have two commits in our Git history, a fact we can verify by examining the output of git log:

```
commit 1e43b6e6731407a810601d973c83b406249f4d59 (HEAD -> main) ❶
Author: Saleem Siddiqui ...
Date:   Sun Mar 7 12:58:47 2021 -0600

    feat: division and multiplication features done ❷

commit bb31b94e90029ddeeee89f3ca0fe099ea7556603 ❸
Author: Saleem Siddiqui ...
Date:   Sun Mar 7 12:26:06 2021 -0600

    feat: first green test
```

❶ New SHA hash for our second commit, which represents the HEAD of the Git repository

❷ The message we used for our second commit

❸ The SHA hash for our previous commit from Chapter 1

Where We Are

In this chapter, we built a second feature, division, and modified our design to deal with numbers with fractions. We have introduced a Money entity that allows us to consolidate how dollars and euros (and potentially other currencies) are multiplied by a number. We have a couple of passing tests. We have also cleaned up our code along the way.

 Depending on the specific data types and language, floating-point arithmetic can cause problems of overflow/underflow. If needed, the problems can be surfaced via tests—and then solved—using the RGR cycle. We also refactored our code to make it succinct and expressive.

With a couple more features crossed off our list, we're ready to look at adding up amounts in *different* currencies—which will get our attention in the next chapter.

Here's where we are in our feature list:

~~5 USD × 2 = 10 USD~~
~~10 EUR × 2 = 20 EUR~~
~~4002 KRW / 4 = 1000.5 KRW~~
5 USD + 10 EUR = 17 USD
1 USD + 1100 KRW = 2200 KRW
Remove redundant Money multiplication tests

 The code for this chapter is in a branch named "chap02" in the GitHub repository (*https://github.com/saleem/tdd-book-code/tree/chap02*).

CHAPTER 3

Portfolio

Penny wise and dollar foolish.[1]

    —Tired proverb

We can multiply and divide amounts in any one currency by numbers. Now we need to add amounts in multiple currencies.

~~5 USD × 2 = 10 USD~~

~~10 EUR × 2 = 20 EUR~~

~~4002 KRW / 4 = 1000.5 KRW~~

5 USD + 10 EUR = 17 USD

1 USD + 1100 KRW = 2200 KRW

Remove redundant Money multiplication tests

In this chapter, we'll deal with the mixed-mode addition of currencies.

Designing Our Next Test

To test-drive the next feature—5 USD + 10 EUR = 17 USD—it's enlightening to first sketch out how our program will evolve. TDD plays nicely with software design, contrary to prevailing myths!

The feature, as described in our feature list, says that 5 dollars and 10 euros should add up to 17 dollars, assuming we get 1.2 dollars for exchanging one euro.

---

1 Or, to unfurl the brows of my many and dear British friends, "Penny wise and pound foolish"!

However, it's equally true that:

```
1 EUR + 1 EUR = 2.4 USD
```

Or, rather obviously:

```
1 EUR + 1 EUR = 2 EUR
```

An epiphany! When we add two (or more) Money entities, the result can be expressed in any currency, as long as we know the exchange rate between all currencies involved (i.e., from the currency of each Money into the currency in which we want to express the result). This is true even if all the currencies involved are the same—as in the last example, which is just one particular case out of many.

 Test-driven development gives us an opportunity to pause after each RGR cycle and design our code intentionally.

We realize that "adding dollars to dollars results in dollars" is an oversimplification. The general principle is that adding Money entities in different currencies gives us a Portfolio, which we can then express in any one currency (given the necessary exchange rates between currencies).

Did we just introduce a new entity: Portfolio? You bet! It's vital to let our code reflect the realities of our domain. We're writing code to represent a collection of stock holdings, for which the correct term is *portfolio*.[2]

When we add two or more Money entities, we should get a Portfolio. We can extend this domain model by saying that we should be able to evaluate a Portfolio in any specific currency. These nouns and verbs give us an idea about the new abstractions in our code, which we'll drive out through tests.

 Analysis of the problem domain is an effective way to discover new entities, relationships, functions, and methods.

Given this new realization, let's add the simpler case of adding two Money entities in the *same* currency first, deferring the case of multiple currencies until later:

---

2 Are there other entities that we should have in addition to "Money"? Possibly. However, the "Money" abstraction meets our current needs. We'll add one more entity in Chapter 11, when its time comes.

~~5 USD × 2 = 10 USD~~
~~10 EUR × 2 = 20 EUR~~
~~4002 KRW / 4 = 1000.5 KRW~~
5 USD + 10 USD = 15 USD
5 USD + 10 EUR = 17 USD
1 USD + 1100 KRW = 2200 KRW

Remove redundant Money multiplication tests

Let's build this feature: adding Money entities together. We'll start with a test to add two Money entities in the same currency, using the Portfolio as a new entity.

Go

Here's our new test, TestAddition, which we add after the existing tests in money_test.go:

```go
func TestAddition(t *testing.T) {
    var portfolio Portfolio ❶
    var portfolioInDollars Money

    fiveDollars := Money{amount: 5, currency: "USD"}
    tenDollars := Money{amount: 10, currency: "USD"}
    fifteenDollars := Money{amount: 15, currency: "USD"}

    portfolio = portfolio.Add(fiveDollars) ❷
    portfolio = portfolio.Add(tenDollars)  ❸
    portfolioInDollars = portfolio.Evaluate("USD") ❹

    assertEqual(t, fifteenDollars, portfolioInDollars) ❺
}
```

❶ Declaring an empty Portfolio struct

❷ Adding a Money struct to the Portfolio struct

❸ Adding a second Money struct

❹ Evaluating the Portfolio struct to get a Money struct

❺ Comparing the result of the evaluation with the expected Money struct

Notice that we have declared the portfolio and portfolioInDollars variables explicitly, to emphasize their types. The verbosity makes things clear to us as we proceed.

Of course, in our current simple case, the currency is always the same, so exchange rates don't (yet) become a concern. Let's walk before we run!

By now, we're very accustomed to errors like undefined: Portfolio. Let's speed ahead and implement the barest possible type Portfolio to get beyond these errors. Here's what it looks like, added to the end of money_test.go:

```go
type Portfolio []Money

func (p Portfolio) Add(money Money) Portfolio {
    return p
}

func (p Portfolio) Evaluate(currency string) Money {
    return Money{amount: 15, currency: "USD"}
}
```

We declare a new type Portfolio as an alias for a slice of Money structs. We then define the two missing methods: Add and Evaluate. The signatures of these methods are suggested by the failing test we wrote. The implementation is the least possible code to get the test to pass—including the "silly" hardcoded Money that Evaluate returns.

In an earlier round of red-green-refactor, we recognized the subtle duplication in the test and production code and used it to change the "silly" implementation to a more correct one. Where is the duplication in this case? Yep: it's the "15" that's in both the test and production code.

We should replace the hardcoded 15 in Evaluate method with code that actually sums up the amount in the Money structs:

```go
func (p Portfolio) Evaluate(currency string) Money {
    total := 0.0
    for _, m := range p {
        total = total + m.amount
    }
    return Money{amount: total, currency: currency}
}
```

Hmm... our TestAddition fails with an assertion failure:

```
... Expected {amount:15 currency:USD} Got {amount:0 currency:USD}
```

Ah! We are iterating over an empty slice. We made the correct change to Evaluate, but our Add method still has a trivial ("silly") implementation. Let's fix that, too:

```go
func (p Portfolio) Add(money Money) Portfolio {
    p = append(p, money)
    return p
}
```

The test is now green.

We know that the currency in the `Money` struct returned by `Evaluate` has the same value as whatever was passed in as the first (and only) parameter to that method. This is obviously not the right implementation: it only works because our test uses two `Money` structs that both have the same currency, and then calls `Evaluate` also with the same currency.

Should we test-drive our way to removing this "silly" behavior of our code or use our "refactoring budget" (now that we have green tests) to do it?

There is no one-size-fits-all answer. TDD allows us to define for *ourselves* how fast we want to go. In our case, we have good reason to defer fixing the "silly" behavior of our code.

We know that when we `Evaluate` a `Portfolio` containing `Money` structs with different currencies, we'll have to use exchange rates—a concept we haven't defined yet. We also know that we have an item on our to-do list—5 USD + 10 EUR = 17 USD—that will compel us to test-drive this mixed-currency feature. Therefore, we can defer the change for a bit: the "silly" implementation survives to see another day. Or maybe another 10 minutes.

JavaScript

Here's our new test for adding two `Money` objects, which we add to the very end of `test_money.js`:

```
let fifteenDollars = new Money(15, "USD");
let portfolio = new Portfolio(); ❶
portfolio.add(fiveDollars, tenDollars); ❷
assert.deepStrictEqual(portfolio.evaluate("USD"), fifteenDollars); ❸
```

❶ Declaring an empty `Portfolio` object

❷ Adding multiple `Money` objects with the same currency to this `Portfolio` object

❸ Evaluating the `Portfolio` in the same currency and comparing the result with an expected `Money` object

In this test case, the currency is the same throughout, so exchange rates don't yet become a concern.

By now, we're very accustomed to errors like `ReferenceError: Portfolio is not defined`. Let's speed ahead and implement the barest possible `class Portfolio` to get beyond the errors and a quick passing test:

```
class Portfolio {
    add(money) {
    }
```

```
        evaluate(currency) {
            return new Money(15, "USD");
        }
    }
```

We define a new `Portfolio` class below the preexisting `Money` class in `test_money.js`. We give it the two methods our test demands: `add` and `evaluate`. The signatures of these methods are also evident from our test. In `evaluate`, we implement the quick-fire solution that gets our test to pass: always return a `Money` object representing "15 USD."

In an earlier round of red-green-refactor, we recognized the subtle duplication in the test and production code and used it to change the trivial ("silly") implementation to a more correct one. Where is the duplication in this case? Yep: it's the "15" that's in both the test and production code.

Now that our tests pass, we should replace the hardcoded 15 in `evaluate` method with code that actually sums up the `amount` in the `Money` objects:

```
        evaluate(currency) {
            let total = this.moneys.reduce( (sum, money) => {
                return sum + money.amount;
            }, 0);
            return new Money(total, currency);
        }
```

We use the reduce function (*https://oreil.ly/sDyXq*) for an array. We declare an anonymous function that adds up the `amount` of each `Money` object, thereby reducing the array `this.moneys` to a single scalar value. We then create a new `Money` object with this `total` and the given `currency` and return it.

 ES6 Arrays are list-like objects (*https://oreil.ly/L0BvQ*) whose prototype defines methods like `map`, `reduce`, and `filter` to facilitate a functional programming style.

The `evaluate` function, predictably, results in an error:

```
        let total = this.moneys.reduce( (sum, money) => {
                         ^

    TypeError: Cannot read properties of undefined (reading 'reduce')
```

Let's define the missing `this.moneys` array in a new `constructor` in the `Portfolio` class:

```
        constructor() {
            this.moneys = [];
        }
```

After adding the constructor, we get an interesting assertion error:

```
AssertionError [ERR_ASSERTION]: Expected values to be strictly deep-equal:
+ actual - expected

  Money {
+   amount: 0,
-   amount: 15,
    currency: 'USD'
  }
```

We are iterating over an empty array. Our evaluate method and constructor are correct, but our add method is still empty. Let's rectify this shortcoming. We'll use the rest parameter syntax (*https://oreil.ly/yo1hG*) to allow multiple Moneys to be added simultaneously:

```
add(...moneys) {
    this.moneys = this.moneys.concat(moneys);
}
```

The test is now green.

Python

Here's our new test for the addition of two Money objects, which we append to our growing list of tests in TestMoney class:

```
def testAddition(self):
    fiveDollars = Money(5, "USD")
    tenDollars = Money(10, "USD")
    fifteenDollars = Money(15, "USD")
    portfolio = Portfolio() ❶
    portfolio.add(fiveDollars, tenDollars) ❷
    self.assertEqual(fifteenDollars, portfolio.evaluate("USD")) ❸
```

❶ Declaring an empty Portfolio object

❷ Adding multiple Money objects with the same currency to this Portfolio object

❸ Evaluating the Portfolio in the same currency and comparing the result with an expected Money object

In this test case, the currency is always the same, so exchange rates don't yet become a concern.

We're now quite accustomed to errors like NameError: name 'Portfolio' is not defined. Let's speed ahead and implement the smallest possible class Portfolio to get beyond these errors to a passing test. We add the new class after the Money class definition in test_money.py:

```
class Portfolio:
    def add(self, *moneys):
        pass

    def evaluate(self, currency):
        return Money(15, "USD")
```

The Portfolio class has a no-op add method and an evaluate method with a "silly" implementation that always returns a Money object that's worth "15 USD." Just enough code to get a passing test.

In an earlier round of red-green-refactor, we recognized the subtle duplication in the test and production code and used it to change the trivial ("silly") implementation to a more correct one. Where is the duplication here? Yep: it's the "15" that's in both the test and production code.

We can replace the hardcoded 15 in the evaluate method with code that actually sums up the amount in the Money objects:

```
import functools ❶
import operator ❷
...
class Portfolio:
...
    def evaluate(self, currency):
        total = functools.reduce(
            operator.add, map(lambda m: m.amount, self.moneys))
        return Money(total, currency)
```

❶ The functools package gives us the reduce function.

❷ The operator package gives us the add function.

This code uses Python's functional programming idioms. The best way to understand how total is derived is to unravel the expression from the inside out:

1. We import the packages we need: functools and operator.

2. Using a lambda expression, we map the self.moneys array to a map of only the amounts in each Money object.

3. We then reduce this map to a single scalar value, using the operator.add operation.

4. We assign this scalar value to the variable named total.

5. We finally create a new Money object using this total and the currency passed in the first (and only) parameter to the evaluate method.

Phew! That one line of functional code sure packs a lot of punch!

Python has rich support for functional programming (*https://oreil.ly/WS1Ul*), including map, reduce, and filter in the func tools package and custom-written lambda functions.

We're not done yet: when we run our test, the error message AttributeError: 'Port folio' object has no attribute 'moneys' reminds us of that. Let's add an __init__ method that initializes this missing attribute in Portfolio:

```
def __init__(self):
    self.moneys = []
```

This gives us a new error: TypeError: reduce() of empty sequence with no ini tial value. We realize two things:

1. The add method in Portfolio is still a no-op. That's why our self.moneys is an empty array.

2. Notwithstanding the above problem, our code should *still* work with an empty array.

We fix these two shortcomings by the following code changes in Portfolio:

```
def add(self, *moneys):
    self.moneys.extend(moneys)

def evaluate(self, currency):
    total = functools.reduce(
        operator.add, map(lambda m: m.amount, self.moneys), 0) ❶
    return Money(total, currency)
```

❶ The last parameter to reduce (0 in our case) is the initial value of the accumulated result.

We give the add method its correct implementation: it accumulates any given Money objects in the self.moneys array. And we add an initial value of 0 to our call to func tools.reduce. This ensures that the code works even when there is an empty array.

All tests are now green.

Committing Our Changes

We have the addition feature implemented for Money entities in the same currency. This suggests the appropriate message for our next commit to our local Git repository:

```
git add .
git commit -m "feat: addition feature for Moneys in the same currency done"
```

We now have three commits in our Git repository.

Where We Are

We started to tackle the problem of adding different representations of Money. This new feature requires us to introduce a new entity to our code, which we named Portfolio. (Addition of Money entities also requires introduction of exchange rates. Since that is too much to take on all at once, we used a divide-and-conquer strategy to first add two Money entities and evaluate the value of the Portfolio all in the same currency. This allows us to gently introduce the concepts of Portfolio and addition of Money entities.

This divide-and-conquer strategy means our Portfolio is far from finished. It needs to be enhanced to evaluate correctly when the Money entities in it have different currencies, as well as when the currency of evaluation is different.

Also, we can't help noticing that our source code is growing as we accrete tests and features. No surprises there! However, it's getting a bit too long to all be in one file. We need to restructure our code: separating the test code from the production code would be a good start.

For now, let's take a deep breath and celebrate crossing one more item from our feature list, before we pick up the next item.

~~5 USD × 2 = 10 USD~~
~~10 EUR × 2 = 20 EUR~~
~~4002 KRW / 4 = 1000.5 KRW~~
~~5 USD + 10 USD = 15 USD~~
5 USD + 10 EUR = 17 USD
1 USD + 1100 KRW = 2200 KRW
Remove redundant Money multiplication tests

The code for this chapter is in a branch named "chap03" in the GitHub repository (*https://github.com/saleem/tdd-book-code/tree/chap03*).

PART II

Modularization

CHAPTER 4

Separation of Concerns

> "Separation of concerns" ... is what I mean by "focusing one's attention upon some aspect": it does not mean ignoring the other aspects, it is just doing justice to the fact that from this aspect's point of view, the other is irrelevant. It is being one- and multiple-track minded simultaneously.
>
> —Edsger Dijkstra, "On the Role of Scientific Thought" (*https://oreil.ly/BS8Uv*)

Our source code has grown. Depending on the language, it's 50–75 lines in one source file. That's more than a screenful on many display monitors, and certainly more than a printed page in this book.

Before we get to the next feature, we'll spend some time refactoring our code. That's the subject of this and the next three chapters.

Test and Production Code

Thus far, we've written two different types of code.

1. Code that *solves our Money problem*. This includes `Money` and `Portfolio` and all the behavior therein. We call this *production code*.
2. Code that *verifies that the problem is correctly solved*. This includes all the tests and the code needed to support these tests. We call this *test code*.

There are similarities between the two types of code: they are in the same language, we write them in quick succession (through the by now familiar red-green-refactor cycle), and we commit both to our code repository. However, there are a few key differences between the two types of code.

Unidirectional Dependency

Test code has to depend on production code—at least on those parts of production code that it tests. However, there should be no dependencies in the other direction.

Currently, all our code for each language is in one file, as shown in Figure 4-1. So it's not easy to ensure that there are no accidental dependencies from production code to test code. There is an implicit dependency from the test code to the production code. This has a couple of implications:

1. When writing code, we have to be careful to not accidentally use any test code in our production code.

2. When reading code, we have to recognize the patterns of usage and also notice the *missing* patterns, i.e., the fact that production code cannot call any test code.

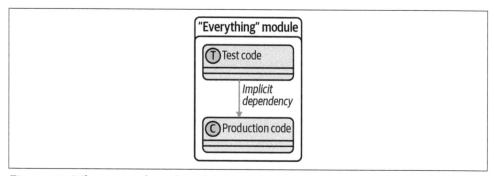

Figure 4-1. When test code and production code are in the same module, the dependency from the former to the latter is implicit

 Test code depends on production code; however, there should be no dependency in the other direction.

If production code is dependent on test code, what are the possible bad results? In particularly bad cases, it can mislead us to a path where the code path that is tested is "pristine" whereas the paths that are not tested are fraught with bugs. Figure 4-2 shows a portion of the pseudocode for the engine control unit in a car. The code works differently if the engine is being tested for emissions compliance than when the engine is being used "in the real world."

```
1   if isEmissionsTest:
2       setEngineControlUnitParams(LOW_EMISSIONS_MODE)
3 · else:
4       setEngineControlUnitParams(HIGH_PERFORMANCE_MODE)
```

Figure 4-2. Accidental dependency of production code on test code can create production code paths that behave differently and in untested ways

If you're skeptical that such a blatant case of "be on your best behavior for tests" could ever happen in reality, you're encouraged to read about the Volkswagen emissions scandal, from which the pseudocode in Figure 4-2 is drawn.[1]

Having a unidirectional dependency—where production code does not depend on test code in any way and is therefore not susceptible to behaving differently when under test—is vital to ensuring defects of this nature (whether accidental or malicious) do not creep in.

Dependency Injection

Dependency injection is a practice to separate the creation of an object from its usage. It increases the cohesion of code and reduces its coupling.[2] Dependency injection requires different code units (classes and methods) to be independent from each other. Separating test and production code is an important prerequisite to facilitating dependency injection.

We'll have more to say about dependency injection in Chapter 11, where we'll use it to improve the design of our code.

Packaging and Deployment

When application code is packaged for deployment, the test code is almost always packaged separately from production code. This allows deploying production and test code independently. Often, only production code is deployed in certain "higher" environments such as the production environment. This is shown in Figure 4-3.

---

1 On the Volkswagen "dieselgate" scandal, Felix Domke has done a lot of work. He's coauthored a whitepaper (*https://oreil.ly/Rhsht*). He also delivered a keynote at the Chaos Computer Club conference (*https://oreil.ly/DA7fd*).

2 Cohesion and coupling are described in more detail in Chapter 14.

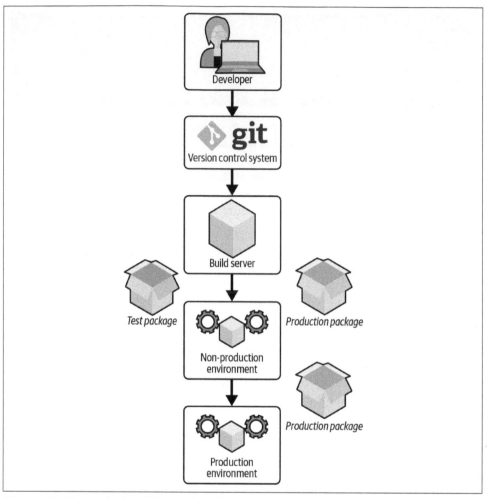

Figure 4-3. Test code should be packaged separately from production code so that they can be deployed independently via the CI/CD pipeline

We'll describe deployment in more detail in Chapter 13, when we build a continuous integration pipeline for our code.

Modularization

The first thing we'll do is to separate the test code from the production code. This will require us to solve the problem of *including*, *importing*, or *requiring* the production code in the test code. It is vital that this should always be a one-way dependency, as shown in Figure 4-4.

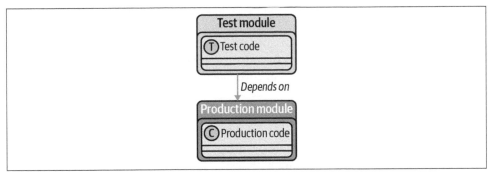

Figure 4-4. Only test code should depend on production code, not the other way around

In practice, this means that the code should be modularized along these lines:

1. The test and production code should be in separate source files. This allows us to read, edit, and focus on test or production code independently.

2. The code should use namespaces to clearly identify which entities belong together. A namespace may be called a "module" or a "package," depending on the language.

3. Insofar as it's possible, there should be an explicit code directive—import, require, or similar, depending on the language—to indicate that one module depends on another. This ensures that we can specify the dependency shown in Figure 4-1 explicitly.

We'll also look for opportunities to make code more self-describing. This would include renaming and reordering entities, methods, and variables to better reflect their intent.

Removing Redundancy

The second thing we'll do is to remove redundancy from our tests.

We have had two multiplication tests for a while now: one for euros and one for dollars. They test the same functionality. In contrast, we have only one test for division. Should we keep both the multiplication tests?

There is seldom an ironclad "yes" or "no" answer to this. We could argue that the two tests protect us from inadvertently hardcoding the currency in the code that does the multiplication—although that argument would be weakened by the fact that we have one test for division and a similar hardcoded currency error could crop up there.

To make our decision making more objective, here is a checklist:

1. Would we have the same code coverage if we delete a test? *Line coverage* is a measure of the number of lines of code that are executed when running a test. In our case, there would be no loss of coverage if we deleted either one of the multiplication tests.

2. Does one of the tests verify a significant edge case? If, for example, we were multiplying a really large number in one of our tests and our goal was to ensure that there was no overflow/underflow on different CPUs and operating systems, we could make the case for keeping both tests. However, that is also not the case for our two multiplication tests.

3. Do the different tests provide unique value as living documentation? For example, if we were using currency symbols from beyond the alphanumeric character set ($, €, ₩), we could say that displaying these disparate currency symbols provides additional value as documentation. However, we are currently using letters drawn from the same 26 letters of the English alphabet (USD, EUR, KRW) for our currencies, so the variation between currencies provides minimal documentation value.

Line (or *statement*) *coverage*, *branch coverage*, and *loop coverage* are three different metrics (*https://oreil.ly/Zs4vN*) that measure how much of a given body of code has been tested.

Where We Are

In this chapter, we reviewed the significance of separation of concerns and removing redundancy. These are the two goals that will garner our attention in the following three chapters.

Let's update our feature list to reflect that:

~~5 USD × 2 = 10 USD~~
~~10 EUR × 2 = 20 EUR~~
~~4002 KRW / 4 = 1000.5 KRW~~
~~5 USD + 10 USD = 15 USD~~
Separate test code from production code
Remove redundant tests
5 USD + 10 EUR = 17 USD
1 USD + 1100 KRW = 2200 KRW

Our goals are clear. The steps to accomplish these—especially the first goal of separation of concerns—will vary significantly from language to language. Therefore, the implementation has been separated into the next three chapters:

- Chapter 5, "Packages and Modules in Go"
- Chapter 6, "Modules in JavaScript"
- Chapter 7, "Modules in Python"

Read these chapters in the order that makes most sense to you. Refer to "How to Read This Book" on page xix for guidance.

Packages and Modules in Go

> Go programs are constructed by linking together packages. A Go package in turn is constructed from one or more source files...
>
> —The Go Programming Language Specification (*https://oreil.ly/YWhHE*)

In this chapter, we'll do a few things that clean up our Go code. We'll look at the Go module we created back in Chapter 0 and see its purpose in separating code. Then we'll do the work to separate our test code from our production code using packages. Finally, we'll remove some redundancy from our code, making things compact and meaningful.

Separating Our Code into Packages

Let's begin by separating our test code from our production code. This entails two separate tasks:

1. Separating test code from production code.
2. Ensuring the dependency is only from the test code to the production code.

We have production code for Money and Portfolio sitting next to our test code in one file—money_test.go. Let's first create two new files named money.go and portfo lio.go. We'll put both these files in the $TDD_PROJECT_ROOT/go folder. Next, we move code for the relevant classes, Money and Portfolio, to their appropriate files. This is how portfolio.go looks:

```
package main

type Portfolio []Money
```

```go
func (p Portfolio) Add(money Money) Portfolio {
    p = append(p, money)
    return p
}

func (p Portfolio) Evaluate(currency string) Money {
    total := 0.0
    for _, m := range p {
        total = total + m.amount
    }
    return Money{amount: total, currency: currency}
}
```

The file money.go, not shown here, similarly contains the Money struct and its methods.

If we run our tests now, they're all green. Yay! Because everything is in the main package, we didn't have to do anything special to access Portfolio and Money code from our tests. In particular, we don't have to add any import statements to our test class, like the one we have to import the testing module.

We have separated the source code into separate *files*, but what about higher-level organization of code? We'd like to group Portfolio and Money together in a namespace to indicate they both pertain to the "stock" market—another term borrowed from our domain.

Before we do this separation, let's take a look at how modules and packages work in Go.

Go Modules

A Go program typically consists of multiple source files. Each Go source file declares the package to which it belongs. That declaration is in the very first line of code in the file. For all three of our source files, the declaration is package main, specifying that all our code currently resides in the main package.

In general, a Go code repository comprises exactly one module. This module includes multiple packages, which in turn contain several files each.

 Module support is a fast-evolving feature and a topic of great interest in Go. This book uses *module mode* (*https://oreil.ly/WyyaQ*), which is the default (and favored) style in Go v1.13 onward. The older style, using GOPATH, is largely incompatible with Go modules. GOPATH-style is not used in this book.

Any program that has to run as an application—i.e., any files with a main() function —*must* be in the main package. There *may* be other files containing structs, functions, types, etc. also in the main package. And there *may* be other packages. This general structure of a Go program is shown in Figure 5-1.

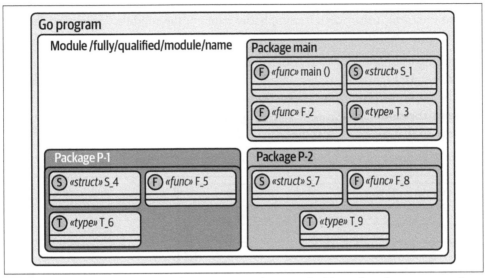

Figure 5-1. Structure of a typical Go program, showing the hierarchy of program module, packages, and files

 We run our tests using go test . command. We do not need to run anything the via the go run command—which would have required a main() method in the main package. That's why we don't have a main() method anywhere.

Our program has these (and only these) files in our go folder:

```
go
├── go.mod
├── money.go
├── money_test.go
└── portfolio.go
```

We generated the go.mod file back in Chapter 0, by running the go mod init tdd command. Here are the contents of the go.mod file, shown in their glorious entirety:

```
module tdd

go 1.17
```

We are reminded of the fact that our module is named tdd every time we run our tests. The last couple of lines of every successful test run are virtually identical:

```
PASS
ok      tdd ...  ❶
```

❶   The execution time, omitted here, is also shown for actual test runs.

That tdd in the last line isn't an appreciation for our newly acquired skill (although it's fine to interpret it that way); it's simply the name of the module declared in the first line of the go.mod file.

Inside this tdd module, all our code is in the main package. Because everything is in the same package, there is no need to import either of our classes—Money or Portfolio—in our test code. The test code is able to "see" these classes by virtue of being in the same package. The only import statement we need is for the testing package so that we may access the struct T defined in it.

Figure 5-2 shows the current structure of our code.

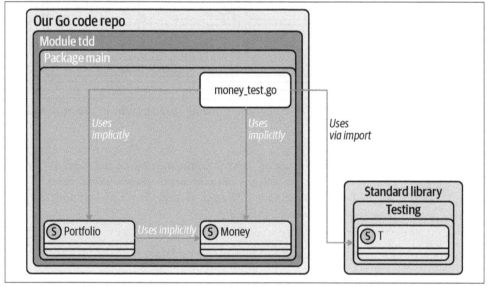

Figure 5-2. The test and production code are in the main package; therefore, the dependencies among them are implicit and do not require import statements

Creating a Package

We have separate source files, but all our code is still in one and the same package—main. Let's now separate our production code into a new package.

We create a subfolder named stocks under go/src folder and move the files money.go and portfolio.go into it. Our folder structure looks like this:

```
go
├── go.mod
├── money_test.go
└── stocks
    ├── money.go
    └── portfolio.go
```

The folder stocks takes on added significance by being a subfolder in a module—it is also a package. This means that the files in it now belong to a package whose name is also stocks. We can see evidence of this if we try to run our tests from the go folder—we get a bunch of undefined: Money and undefined: Portfolio errors. We need to modify our source files to reflect the new package structure.

In portfolio.go and money.go, we replace the top line, which currently says package main, with the correct package name:

```
package stocks
```

In money_test.go, we add an import statement for our newly created package using its fully qualified name: tdd/stocks. The import section in test_money now looks like this:

```
import (
    "testing"
    "tdd/stocks"
)
```

The fully qualified name of a package starts with the module name containing the package.

Hmm...we still have all the errors we got last time, plus an additional one: imported and not used: "tdd/stocks". In fact, the go test tool seems to give up after printing a handful of errors and politely tells us too many errors at the end. Things are not trending in the right direction, as they say in the stock market!

We spot a hint: the *other* package we have imported since the very beginning, test ing, requires us to prefix the package name before referring to the struct T. We need to do the same to refer to the structs within our stocks folder. Since tdd/stocks is a long and rather unwieldy name, we first give it an alias s.

```
import (
    "testing"
    s "tdd/stocks" ❶
)
```

❶ We use s as an alias for the tdd/stocks package.

We change all references to Money and Portfolio in test_money.go to s.Money and s.Portfolio. For example, here's the signature of the assertEqual method:

```
func assertEqual(t *testing.T, expected s.Money, actual s.Money) { ❶
    ...
}
```

❶ Prefixing all occurrences of Money and Portfolio with s.—the package name alias

Are we done? Let's run our tests and see.

Yelp! There are "too many errors," repeatedly informing us that amount and currency are no longer accessible:

```
... cannot refer to unexported field 'amount'
        in struct literal of type stocks.Money
... cannot refer to unexported field 'currency'
        in struct literal of type stocks.Money
...
... too many errors
```

Looks like moving the Money struct into its own package has caused reference errors because Money's fields are no longer in scope. What should we do?

Encapsulation

This is exactly where we wanted to be! Previously, because all the code was in the same (i.e., main) package, everything was freely accessible to everything else. By packaging Money and Portfolio in the stocks package, we are now compelled to think about encapsulation.

We'd like to specify the amount and currency fields in the Money struct *once* when creating the struct, but they will not be modifiable thereafter. In software parlance, we'd like to make the Money struct *immutable*. The way to do this is to provide some additional behavior to Money:

~~Make amount and currency accessible only from within Money struct and not from outside~~

Create a public New function to initialize the Money struct

We have already—and somewhat inadvertently—accomplished the first item on this list. Let's do the other one.

"Immutability" is a design dictum that requires that the state of an entity be defined exactly once—when it's created—and not modified thereafter. It's a cornerstone of functional programming and a useful idiom across programming languages.

To the `money.go` file, let's add a function named `NewMoney`. It takes an `amount` and a `currency`, creates a `Money` struct from these two values, and returns it:

```go
func NewMoney(amount float64, currency string) Money {
    return Money{amount, currency}
}
```

Notice that we *can* access the fields of the `Money` struct in `NewMoney`, because this function is in the same package as `Money`.

Now let's change all the occurrences in `money_test.go` where `Money` is created to call `NewMoney` instead:

```go
fiveDollars := s.NewMoney(5, "USD")
```

We change all occurrences, taking extra care to keep the same parameter values for all these calls to `NewMoney`!

After correctly changing all such occurrences, we get back to green tests. Splendid!

That's all fine and dandy, but there is a bit of curious behavior. We cannot *access* the fields in the `Money` struct from outside the `stocks` package, so how are we able to successfully *compare* different `Money` structs in the `assertEqual` method?

The answer lies in the way Go compares two different structs when the `==` and `!=` operators are used. Two structs are equal if all the corresponding fields of both are equal. Thus, it is possible to compare `Money` structs without being able to directly access their fields from outside the package where the struct is defined.

Some Go types, like slices, maps, and functions, are inherently non-comparable and will raise a compilation error if we attempt to compare Go structs (*https://oreil.ly/bdftH*) containing them.

Removing Redundancy in Tests

We have two tests for multiplication, and one each for division and addition.

Given the criteria in Chapter 4, let's delete the `TestMultiplicationInDollars`. This way, we have three tests, each one for a different currency. We'll rename the remaining multiplication test as `TestMultiplication`.

Committing Our Changes

We have added code and moved files around. It's particularly important to commit our changes to our Git repo:

```
git add .
git commit -m "refactor: moved Money and Portfolio to stocks Go package"
```

The output should verify that three files were changed:

```
[main b67ab66] refactor: moved Money and Portfolio to stocks Go package
 3 files changed, 75 insertions(+), 71 deletions(-)
 rewrite go/money_test.go (69%) ❶
 create mode 100644 go/stocks/money.go
 create mode 100644 go/stocks/portfolio.go
```

❶ The 69% is the similarity index: the percentage of the file that's unchanged.

Where We Are

We revisited the `tdd` module we generated in Chapter 0. We created a new package named `stocks` and moved all the production code into this package. Partitioning code this way forced us to explicitly indicate the dependency from test code to production code—and ensure that there is no dependency in the other direction. We also deleted one of the tests that didn't add much value.

Figure 5-3 shows the resulting structure of our code.

> The code for this chapter is in a branch named "chap05" in the GitHub repository (*https://github.com/saleem/tdd-book-code/tree/chap05*).

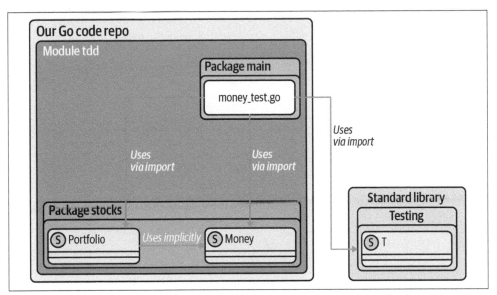

Figure 5-3. The production code is now in its own package; therefore, the dependency from test code to production code is explicitly declared

CHAPTER 6

Modules in JavaScript

A module is a function or object that presents an interface but that hides its state and implementation.

—Douglas Crockford, *JavaScript: The Good Parts* (O'Reilly, 2008)

In this chapter, we'll take several actions that clean up and improve our JavaScript code. We'll separate our test code from our production code using JavaScript modules. There are several ways to write modules in JavaScript—we'll look at four different styles and their applicability to our code. We'll turn our attention to how our test code is organized, then improve how it runs and the output it produces. Finally, we'll remove some redundancy in our tests. That's a lot of work, so let's get to it!

Separating Our Code into Modules

Let's separate the `Money` and `Portfolio` classes from the test code. We create two new files named `money.js` and `portfolio.js` in the same folder as `test_money.js` and move the relevant code there. Here's our new folder structure:

```
js
├── money.js
├── portfolio.js
└── test_money.js
```

This is how `portfolio.js` looks:

```
class Portfolio {
    constructor() {
        this.moneys = [];
    }

    add(...moneys) {
        this.moneys = this.moneys.concat(moneys);
```

```
        }

        evaluate(currency) {
            let total = this.moneys.reduce((sum, money) => {
                return sum + money.amount;
            }, 0);
            return new Money(total, currency);
        }
    }
```

The file money.js, not shown here, similarly contains the Money class and its methods.

When we now run our tests by executing node js/test_money.js from the TDD_Project_Root folder, we get our old friend, ReferenceError:

```
ReferenceError: Money is not defined
```

Now that the classes Money and Portfolio are in their own files, they are no longer accessible from the test code. What to do?

We take a hint from our test code: we use the require statement to access the assert library. Can we require both Money and Portfolio?

Yes, we can! However, before we do that, we first have to export those classes from their respective files.

At the very end of money.js, let's add a line to export the Money class:

```
module.exports = Money;
```

Similarly, we add a module.exports statement at the end of portfolio.js file:

```
module.exports = Portfolio;
```

Now, at the top of test_money.js, let's add two require statements:

```
const Money = require('./money');
const Portfolio = require('./portfolio');
```

What happens when we run our tests now? We get the ReferenceError again:

```
.../portfolio.js:14
            return new Money(total, currency);
            ^

ReferenceError: Money is not defined
```

Wait: the error is now being reported in the portfolio.js file. Of course! Portfolio depends on Money, so we need to specify this dependency at the top of portfolio.js file, too:

```
const Money = require('./money');
```

After all these changes, our tests are passing again. Yay!

Separating our code into modules makes the dependency tree of our code clearer. Figure 6-1 shows the dependencies.

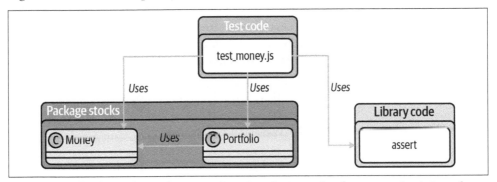

Figure 6-1. The dependency diagram of our JavaScript code after separating it into three source files

A Segue into JavaScript Modules

Modules—components of code packaged as a unit to promote reuse—are a well-understood concept in many programming languages. JavaScript is no different. Except, perhaps, in having multiple ways in which modules can be specified and (re)used.

ES5 and earlier editions of ECMAScript did not define modules. However, the need to modularize code was very pressing and very real; therefore, different flavors of modules emerged over time.

CommonJS

CommonJS (*https://oreil.ly/XxydR*) is the style favored by Node.js. It's also the style used in the JavaScript code shown in this chapter.

CommonJS uses a `module.exports` statement in each source file (i.e., module) containing an object—which could be a class, a function, or a constant—that other modules need. Those other modules then have a `require` statement before they can use that dependent object. Although the `require` statement can be put anywhere before the first use of the dependency, it's customary to put all `require` statements in a group at the top of the file.

Asynchronous Module Definition (AMD)

The asynchronous module definition (AMD) specification (*https://oreil.ly/wvpS9*), as its name implies, facilitates the asynchronous loading of multiple modules. This means modules can be loaded separately (and many at a time, if possible) instead of sequentially (one after the other). This asynchronous loading is highly desirable when JavaScript code runs in a web browser, as it can noticeably improve the responsiveness of web pages and websites. This is shown in Figure 6-2.

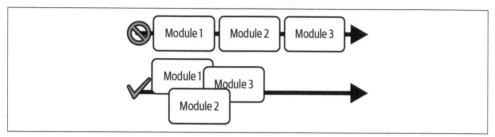

Figure 6-2. Asynchronous module definition allows modules to be loaded separately and concurrently (image from Wikipedia.org, courtesy Ле Лой)

AMD is not supported out of the box by Node.js. A couple of popular implementations of AMD are RequireJS (*https://requirejs.org*) and Dojo Toolkit (*https://oreil.ly/t0kYT*). RequireJS is available as a Node.js package, whereas Dojo Toolkit can be installed via Bower (*https://bower.io*), which is yet *another* package management system (similar to Node.js).

From the previous paragraph, it may appear that grafting AMD on top of a Node.js app is a bit of work. That is because of a couple of fundamental decisions that the designers of Node.js and AMD have taken about the respective styles:

Server-side module management: optimized for correctness
> Node.js, whose runtime is designed for building server-side apps outside the confines of a web browser,[1] strongly favors the CommonJS style of defining module dependencies. CommonJS ensures deterministic loading of modules, which means that modules may wait on other modules to load. This is best illustrated by the way Node.js's CommonJS implementation ensures that even cyclical dependencies—which are, in general, a bad choice—are resolved predictably (*https://oreil.ly/HNLyS*). This waiting is less of a concern on the server, because there are other mechanisms to improve application performance (e.g., statelessness and horizontal scaling).

---

1 The "Hello World" example on Node.js is an HTTP server, betraying its preference for backend apps (*https://oreil.ly/fddE8*).

Client-side module management: optimized for speed

The AMD style, which is optimized for use in browsers, is built around the idea of asynchronous loading—it's right there in the name! Loading modules *as fast as possible* is vital in JavaScript code that runs in a web browser, because any latency due to slow loading is painfully obvious to the human user.

Because of the contrasting needs of running JavaScript on a server versus running it inside a web browser, the two module-definition styles—CommonJS and AMD—are optimized in different ways.

This book does not show the AMD style of module management because its Java-Script code is of a client-side flavor—it's intended to be run inside a web browser.

Universal Module Definition (UMD)

Universal module definition (UMD) is a design pattern and not an official specification. Think of it as a societal convention (like shaking hands with the right hand) and not a law (like driving on the left side of the road in Ireland). The pattern consists of two parts: an immediately invoked function expression (IIFE) and an anonymous function that creates a module. A robust implementation of this design pattern accounts for different libraries (such as AMD or CommonJS) and exports the function accordingly. Implementing AMD with such fallback features usually results in more lines of code. The code snippet below shows how to use UMD to export and import the Money class:[2]

```
// -----------------------------------
// money.js (entire file)
// -----------------------------------
(function (root, factory) {
    if (typeof define === "function" && define.amd) {
        define("Money", [], factory);
    } else {
        root.Money = factory();
    }
}(this, function () {
    class Money {
        constructor(amount, currency) {
            this.amount = amount
            this.currency = currency
        }
        times(multiplier) {
            return new Money(this.amount * multiplier, this.currency)
        }
        divide(divisor) {
            return new Money(this.amount / divisor, this.currency)
```

---

2 This UMD pattern is inspired by this code sample (*https://oreil.ly/ZQfRl*).

```
        }
    };

    return Money;
}));

// ------------------------------------
// test_money.js (one example usage)
// ------------------------------------
const m = require('./money');
let fiveDollars = new m.Money(5, "USD");
```

Because of the relative verbosity of the UMD pattern, this book eschews its use.

ESModules

As the name implies, ESModules (*https://oreil.ly/qNbsc*) is the standard promoted by ECMAScript. It is syntactically similar to CommonJS with a few differences. There is an `export` keyword, which can be used to export anything—e.g., a `class`, `var`, or `function`—from a module. Instead of `require`, an `import` statement allows a dependent module to import and use another module that it needs.

Node.js has supported ESModules for a few versions. Versions v14 and v16, referenced in this book, support it fully. To use ESModules instead of the default CommonJS, we need to do the following steps:

1. *Either* rename our source files to end in `.mjs` instead of `.js` *or* add a `package.json` file with `{ "type": "module" }` in our source folder.

2. Declare and export modules using directives like `export class Money`.

3. Import modules using directives like `import {Money} from './money.mjs';`.

This code snippet shows how to use ESModules. It shows the files as renamed to end with `.mjs` (which is simpler because it does not require the creation of a `package.json` file):

```
// -----------------------------------
// portfolio.mjs (entire file)
// -----------------------------------
import {Money} from './money.mjs';

export class Portfolio {
    constructor() {
        this.moneys = [];
    }
    add() {
        this.moneys = this.moneys.concat(Array.prototype.slice.call(arguments));
    }
```

```
    evaluate(currency) {
        let total = this.moneys.reduce( (sum, money) => {
            return sum + money.amount;
          }, 0);
        return new Money(total, currency);
    }
}

// ----------------------------------
// test_money.mjs (example usage only)
// ----------------------------------
import * as assert from 'assert';
import {Money} from './money.mjs';
import {Portfolio} from './portfolio.mjs';

let fifteenDollars = new Money(15, "USD");
let portfolio = new Portfolio();
portfolio.add(fiveDollars, tenDollars);
assert.deepStrictEqual(portfolio.evaluate("USD"), fifteenDollars);
```

Improving Our Tests

The most obvious problem plaguing our tests is that they have a loose, almost accidental structure. There is no organization in test functions, no encapsulation of data used by each test. We have one JavaScript file with almost two dozen statements, four of which happen to be calls to `assert` methods. That's about it.

Another smaller problem is that we have two tests for multiplication, and one each for division and addition. The two tests for multiplication test the same feature, albeit with different currencies.

JavaScript has several test libraries and frameworks. Appendix B describes a few of them. As stated in Chapter 0, we shun all of these, settling on using the `assert` package within Node. Without the structure enforced by a library or framework, how can we add structure to our code to make it modular?

In particular, we'd like the items listed in Table 6-1.

Table 6-1. List of improvements to our tests

Item	Description
1	Remove one of the two multiplication tests.
2	Organize tests in a class comprising test methods with names that reflect the intent of each test.
3	Allow us to run all the test methods automatically, including any future tests we write.
4	Produce succinct output when tests run successfully (while preserving the verbose messages we already get when tests fail).
5	Run all subsequent tests even if an earlier one fails with an `AssertionError`.

Let's take a brief sojourn to make these improvements to our test code. What's more, we'll use TDD to accomplish the aforementioned goals. (That should come as no surprise, since we're roughly halfway into a book on TDD!)

Removing Redundancy in Tests

Let's first delete the line of code that asserts multiplication in dollars, taking care to *not* delete the variables named fiveDollars and tenDollars, which we need for our Portfolio test. Let's move these variables closer to that test. We now have three tests, segmented out by empty lines:

```
const assert = require('assert');
const Money = require('./money');
const Portfolio = require('./portfolio');

let tenEuros = new Money(10, "EUR");
let twentyEuros = new Money(20, "EUR");
assert.deepStrictEqual(tenEuros.times(2), twentyEuros);

let originalMoney = new Money(4002, "KRW");
let actualMoneyAfterDivision = originalMoney.divide(4);
let expectedMoneyAfterDivision = new Money(1000.5, "KRW");
assert.deepStrictEqual(actualMoneyAfterDivision, expectedMoneyAfterDivision);

let fiveDollars = new Money(5, "USD");
let tenDollars = new Money(10, "USD");
let fifteenDollars = new Money(15, "USD");
let portfolio = new Portfolio();
portfolio.add(fiveDollars, tenDollars);
assert.deepStrictEqual(portfolio.evaluate("USD"), fifteenDollars);
```

This is a good starting point for adding some structure.

Adding a Test Class and Test Methods

How should we make changes to our test code, using the principles of test-driven development?

We have one thing going for us: we have green tests right now. We can refactor either our production code or our test code using TDD as long as we run our tests frequently. The current behavior of tests is that if we don't get *any* output, it could indicate one of these scenarios:

- All tests ran successfully.

or

- One or more broken tests didn't run.

That's why item 3 in Table 6-1 is important.

Since silence ≠ success, we'll adopt a TDD strategy tailored to our situation, as shown in Table 6-2.

Table 6-2. Modified RGR strategy to improve the behavior of our tests

Step	Description	RGR phase
1	Run our tests *first* before we make any changes, verifying that all tests pass.	*GREEN*
2	Improve our test code, with a preference for keeping all changes small. Run our tests *again*, observing if there are any failures.	*REFACTOR*
3	If there are no failures, we *deliberately* break our tests one at a time by modifying the `assert` statements. We'll run the tests *a third time* to verify that the expected error messages are in the output.	*RED*
4	When we are satisfied that the tests indeed produce output when broken, we revert the deliberately induced errors. This ensures the tests pass again. We're ready to recommence the RGR cycle.	*GREEN*

Notice that the three phases of RGR still occur, and in the same order. The only difference is that, because our tests are currently silent when they pass, we will *deliberately* break them in the *red* phase to ensure that we're making progress.

Does the third step, where we *deliberately* break the tests, seem odd? It's appropriate to remember the purpose of tests, so aptly captured by Dijkstra in *Software Engineering Techniques* (*https://oreil.ly/PsRDt*):

> Testing shows the presence, not the absence of bugs.

Temporarily changing production code to *deliberately* break a unit test is a nifty trick. It reassures us that the test is reliably run as part of the suite and that it indeed executes the particular line(s) of production code. Remember to revert the code so the test returns to green!

We'll repeat the steps listed in Table 6-2 until we accomplish all remaining items in Table 6-1.

Let's add a class named `MoneyTest` in `test_money.js`. Let's also move the three code blocks into three methods named `testMultiplication`, `testDivision`, and `testAddition` respectively. Here's how our newly minted class looks:

```
const assert = require('assert');
const Money = require('./money');
const Portfolio = require('./portfolio');

class MoneyTest {
  testMultiplication() {
    let tenEuros = new Money(10, "EUR");
    let twentyEuros = new Money(20, "EUR");
    assert.deepStrictEqual(tenEuros.times(2), twentyEuros);
```

```
    }
    testDivision() {
      let originalMoney = new Money(4002, "KRW")
      let expectedMoneyAfterDivision = new Money(1000.5, "KRW")
      assert.deepStrictEqual(originalMoney.divide(4), expectedMoneyAfterDivision)
    }

    testAddition() {
      let fiveDollars = new Money(5, "USD");
      let tenDollars = new Money(10, "USD");
      let fifteenDollars = new Money(15, "USD");
      let portfolio = new Portfolio();
      portfolio.add(fiveDollars, tenDollars);
      assert.deepStrictEqual(portfolio.evaluate("USD"), fifteenDollars);
    }
}
```

This runs so silently that we wonder if it's running at all! Let's follow the modified RGR cycle described in Table 6-2 and break one of the assertions deliberately. In `test Multiplication`, we change the 2 to 2000:

```
      assert.deepStrictEqual(tenEuros.times(2000), twentyEuros);
```

There is still no output. This proves that we're not running any of the tests. Let's add a `runAllTests()` method to the class and call it outside the class:

```
class MoneyTest {
  testMultiplication() {
...
  }
  testDivision() {
...
  }

  testAddition() {
...
  }

  runAllTests() {
    this.testMultiplication();
    this.testDivision();
    this.testAddition();
  }
}

new MoneyTest().runAllTests();
```

Now we get the expected error from our deliberately broken test:

```
    code: 'ERR_ASSERTION',
    actual: Money { amount: 20000, currency: 'EUR' },
    expected: Money { amount: 20, currency: 'EUR' },
```

Let's revert the deliberately broken test back to its correct form.

When we run our class now, the tests run. We've accomplished item 2 in Table 6-1.

Discovering and Running Tests Automatically

We'd like to create a mechanism whereby we can automatically discover all the tests and then run them. This can be broken down into two parts:

1. Discover the names of all the test methods in our class (i.e., methods that start with **test** because that's our naming convention).

2. Execute these methods one by one.

Let's tackle part 2 first. If we had the names of all our test methods in an array, we could use the `Reflect` object in standard library to execute them.

 The Reflect object (*https://oreil.ly/qrYw7*) in ES6 provides Reflection capabilities (*https://oreil.ly/wM6P3*). It allows us to write code that can inspect, execute, and even modify itself.

Let's add a new method to `MoneyTest` that simply returns an array of strings, where each string is the name of one of our test methods:

```
getAllTestMethods() {
  let testMethods = ['testMultiplication', 'testDivision', 'testAddition'];
  return testMethods;
}
```

Yes, this is not "discovering the names of all the test methods" that we said in part 1! We'll get to this shortly.

We can now call `Reflect.get` and `Reflect.apply` in `runAllTests` to call our test methods in succession:

```
runAllTests() {
  let testMethods = this.getAllTestMethods(); ❶
  testMethods.forEach(m => {
    let method = Reflect.get(this, m); ❷
    Reflect.apply(method, this, []); ❸
  });
}
```

❶ Get names of all test methods.

❷ Get the `method` object for each test method name via reflection.

❸ Invoke the test method with no arguments on this object.

We first call the getAllTestsMethods to get the test method names. For each name, we get the method object by calling Reflect.get. We invoke this method by calling Reflect.apply. The second parameter to Reflect.apply is the object on which the method is invoked, which is this instance of TestMoney. The last parameter to Reflect.apply is an array of any parameters required to invoke method—which, in our case, is always an empty array because none of our tests methods require any parameters.

When we run our tests now, they still run. Deliberately breaking the tests one by one—pursuant to the strategy described in Table 6-2—yields the expected error messages.

Turning our attention to part 1: we're *executing* our tests methods using reflection, but we're not *finding* their names automatically. Let's improve our getAllTest Methods method to discover all methods whose names start with test:

```
getAllTestMethods() {
  let moneyPrototype = MoneyTest.prototype; ❶
  let allProps = Object.getOwnPropertyNames(moneyPrototype); ❷
  let testMethods = allProps.filter(p => {
    return typeof moneyPrototype[p] === 'function' && p.startsWith("test"); ❸
  });
  return testMethods;
}
```

❶ Get the prototype for this MoneyTest object.

❷ Get all the properties defined on the MoneyTest prototype (but not any inherited ones).

❸ Retain only those functions whose names start with test, filtering out all the rest.

 The Object.getOwnPropertyNames (*https://oreil.ly/LAAsj*) method returns an array of all properties—including methods—found directly in a given object. It does not return inherited properties (*https://oreil.ly/vN029*).

We call the Object.getOwnPropertyNames to get all the properties defined for Money Test.prototype. Why the prototype and not simply MoneyTest? It is because *Java-Script (as well as ES6) has prototype-based inheritance*, not class-based inheritance as in many other languages. The methods declared within the MoneyTest class are in reality attached to the object reachable via the prototype property of MoneyTest.

ECMAScript is a language with prototype-based inheritance (*https://oreil.ly/Hxdrj*).

Next, we iterate over all the properties of MoneyTest and select all (and only) those that are of type function and start with test. Because of our naming convention, these are our test methods. We return this array of test method names.

Running our tests validates that all of them are indeed still executing. We verify this by deliberately breaking each of them and observing the assertion failures that show up. That's the top three items in Table 6-1 accomplished.

Produce Output When Tests Run Successfully

Throughout this section, as we worked through the items described in Table 6-1, we had to deliberately break our tests to verify that they were still running as we made changes to test_money.js. This is the modified RGR cycle described in Table 6-2. It would be really nice if we got a brief output upon success, instead of the absolute silence we currently have when the tests are green. (There is a "Soylent Green" joke in there somewhere!)

Let's add a simple output line to the runAllTests method that prints the name of each test before executing it:

```
runAllTests() {
    let testMethods = this.getAllTestMethods();
    testMethods.forEach(m => {
        console.log("Running: %s()", m); ❶
        let method = Reflect.get(this, m);
        Reflect.apply(method, this, []);
    });
}
```

❶ Print the name of the method before invoking it.

Now, when we run our tests, we get a short and meaningful message even when tests are green:

```
Running: testMultiplication()
Running: testDivision()
Running: testAddition()
```

Run All Tests Even When an Earlier Test Assertion Fails

As we were following the modified RGR cycle described in Table 6-2, we noticed that when we deliberately break a test that runs first (e.g., `TestMultiplication`), the subsequent tests don't run at all. This can be misleading because the first failing test may not be the only failing test. When test-driving code, it's vital to be aware of the broad impact of any change, not a myopic perspective that gets us fixated on the first problem that shows up.

We'd like our test class to run *all* the tests, even when one or more of them fail.

The reason the first assertion failure stops the test execution is that we're not handling the `AssertionError`s that are thrown. We could catch `AssertionError`s and log them to the console. Let's add a `try ... catch` block around the `Reflect.apply` call in our `runAllTests` method to do just that:

```
runAllTests() {
  let testMethods = this.getAllTestMethods();
  testMethods.forEach(m => {
    console.log("Running: %s()", m);
    let method = Reflect.get(this, m);
    try { ❶
      Reflect.apply(method, this, []);
    } catch (e) {
      if (e instanceof assert.AssertionError) { ❷
        console.log(e);
      } else {
        throw e; ❸
      }
    }
  });
}
```

❶ Surround the method invocation in a `try ... catch` block.

❷ Log only `AssertionError`s.

❸ Rethrow all other errors.

We catch all errors. However, we only output `AssertionError`s to the console; we rethrow the rest. (We do not want to inadvertently interfere with other errors, such as the `TypeError`s and `ReferenceError`s we've already seen.)

After this change, all our tests run every time we run `MoneyTest`. For example, when we deliberately break `testMultiplication`, the other tests—`testDivision` and `testAddition`—run successfully after the assertion error.

```
Running: testMultiplication()
AssertionError [ERR_ASSERTION]: Expected values to be strictly deep-equal:
+ actual - expected

  Money {
+   amount: 20,
-   amount: 2000,
    currency: 'EUR'
  }
...
Running: testDivision()
Running: testAddition()
```

Sweet! We've accomplished all the items in Table 6-1.

Committing Our Changes

We have added new files and redistributed code among them. This is a particularly good time to commit our changes to our local Git repository:

```
git add .
git commit -m "refactor: created Money and Portfolio modules; improved tests"
```

The output should validate our changes:

```
[main 5781251] refactor: created Money and Portfolio modules; improved tests
 3 files changed, 84 insertions(+), 50 deletions(-)
 create mode 100644 js/money.js
 create mode 100644 js/portfolio.js
 rewrite js/test_money.js (95%) ❶
```

❶ The 95% is the similarity index: the percentage of the file that's unchanged.

Where We Are

In this chapter, we separated our code by creating modules for Money and Portfolio. The separation allowed us to explicitly specify our dependencies and to ensure there are no dependencies from production code to test code.

Of the several module definition styles and standards available in JavaScript, we chose the CommonJS style—which is the default for NodeJS apps. Going forward, we'll keep this style of module definition for the remainder of this book.

We also saw how to adopt the UMD and ESModules styles in our code.

We improved the organization of our tests by introducing a test class, test methods, and a mechanism to run all tests automatically. The tests now produce output when they pass (succinctly) and when they fail (verbosely). We also ensured that all tests run even when some of them fail early due to assertion errors. Finally, we cleansed our code by removing a redundant multiplication test.

 The code for this chapter is in a branch named "chap06" in the GitHub repository (*https://github.com/saleem/tdd-book-code/tree/chap06*).

CHAPTER 7

Modules in Python

> A module is a file containing Python definitions and statements.
>
> —The Python Tutorial (*https://oreil.ly/NiHEn*)

In this chapter, we'll do a few things to improve the organization of our Python code. We'll separate our test code from our production code using modules. We'll see how the scoping and import rules in Python help us ensure the dependencies in our code are correct. Finally, we'll remove a redundant test from our code, making things compact and meaningful.

Separating Our Code into Modules

We have production code for `Money` and `Portfolio` right next to our test code in the same file. We need to separate this code into individual source files.

Let's first create two new files named `money.py` and `portfolio.py` in the same folder as `test_money.py`. Our folder structure looks like this:

```
py
├── money.py
├── portfolio.py
└── test_money.py
```

We move the code for `Money` and `Portfolio` classes to `money.py` and `portfolio.py`, respectively. This code segment shows the complete contents of `portfolio.py` after this code relocation:

```
import functools
import operator

class Portfolio:
    def __init__(self):
        self.moneys = []

    def add(self, *moneys):
        self.moneys.extend(moneys)

    def evaluate(self, currency):
        total = functools.reduce(operator.add,
                                 map(lambda m: m.amount, self.moneys), 0)
        return Money(total, currency)
```

Notice that we carry the two `import` statements along with the code for the Portfolio class, because `Portfolio` uses `functools` and `operator`.

The file `money.py`, not shown here, similarly contains the `Money` class and its methods.

When we run our tests now, we get our old friend, `NameError` arising from our tests:

```
File "/Users/saleemsiddiqui/code/github/saleem/tdd-project/py/test_money.py",
      line 22, in testAddition
   fiveDollars = Money(5, "USD")
NameError: name 'Money' is not defined
```

We realize that the test class is dependent on both `Money` and `Portfolio`, so we add these `import` statements at the top of `test_money.py`:

```
from money import Money
from portfolio import Portfolio
```

Ah—we now get `NameError: name 'Money' is not defined` from within `Portfolio`! A quick look at `portfolio.py` shows that it depends on `Money`, too. So we add `from money import Money` to the top of `portfolio.py` and all tests become green. Yay!

Moving code around and adding `import` statements makes the dependency tree of our code clearer. Figure 7-1 shows the dependency diagram of our code.

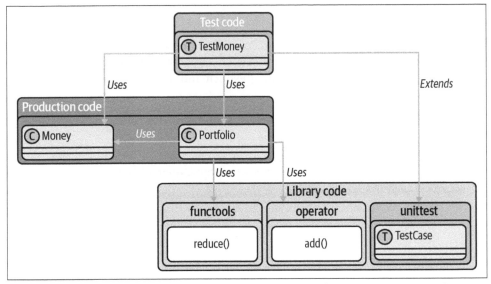

Figure 7-1. The dependency diagram of our Python code after separating it into three source files

Removing Redundancy in Tests

We currently have two tests for multiplication, and one each for division and addition. The two tests for multiplication test the same functionality in the Money class. This is a bit of duplication we can do without. Let's delete the testMultiplicationIn Dollars and shorten the name of the other test to testMultiplication. The resulting symmetry—three tests for the three features (multiplication, division, and addition) where each test uses a different currency (euros, wons, and dollars respectively)—is both compact and elegant.

Committing Our Changes

We have added a couple of new files and partitioned code among them. This is an especially opportune moment to commit our changes to our local Git repository:

```
git add .
git commit -m "refactor: moved Money and Portfolio classes their own Python files"
```

The output of these two commands should validate our changes:

```
[main c917e7c] refactor: moved Money and Portfolio classes their own Python files
 3 files changed, 30 insertions(+), 33 deletions(-)
 create mode 100644 py/money.py
 create mode 100644 py/portfolio.py
```

Where We Are

In this chapter, we separated `Money` and `Portfolio` into their own source files, which in Python, makes them their own modules. The separation ensures that the dependency from test code to production code is explicit and that there is no dependency in the other direction.

We also removed an extraneous test, thereby simplifying our code.

 The code for this chapter is in a branch named "chap07" in the GitHub repository (*https://github.com/saleem/tdd-book-code/tree/chap07*).

PART III

Features and Redesign

CHAPTER 8

Evaluating a Portfolio

Money itself isn't lost or made. It's simply transferred from one perception to another. Like magic.

—Gordon Gekko, *Wall Street* (the movie)

We've dallied around the question of how to convert the several Money entities in a Portfolio into a single currency. Let's dally no longer!

The next feature on our list is the one dealing with mixed currencies:

~~5 USD × 2 = 10 USD~~
~~10 EUR × 2 = 20 EUR~~
~~4002 KRW / 4 = 1000.5 KRW~~
~~5 USD + 10 USD = 15 USD~~
~~Separate test code from production code~~
~~Remove redundant tests~~
5 USD + 10 EUR = 17 USD
1 USD + 1100 KRW = 2200 KRW

Mixing Money

A heterogeneous combination of currencies demands that we create a new abstraction in our code: the conversion of money from one currency to another. This requires establishing some ground rules about currency conversions, drawn from our problem domain:

Conversion always relates a pair of currencies.

This is important because we want all conversions to be independent. It does happen in reality that multiple currencies are "pegged" to one single currency—which means that a particular exchange rate is fixed de jure.[1] Even in such cases, it's important to treat each pegged relationship as a distinct pair.

Conversion is from one currency to another with a well-defined exchange rate.

The exchange rate—the number of units of the "to" currency we get for one unit of the "from" currency—is a key component of currency conversion. The exchange rate is represented by a fractional number.

The two exchange rates between a pair of currencies may or may not be arithmetical reciprocals of each other.

For example: the exchange rate from EUR to USD may or may not be the mathematical reciprocal (i.e., $1/_x$) of the exchange rate from USD to EUR.

It is possible for a currency to have no defined exchange rate to another currency.

This could be because one of the two currencies is an inconvertible currency.[2]

Given that currency conversion involves all the above considerations, how should we implement it? The answer is: one test-driven scenario at a time!

We'll start by test-driving the scenario listed in the next item on our feature list: the conversion from EUR to USD. This will help us set up the scaffolding for the "convert" method and a single exchange rate from EUR to USD. Because exchange rates are unidirectional, we'll represent this particular one as "EUR→USD."

Starting with this one scenario means it's likely that we'll add more items to our feature list. That's all right—making controlled progress at a measured pace isn't a bad deal!

Go

Let's write our new test in `money_test.go` to represent addition of dollars and euros:

```
func TestAdditionOfDollarsAndEuros(t *testing.T) {
    var portfolio s.Portfolio

    fiveDollars := s.NewMoney(5, "USD")
    tenEuros := s.NewMoney(10, "EUR")
```

---

1 For an economic discussion of currency pegging, see Investopedia (*https://oreil.ly/MLoWf*).

2 Currencies can be inconvertible for a variety of reasons: economic, political, or martial (*https://oreil.ly/1IKvM*).

```
    portfolio = portfolio.Add(fiveDollars)
    portfolio = portfolio.Add(tenEuros)

    expectedValue := s.NewMoney(17, "USD") ❶
    actualValue := portfolio.Evaluate("USD")

    assertEqual(t, expectedValue, actualValue)
}
```

❶ The expected value of 17 USD assumes that we get 1.2 dollars for every euro we convert.

The test creates two Money structs representing 5 USD and 10 EUR, respectively. They are added to a newly created Portfolio struct. The actualValue from evaluating the Portfolio in dollars is compared with the expectedValue struct of 17 USD.

The test fails as expected:

```
... Expected {amount:17 currency:USD} Got {amount:15 currency:USD}
```

This validates what we know: the evaluate method simply adds the amounts of all Money structs (5 and 10 in our test) to get the result, regardless of the currencies involved (USD and EUR in our test).

What we need is to *first* convert the amount of each Money into the target currency and *then* add it:

```
    for _, m := range p { ❶
        total = total + convert(m, currency)
    }
```

❶ In Evaluate method

How should we write the convert method? The simplest thing that works is to return the amount when the currencies match and to arbitrarily multiply by the conversion rate required by our test otherwise:

```
func convert(money Money, currency string) float64 { ❶
    if money.currency == currency {
        return money.amount
    }
    return money.amount * 1.2 ❷
}
```

❶ New function in portfolio.go file

❷ Hardcoded exchange rate

The test turns green, but something doesn't seem right about our code! Specifically:

1. The exchange rate is hardcoded. It should be declared as a variable.
2. The exchange rate isn't dependent on the currency. It should be looked up based on the two currencies involved.
3. The exchange rate should be modifiable.

Let's address the first of these and add the remaining two to our feature list. We define a variable named eurToUsd in our convert method and use it:

```go
func convert(money Money, currency string) float64 {
    eurToUsd := 1.2 ❶
    if money.currency == currency {
        return money.amount
    }
    return money.amount * eurToUsd ❷
}
```

❶ Exchange rate is defined as an appropriately named variable.

❷ The exchange rate variable is used to convert currency.

The test is still green.

JavaScript

Let's start by adding a new test in MoneyTest to test the addition of dollars and euros:

```javascript
testAdditionOfDollarsAndEuros() {
  let fiveDollars = new Money(5, "USD");
  let tenEuros = new Money(10, "EUR");
  let portfolio = new Portfolio();
  portfolio.add(fiveDollars, tenEuros);
  let expectedValue = new Money(17, "USD"); ❶
  assert.deepStrictEqual(portfolio.evaluate("USD"), expectedValue);
}
```

❶ The expected value of 17 USD assumes that we get 1.2 dollars for every euro we convert.

The test creates two Money objects representing 5 USD and 10 EUR each. These are added to a Portfolio object. The value from evaluating the Portfolio in USD is compared with a Money object representing 17 USD.

The test fails as expected:

```
AssertionError [ERR_ASSERTION]: Expected values to be strictly deep-equal:
+ actual - expected
```

```
  Money {
+   amount: 15,
-   amount: 17,
    currency: 'USD'
  }
```

We expect this failure because the current implementation of the evaluate method simply adds the amount attribute of all Money objects, regardless of their currencies.

We need to *first* convert the amount of each Money into the target currency and *then* sum it:

```
evaluate(currency) {
    let total = this.moneys.reduce((sum, money) => {
        return sum + this.convert(money, currency);
    }, 0);
    return new Money(total, currency);
}
```

How should the convert method work? For now, the simplest implementation that works is one that returns amount when the currencies match and otherwise multiplies the amount by the conversion rate required by our test:

```
convert(money, currency) { ❶
    if (money.currency === currency) {
        return money.amount;
    }
    return money.amount * 1.2; ❷
}
```

❶ New method in Portfolio class

❷ Hardcoded exchange rate

The test is now green. That's progress, but not everything is hunky-dory. In particular:

1. The exchange rate is hardcoded. It should be declared as a variable.

2. The exchange rate isn't dependent on the currency. It should be looked up based on the two currencies involved.

3. The exchange rate should be modifiable.

Let's address the first of these right away and add the remaining to our feature list.

We define a variable named eurToUsd and use it in our convert method:

```
convert(money, currency) {
    let eurToUsd = 1.2; ❶
    if (money.currency === currency) {
```

```
        return money.amount;
    }
    return money.amount * eurToUsd; ❷
}
```

❶ Exchange rate is defined as an appropriately named variable.

❷ The exchange rate variable is used to convert currency.

All tests are green.

Python

Let's write a new test in `test_money.py` that validates adding dollars to euros:

```
def testAdditionOfDollarsAndEuros(self):
    fiveDollars = Money(5, "USD")
    tenEuros = Money(10, "EUR")
    portfolio = Portfolio()
    portfolio.add(fiveDollars, tenEuros)
    expectedValue = Money(17, "USD") ❶
    actualValue = portfolio.evaluate("USD")
    self.assertEqual(expectedValue, actualValue)
```

❶ The expected value of 17 USD assumes that we get 1.2 dollars for every euro we convert.

The test creates two `Money` objects representing 5 USD and 10 EUR, respectively. They are added to a pristine `Portfolio` object. The `actualValue` from evaluating the `Portfolio` in dollars is compared with a newly minted `expectedValue` of 17 USD.

We expect the test to fail, of course, because we are in the *red* phase of our of RGR cycle. However, the error message from the assertion failure is rather cryptic:

```
AssertionError:
    <money.Money object at 0x10f3c3280> != <money.Money object at 0x10f3c33a0>
```

Who on earth knows what mysterious goblins reside at those obscure memory addresses!

This is one of those times where we must slow down and write a better failing test before we attempt to get to *green*. Can we make the assertion statement print a more helpful error message?

The `assertEqual` method—like most other assertion methods in the `unittest` package—takes an optional third parameter, which is a custom error message. Let's provide a formatted string showing the stringified representation of `expectedValue` and `actualValue`:

```
        self.assertEqual(
            expectedValue, actualValue, "%s != %s" % (expectedValue, actualValue)
        ) ❶
```

❶ Last line of `testAdditionOfDollarsAndEuros` test method

Nope! That simply prints the obscure memory addresses *twice*:

```
AssertionError:
    <money.Money object at 0x1081111f0> != <money.Money object at 0x108111310> :
    <money.Money object at 0x1081111f0> != <money.Money object at 0x108111310>
```

What we need to do is to override the __str__ method in the Money class and make it return a more human-readable representation, something like "USD 17.00."

```
        def __str__(self): ❶
            return f"{self.currency} {self.amount:0.2f}"
```

❶ In Money class

We format Money's `currency` and `amount` fields, printing the latter up to two decimal places.

After adding the __str__ method, let's run our test suite again:

```
AssertionError: ... USD 17.00 != USD 15.00
```

Ah, *much* better! Seventeen dollars certainly isn't the same thing as 15 dollars!

 Python's F-strings interpolation provides a succinct and neat way to format strings with a mixture of fixed text and variables. F-strings were defined in PEP-498 (*https://oreil.ly/2n7xJ*) and have been a part of Python since version 3.6.

This validates our belief that the `evaluate` method, as currently implemented, mindlessly adds the amounts of all Money objects (5 and 10 in our test) to get the result, with no regard to the currencies (USD and EUR, respectively, in our test).

A closer examination of the `evaluate` method shows that the mindlessness is in the lambda expression. It maps every Money object to its `amount`, regardless of its currency. These amounts are then added up by the `reduce` function using the `add` operator.

What if the lambda expression mapped every Money object to its converted value? The target currency for the conversion would be the currency in which the Portfolio is being evaluated:

```
total = functools.reduce(
    operator.add, map(lambda m: self.__convert(m, currency), self.moneys), 0
) ❶
```

❶ In `Portfolio.evaluate` method

 Python doesn't have truly "private" scope for variables or functions. The naming convention and something called "name mangling" ensure that names with two leading underscores are treated as private (*https://oreil.ly/SSu9D*).

How should we implement the __convert method? Converting to the same `currency` as that of the `Money` is trivial: the `Money`'s amount doesn't change in this case. When converting to a different currency, we'll multiply `Money`'s amount with the (for now) hardcoded exchange rate between USD and EUR:

```
def __convert(self, aMoney, aCurrency): ❶
    if aMoney.currency == aCurrency:
        return aMoney.amount
    else:
        return aMoney.amount * 1.2 ❷
```

❶ New method in `Portfolio` class

❷ Hardcoded exchange rate

The test is green. Yay…and hmm! We should do the refactoring to remove the ugliness of this code. Here are some problems with it:

1. The exchange rate is hardcoded. It should be declared as a variable.

2. The exchange rate isn't dependent on the currency. It should be looked up based on the two currencies involved.

3. The exchange rate should be modifiable.

Let's address the first of these three items in the *refactor* phase and add the remaining two to our feature list.

We define a private variable named _eur_to_usd in the __init__ method and use it instead of the hardcoded value in the __convert method:

```
class Portfolio:
    def __init__(self):
        self.moneys = []
        self._eur_to_usd = 1.2 ❶
    ...
    def __convert(self, aMoney, aCurrency):
        if aMoney.currency == aCurrency:
            return aMoney.amount
        else:
            return aMoney.amount * self._eur_to_usd ❷
```

❶ Exchange rate is defined as an appropriately named variable.

❷ The exchange rate variable is used to convert currency.

All tests are green.

Committing Our Changes

We have our first implementation of converting money between two different currencies, specifically USD → EUR. Let's commit our changes to our local Git repository:

```
git add .
git commit -m "feat: conversion of Money from EUR to USD"
```

Where We Are

We have solved the conversion of Money entities in different currencies for the scenario of converting USD to EUR. However, we cut a few corners while doing so. The conversion only works for one specific case (USD → EUR). Furthermore, there is no way to add or modify exchange rates.

Let's update our feature list to cross out the accomplished items and add the new ones:

~~5 USD × 2 = 10 USD~~

~~10 EUR × 2 = 20 EUR~~

~~4002 KRW / 4 = 1000.5 KRW~~

~~5 USD + 10 USD = 15 USD~~

~~Separate test code from production code~~

~~Remove redundant tests~~

~~5 USD + 10 EUR = 17 USD~~

1 USD + 1100 KRW = 2200 KRW

Determine exchange rate based on the currencies involved (from → to)

Allow exchange rates to be modified

> The code for this chapter is in a branch named "chap08" in the GitHub repository (*https://github.com/saleem/tdd-book-code/tree/chap08*).

CHAPTER 9

Currencies, Currencies, Everywhere

Small change, small wonders—these are the currency of my endurance and ultimately of my life.

—Barbara Kingsolver

Here's the current state of our evaluate feature vis-à-vis Money entities in a Portfolio:

1. When converting a Money in a currency to the *same* currency, it returns the amount of the Money. This is correct: the exchange rate for any currency to itself is 1.

2. In all other cases, the amount of the Money is multiplied by a fixed number (1.2). This is correct in a very limited sense: this rate ensures conversions from USD to EUR only. There is no way to modify this exchange rate or specify any other rate.

Our currency conversion code does one thing correctly and another thing almost correctly. It's time to make it work correctly in both cases. In this chapter, we'll introduce—at long last—the conversion of money from one currency into another using currency-specific exchange rates.

Making a Hash(map) of Things

What we need is a hashmap that allows us to look up exchange rates given a "from" currency and a "to" currency. The hashmap would be a representation of an exchange rate table we regularly see in banks and currency exchange counters at airports, as shown in Table 9-1.

Table 9-1. Exchange rate table

From	To	Rate
EUR	USD	1.2
USD	EUR	0.82
USD	KRW	1100
KRW	USD	0.00090
EUR	KRW	1344
KRW	EUR	0.00073

To read this table, use this pattern: given an amount in the "from" currency, multiply by the "rate" to get the equivalent amount in the "to" currency.

As noted in Chapter 8, the mutual rates for any pair of currencies are *not* arithmetical reciprocals of each other.[1] Let's use an example to illustrate this point: based on the rates given in Table 9-1, if we convert 100 EUR to USD and back to EUR, we'll get 98.4 EUR, not the original 100 EUR we started with. This is common for exchange rate tables; it's one way that banks make money![2]

The next couple of items on our feature list give us the opportunity to build out an implementation of the exchange rate table in our code. We'll do this by introducing a new currency:

~~5 USD × 2 = 10 USD~~

~~10 EUR × 2 = 20 EUR~~

~~4002 KRW / 4 = 1000.5 KRW~~

~~5 USD + 10 USD = 15 USD~~

~~Separate test code from production code~~

~~Remove redundant tests~~

~~5 USD + 10 EUR = 17 USD~~

1 USD + 1100 KRW = 2200 KRW

Determine exchange rate based on the currencies involved (from → to)

Allow exchange rates to be modified

---

1 The arithmetic reciprocal of a fraction *a/b* is the fraction *b/a*, assuming that neither *a* nor *b* is zero. For example, the reciprocal of 6/5 (i.e., 1.2) is 5/6 (~0.833).

2 This is putatively more legal than the "penny-rounding subroutine" that the three protagonists use to make money in the now-classic movie *Office Space*!

As we introduce the additional currency, we'll see the *transformation priority premise* *(TPP)* in action. That is, instead of adding more conditional code in a Tower of Babel style if-else chain, we'll introduce a new data structure that allows us to *look up* the exchange rate.[3]

The transformation priority premise (*https://oreil.ly/p2WQt*) states that as tests get more specific, the production code gets more generic through a series of transformations.

Go

Let's write a new test. This test will also involve multiple currencies—like our last one. We'll name it after the two currencies used in this case:

```go
func TestAdditionOfDollarsAndWons(t *testing.T) {
    var portfolio s.Portfolio

    oneDollar := s.NewMoney(1, "USD")
    elevenHundredWon := s.NewMoney(1100, "KRW")

    portfolio = portfolio.Add(oneDollar)
    portfolio = portfolio.Add(elevenHundredWon)

    expectedValue := s.NewMoney(2200, "KRW") ❶
    actualValue := portfolio.Evaluate("KRW")

    assertEqual(t, expectedValue, actualValue)
}
```

❶ The expected value of 2,200 KRW assumes that we get 1,100 won for every dollar we convert.

The test fails, of course. The error message is interesting:

```
... Expected {amount:2200 currency:KRW} Got {amount:1101.2 currency:KRW}
```

Since we don't yet have any mechanism to choose the correct exchange rates, our con vert method chose the incorrect eurToUsd rate, producing the odd result of 1101.2 KRW.

---

3 Fred Brooks has analyzed the biblical Tower of Babel narrative in a chapter of his classic book *The Mythical Man-Month* (Addison-Wesley, 1975). Brooks said that the Tower project failed because of lack of clear *communication* and *organization*—two things that are also missing from a long chain of if-else statements.

Let's introduce a `map[string]float64` to represent the exchange rates. We will initialize this map with the two exchange rates needed by our tests: EUR->USD: 1.2 and USD->KRW: 1100. For now, let's keep this map local to the `convert` method:

```
exchangeRates := map[string]float64{ ❶
    "EUR->USD": 1.2,
    "USD->KRW": 1100,
}
```

❶ In the `convert` method, at the very top

Instead of always multiplying `money.amount` by `eurToUsd` (which is 1.2) in `convert`, we can use the "from" and "to" currencies to create a key and look up the exchange rate. We delete the line defining the `eurToUsd` variable and replace the final `return` statement with this lookup and calculation:

```
key := money.currency + "->" + currency ❶
return money.amount * exchangeRates[key]
```

❶ In the `convert` method, at the very bottom

With these changes to the `convert` method, all our tests pass.

Out of curiosity: what will happen if we try to evaluate a `Portfolio` in a currency for which the relevant exchange rates are not specified? Let's momentarily comment out both the entries in the `exchangeRates` map:

```
exchangeRates := map[string]float64{ ❶
    // "EUR->USD": 1.2,
    // "USD->KRW": 1100,
}
```

❶ Temporarily comment out all entries in `exchangeRates` as an experiment.

When we run the tests now, we get assertion errors in both of our addition tests:

```
=== RUN    TestAdditionOfDollarsAndEuros
    ...    Expected {amount:17 currency:USD} Got {amount:5 currency:USD} ❶
--- FAIL: TestAdditionOfDollarsAndEuros (0.00s)
=== RUN    TestAdditionOfDollarsAndWons
    ...    Expected {amount:2200 currency:KRW} Got {amount:1100 currency:KRW} ❶
--- FAIL: TestAdditionOfDollarsAndWons (0.00s)
```

❶ With no entries in `exchangeRates`, a value of 0 is used in every call to the `convert` method.

It's clear from the actual values (printed after `Got`) that when an entry isn't found in our map, an exchange rate of 0 is used, effectively burning the `Money` that needs to be converted into an ash pile!

In Go, an attempt to get a map entry with a nonexistent key will return the "default zero" value (*https://oreil.ly/ePwNY*)—e.g., 0 (or 0.0) for `int` or `float`, `false` for `boolean`, `""` for `string`, etc.

Looks like we need better error handling. We'll add this to our feature list. (Let's not forget to revert the two commented out lines of code!)

JavaScript

Let's write a test in `test_money.js` for our new scenario, converting dollars to wons:

```
testAdditionOfDollarsAndWons() {
  let oneDollar = new Money(1, "USD");
  let elevenHundredWon = new Money(1100, "KRW");
  let portfolio = new Portfolio();
  portfolio.add(oneDollar, elevenHundredWon);
  let expectedValue = new Money(2200, "KRW"); ❶
  assert.deepStrictEqual(portfolio.evaluate("KRW"), expectedValue);
}
```

❶ The expected value of 2,200 KRW assumes that we get 1,100 won for every dollar we convert.

The test fails with an interesting error message:

```
Running: testAdditionOfDollarsAndWons()
AssertionError [ERR_ASSERTION]: Expected values to be strictly deep-equal:
+ actual - expected

  Money {
+   amount: 1101.2,
-   amount: 2200,
    currency: 'KRW'
  }
```

The `convert` method is using the incorrect `eurToUSD` rate, even though we don't have any euros in our test. That's how we ended up with the funny amount of `1101.2`.

Let's introduce a `Map` to represent the exchange rates. The two entries we define in the map are those needed by our tests: EUR->USD is `1.2` and USD->KRW is `1100`. For now, we'll keep this map inside the `convert` method:

```
let exchangeRates = new Map(); ❶
exchangeRates.set("EUR->USD", 1.2);
exchangeRates.set("USD->KRW", 1100);
```

❶ In the `convert` method, at the top

We can delete the line defining the eurToUsd variable and use this exchangeRates map instead. We use the "from" and "to" currencies to create a key and look up the exchange rate. The last two lines of convert embody this logic:

```
let key = money.currency + "->" + currency; ❶
return money.amount * exchangeRates.get(key);
```

❶ In the convert method, at the bottom

With this improvement, all our tests are green again.

What if we try to evaluate a Portfolio in a currency for which the relevant exchange rates are unspecified? Let's momentarily comment out both the entries in the exchangeRates map:

```
// exchangeRates.set("EUR->USD", 1.2); ❶
// exchangeRates.set("USD->KRW", 1100);
```

❶ Temporarily comment out all entries in exchangeRates as an experiment.

Both of our addition tests fail with assertion errors:

```
Running: testAdditionOfDollarsAndEuros()
AssertionError [ERR_ASSERTION]: Expected values to be strictly deep-equal:
+ actual - expected

  Money {
+   amount: NaN,
-   amount: 17,
    currency: 'USD'
  }
...
Running: testAdditionOfDollarsAndWons()
AssertionError [ERR_ASSERTION]: Expected values to be strictly deep-equal:
+ actual - expected

  Money {
+   amount: NaN,
-   amount: 2200,
    currency: 'KRW'
  }
```

When an entry isn't found in our map, the exchangeRate lookup value is undefined. The arithmetic operation of multiplying a number (money.amount) with this undefined is "not a number" (i.e., NaN).

 In JavaScript, an attempt to get a map entry with a nonexistent key will always return undefined (*https://oreil.ly/B9p4K*) as the value.

Let's revert the two commented out lines to get back to a green test suite. We'll add the need for better error handling to our feature list.

Python

Let's write a test in `test_money.py` to reflect our new feature—converting dollars to wons:

```python
def testAdditionOfDollarsAndWons(self):
    oneDollar = Money(1, "USD")
    elevenHundredWon = Money(1100, "KRW")
    portfolio = Portfolio()
    portfolio.add(oneDollar, elevenHundredWon)
    expectedValue = Money(2200, "KRW") ❶
    actualValue = portfolio.evaluate("KRW")
    self.assertEqual(
        expectedValue, actualValue, "%s != %s" % (expectedValue, actualValue)
    )
```

❶ The expected value of 2,200 KRW assumes that we get 1,100 won for every dollar we convert.

This test predictably fails. The error message gives an insight into what's wrong:

```
AssertionError: ... KRW 2200.00 != KRW 1101.20
```

The __convert method is using the rate `eurToUsd`, which is incorrect for this case. That's where the peculiar amount `1101.20` comes from.

Let's introduce a dictionary to store exchange rates. We'll add the two entries we need currently: `EUR->USD: 1.2` and `USD->KRW: 1100`. We'll keep this dictionary in the __convert method to begin with:

```python
exchangeRates = {'EUR->USD': 1.2, 'USD->KRW': 1100} ❶
```

❶ In the __convert method, at the top

We can delete the `self.eur_to_usd` variable and use the values in this dictionary instead. We create a key using the "from" and "to" currencies and look up the exchange rate. The `else:` block in __convert changes to the code shown below:

```python
else:
    key = aMoney.currency + '->' + aCurrency ❶
    return aMoney.amount * exchangeRates[key]
```

❶ In the __convert method, at the bottom

With these changes, all our tests turn green again.

Out of curiosity: what if we try to evaluate a `Portfolio` in a currency when the necessary exchange rates are not specified? Let's temporarily remove all entries from the `exchangeRates` map in the `convert` method, making it empty:

```
exchangeRates = {} ❶
```

❶ Temporarily delete all entries in `exchangeRates` as an experiment.

When we run our tests, both the addition tests fail with `KeyErrors`:

```
ERROR: testAdditionOfDollarsAndEuros (__main__.TestMoney)
...
KeyError: 'EUR->USD'
...
ERROR: testAdditionOfDollarsAndWons (__main__.TestMoney)
...
KeyError: 'USD->KRW'
```

In Python, a missing key in a dictionary causes a `KeyError` when a lookup is performed.

> In Python, an attempt to get a dictionary entry via the key-lookup operator [] with a nonexistent key will always raise a KeyError (*https://oreil.ly/P6fHs*).

We need to improve error handling in our code. We'll add this to our feature list. (Let's not forget to restore two values to the `exchangeRates` dictionary!)

Committing Our Changes

We now have the ability to define multiple exchange rates and convert between arbitrary currencies accordingly. Our Git commit message should reflect this new feature:

```
git add .
git commit -m "feat: conversion between currencies with defined exchange rates"
```

Where We Are

Our code has progressed to the point where we can maintain a `Portfolio` of disparate `Money` entities and evaluate it in multiple currencies, as long as the necessary exchange rates are known. That's nothing to sneer at!

We've also identified a need for more robust error handling, particularly when exchange rates are not specified. We'll add this to our list and turn our attention to it in Chapter 10:

~~5 USD × 2 = 10 USD~~

~~10 EUR × 2 = 20 EUR~~

~~4002 KRW / 4 = 1000.5 KRW~~

~~5 USD + 10 USD = 15 USD~~

~~Separate test code from production code~~

~~Remove redundant tests~~

~~5 USD + 10 EUR = 17 USD~~

~~1 USD + 1100 KRW = 2200 KRW#~~

~~Determine exchange rate based on the currencies involved (from → to)~~

Improve error handling when exchange rates are unspecified

Allow exchange rates to be modified

 The code for this chapter is in a branch named "chap09" in the GitHub repository (*https://github.com/saleem/tdd-book-code/tree/chap09*).

CHAPTER 10

Error Handling

What error drives our eyes and ears amiss?

> —William Shakespeare (through the tongue of Antipholus of Syracuse),
> *The Comedy of Errors*

Mistakes are a part of life. One of the reasons for adopting test-driven development is to ensure that we can go as fast as we *safely* can, minimizing bugs in code.

The next item on our feature list is to improve error handling:

~~5 USD × 2 = 10 USD~~

~~10 EUR × 2 = 20 EUR~~

~~4002 KRW / 4 = 1000.5 KRW~~

~~5 USD + 10 USD = 15 USD~~

~~Separate test code from production code~~

~~Remove redundant tests~~

~~5 USD + 10 EUR = 17 USD~~

~~1 USD + 1100 KRW = 2200 KRW#~~

~~Determine exchange rate based on the currencies involved (from → to)~~

Improve error handling when exchange rates are unspecified

Allow exchange rates to be modified

Error Wish List

The way our code currently handles missing exchange rates is buggy. Let's address this shortcoming. Table 10-1 shows our wish list for handling errors due to missing exchange rates.

Table 10-1. Wish list for handling errors due to missing exchange rates

Item	Description
1	The Evaluate method should signal an explicit error when one or more necessary exchange rates are missing.
2	The error message should be "greedy"—that is, it should indicate *all* the missing exchange rates that prevent a Portfolio from being evaluated, not just the first missing exchange rate.
3	To prevent the error from being ignored by the caller, no valid Money should be returned when an error happens due to missing exchange rates.

For instance, if we try to evaluate a portfolio in the currency "Kalganid,"[1] for which there are no defined exchange rates, we should get a detailed error message listing all the missing exchange rates.

Go

We'll need to change the signature of our convert and Evaluate methods when there is a missing exchange rate. We are currently returning only one value from these methods. To indicate an error—the inability to find an exchange rate—we need a second return value.

 In Go, the idiomatic way to indicate failure is to return an error as the last return value (*https://oreil.ly/aJgeV*) from a function or method so the caller can check for it.

Here is the pseudocode for how Evaluate and convert should collaboratively work using Go's idioms:

```
Evaluate:
    For each Money struct:
        Try to convert Money to target currency and add it to the total amount
            If convert returns an error:
                Capture the "from" and "to" currencies in "failures"
    If there are no failures:
        Return a Money struct with the total amount and target currency;
            return nil for error
    Otherwise:
        Return an empty Money struct; return an error message
            including all the failures
```

---

1 "Kalganid" is a fictitious currency in Isaac Asimov's Foundation series.

With this pseudocode sketched out, let's write a failing test in money_test.go. This test will be slightly different from the existing tests: it expects an error to be returned and compares the error message with an expected message:

```
func TestAdditionWithMultipleMissingExchangeRates(t *testing.T) {
    var portfolio s.Portfolio

    oneDollar := s.NewMoney(1, "USD")
    oneEuro := s.NewMoney(1, "EUR")
    oneWon := s.NewMoney(1, "KRW")

    portfolio = portfolio.Add(oneDollar)
    portfolio = portfolio.Add(oneEuro)
    portfolio = portfolio.Add(oneWon)

    expectedErrorMessage := ❶
        "Missing exchange rate(s):[USD->Kalganid,EUR->Kalganid,KRW->Kalganid,]"
    _, actualError := portfolio.Evaluate("Kalganid") ❷

    if expectedErrorMessage != actualError.Error() {
        t.Errorf("Expected %s Got %s",
            expectedErrorMessage, actualError.Error())
    }
}
```

❶ Expected error message should list each missing exchange rate; note the terminating comma.

❷ We don't care about the first return value, so we assign it to the blank identifier.

 Go's implicit semicolon rule requires a trailing comma in composite literals (*https://oreil.ly/7VQWS*). The trailing comma after the last exchange rate in our error message reflects this syntactic preference of Go.

This test is similar to the two existing tests for addition. We expect an error with the detailed message as the *second* return value from Evaluate method. We ignore the first return value by assigning it to the blank identifier.

We compare the expected and actual error messages directly in our test. We cannot use our assertEqual function, as it currently exists, because it can only compare Money structs. We should improve this assertEqual function; we'll defer it until the *refactor* phase.

In Go, we can assign any return value from a function to an underscore (_). This is the "blank identifier" (*https://oreil.ly/zC6pg*)—it effectively means "we don't care about this value."

This code doesn't compile. If we try to run it, we'll get an error in `money_test.go`:

```
... assignment mismatch: 2 variables but portfolio.Evaluate returns 1 values
```

To get this test to pass, we first have to change the signature of the `Evaluate` method to return two values, the second one being an `error`. How would `Evaluate` know when to return an `error`? It would know if one (or more) of the calls to `convert` failed, because `convert` is where any missing exchange rates would be detected. This means that we have to change the signature of the `convert` method, too.

Let's redesign the `convert` method first so that it returns a Boolean to indicate whether the rate was found or not:

```go
func convert(money Money, currency string) (float64, bool) { ❶
    exchangeRates := map[string]float64{
        "EUR->USD": 1.2,
        "USD->KRW": 1100,
    }
    if money.currency == currency {
        return money.amount, true
    }
    key := money.currency + "->" + currency
    rate, ok := exchangeRates[key]
    return money.amount * rate, ok
}
```

❶ Method signature changed to return two values

We modify the signature of `convert` to add a second return type: a `bool`. If the "from" and "to" currencies are the same, the conversion is trivial as before: we return the `money.amount` unchanged and a `true` as the second return value to indicate success. If the "from" and "to" currencies are different, we look up the exchange rate in our map. We use the success or failure of this lookup, captured in the ok variable, as the second return value of `convert` method.

In Go, when we look for a key in a map, the second return value is true if the key was found, false otherwise. Conventionally, the second return value is assigned to a variable named ok—hence the name of this idiom: "comma, ok" (*https://oreil.ly/AajSQ*).

We have modified convert's signature; we need to redesign Evaluate too:

```go
import "errors" ❶
...
func (p Portfolio) Evaluate(currency string) (Money, error) { ❷
    total := 0.0
    failedConversions := make([]string, 0)
    for _, m := range p {
        if convertedAmount, ok := convert(m, currency); ok {
            total = total + convertedAmount
        } else {
            failedConversions = append(failedConversions,
                m.currency+"->"+currency)
        }
    }
    if len(failedConversions) == 0 { ❸
        return NewMoney(total, currency), nil
    }
    failures := "["
    for _, f := range failedConversions {
        failures = failures + f + ","
    }
    failures = failures + "]"
    return NewMoney(0, ""),
        errors.New("Missing exchange rate(s):" + failures) ❹
}
```

❶ The errors package is needed to create errors.

❷ Method signature changed to return two values.

❸ If there are no failed conversions, a nil error is returned as the second value.

❹ If there are failed conversions, an error listing all the failed conversions is returned as the second value.

There are several new lines of code; however, they are a faithful representation of the pseudocode we sketched out earlier. Manufacturing the error message string from the failedConversions slice requires a second for loop, but is conceptually straightforward.

With these changes, we get compilation failures in the three *other* tests we have for addition. We get this error message, in triplicate:

```
... assignment mismatch: 1 variable but portfolio.Evaluate returns 2 values
```

Because we have changed the signature of Evaluate to return two values, we must also change the existing calls to this method to receive the second value, albeit with a "talk to the hand" blank identifier! One example is shown below:

```
actualValue, _ := portfolio.Evaluate("USD")  ❶
```

❶ Assigning the second return value to the blank identifier indicates we don't care about errors here.

With these changes, all the tests now pass.

Time to refactor: let's address the assertion if block in our newest test. We'd like to call the assertEqual method, but its signature currently requires two Money objects, whereas we want to compare two strings. The body of the method is fine as it is: it compares the two things it's given and prints a formatted error message if they're unequal.

Is there a way we could declare the two parameters to assertEqual in a more generic fashion?

Yes, there is. In Go, structs can implement one or more interfaces. The mechanism of this implementation is rather sublime: if a struct happens to be the receiver for all the methods defined in an interface, then it *automatically* implements that interface. There is no declaration in code explicitly saying "Hear ye! This struct hereby implements that interface." (There isn't a programmatic version of this town crier announcement, either.) Go's interfaces are an interesting blend of static typechecking and dynamic dispatch.

An interface in Go (*https://oreil.ly/Pclu0*) is implemented by anything—user-defined struct or built-in type—that implements all the methods in the interface.

Of particular interest is the *empty interface*, which defines exactly zero methods. Because the empty interface has no methods, it is implemented by *every type*.

In Go, the empty interface{} is implemented by *every* type.[2]

Since the empty interface is implemented by *every* type, we can change the signature of the assertEqual method to accept an expected value and an actual value, both of which are of the type interface{}. We can then happily pass in two strings or two Moneys, as we need:

---

2 To test empty Go interfaces, try this useful example in your browser (*https://tour.golang.org/methods/14*).

```
func assertEqual(t *testing.T, expected interface{}, actual interface{}) { ❶
    if expected != actual {
        t.Errorf("Expected %+v Got %+v", expected, actual)
    }
}
```

❶ The signature of this method is changed to accept two interface{}s, instead of two Moneys.

We can now replace the if block in TestAdditionWithMultipleMissingExchange Rates with a call to this modified assertEqual method:

```
func TestAdditionWithMultipleMissingExchangeRates(t *testing.T) {
...
    assertEqual(t, expectedErrorMessage, actualError.Error()) ❶
}
```

❶ Call to the modified assertEqual method; note that the last parameter is now actualError.Error(), to ensure type consistency with the second parameter.

Neat! The tests are still green, and we have fewer lines of code. We have accomplished the three items listed in Table 10-1.

There is still duplication in the code: the bits where we create the key in both convert and Evaluate. We need to simplify our code. We'll add this to our feature list.

JavaScript

We'd like to throw an error from evaluate with a detailed message when one or more exchange rates are not found. Let's write a test in test_money.js to describe the specific message this exception should have:

```
testAdditionWithMultipleMissingExchangeRates() {
    let oneDollar = new Money(1, "USD");
    let oneEuro = new Money(1, "EUR");
    let oneWon = new Money(1, "KRW");
    let portfolio = new Portfolio();
    portfolio.add(oneDollar, oneEuro, oneWon);
    let expectedError = new Error( ❶
        "Missing exchange rate(s):[USD->Kalganid,EUR->Kalganid,KRW->Kalganid]");
    assert.throws(function() {portfolio.evaluate("Kalganid")}, expectedError);
}
```

❶ Expected error message should list each missing exchange rate

This test is similar to the existing tests for addition, with the notable difference that we are trying to evaluate the Portfolio in "Kalganid." The assert.throws takes a reference to an anonymous function that calls the `evaluate` function as the first parameter and the `expectedError` as the second parameter.

 In JavaScript, we don't call the method under test as part of the `assert.throws` when we expect an exception to be thrown; otherwise the assert statement would itself fail to execute successfully. Instead, we pass an anonymous function object as the first parameter, which calls the method under test.

This test fails because our `evaluate` method currently doesn't throw the expected exception:

```
AssertionError [ERR_ASSERTION]: Missing expected exception (Error).
...
  code: 'ERR_ASSERTION',
  actual: undefined,
  expected: Error:
    Missing exchange rate(s):[USD->Kalganid,EUR->Kalganid,KRW->Kalganid]
```

We *could* write a trivial ("silly") conditional statement at the top of the `evaluate` method to get the test to pass. We *could* then write yet another test to force us toward the non-trivial ("better") implementation:

```
evaluate(currency) {
  ////////////////////////////////////////
  // We *could* do this; but let's not!
  ////////////////////////////////////////
  if (currency === "Kalganid") {
      throw new Error(
        "Missing exchange rate(s):[USD->Kalganid,EUR->Kalganid,KRW->Kalganid]");
  }
  ...
}
```

Let's see if we can speed things up by aiming for the non-trivial implementation right away.

In Chapter 9, we saw that when we query a `Map` in JavaScript with a key that doesn't exist, we get an `undefined` return value. We could implement `convert` in a similar way: return the converted amount when the rate is found, `undefined` otherwise.

```
convert(money, currency) {
    let exchangeRates = new Map();
    exchangeRates.set("EUR->USD", 1.2);
    exchangeRates.set("USD->KRW", 1100);
    if (money.currency === currency) {
        return money.amount;  ❶
    }
    let key = money.currency + "->" + currency;
    let rate = exchangeRates.get(key);
```

```
    if (rate === undefined) {
        return undefined; ❷
    }
    return money.amount * rate; ❸
}
```

❶ When "converting" Money from a currency to the same currency, simply return the amount as the result.

❷ When no exchange rate is found, return undefined as the result.

❸ When an exchange rate exists, use it to compute the converted amount.

In evaluate, we can check each call to convert while reducing the moneys array. If any conversions result in an undefined value, we note down the missing conversion key (i.e., the "from" and "to" currencies) in an array. At the end, we either return a new Money object as before if every conversion worked, or throw an error whose message contains the missing conversion keys if there were failures:

```
evaluate(currency) {
    let failures = [];
    let total = this.moneys.reduce( (sum, money) => {
        let convertedAmount = this.convert(money, currency);
        if (convertedAmount === undefined) {
            failures.push(money.currency + "->" + currency);
            return sum;
        }
        return sum + convertedAmount;
    }, 0);
    if (!failures.length) { ❶
        return new Money(total, currency); ❷
    }
    throw new Error("Missing exchange rate(s):[" + failures.join() + "]"); ❸
}
```

❶ Checking if there are no failures.

❷ If there are no failures, a new Money object with the correct amount and currency is returned.

❸ If there are conversion failures, an error listing all the failed conversions is returned.

The tests are all green and we've accomplished the items in Table 10-1.

There is a subtle unpleasant odor in our code, however. The duplication where we create the conversion key in both convert and evaluate is the source of this odor. We'll add this cleanup item to our feature list.

Python

We'd like to raise an `Exception` when `evaluate` fails due to missing exchange rates. In its message, the exception should describe all the missing exchange rate keys (i.e., the "from" and "to" currencies). Let's start with a test that validates this behavior.

Python has a refined class hierarchy for exceptions, errors, and warnings (*https://oreil.ly/TFi6D*). All user-defined exceptions should extend `Exception`.

```python
def testAdditionWithMultipleMissingExchangeRates(self):
    oneDollar = Money(1, "USD")
    oneEuro = Money(1, "EUR")
    oneWon = Money(1, "KRW")
    portfolio = Portfolio()
    portfolio.add(oneDollar, oneEuro, oneWon)
    with self.assertRaisesRegex(
        Exception,
        "Missing exchange rate\(s\):\[USD\->Kalganid,EUR->Kalganid,KRW->Kalganid]",
    ):
        portfolio.evaluate("Kalganid")
```

This test is similar to the existing tests for addition, with a couple of differences. First, we are attempting to `evaluate` a `Portfolio` in "Kalganid," for which no exchange rates exist. Second, we expect the `evaluate` method to throw an exception with a specific error message that we verify in the `assertRaisesRegex` statement.

`assertRaisesRegex` is one of the many useful assertion methods (*https://oreil.ly/Sg5KI*) defined in Python's `TestCase` class. Since our exception string has several characters that have special meaning in regular expressions (*https://oreil.ly/qtnQI*), we escape them using the backslash character.

The test fails with *two* exceptions. First, there's the `KeyError` that we expect: there is no exchange rate key involving the "Kalganid" currency. The second error is the assertion failure we sought to cause:

```
FAIL: testAdditionWithMultipleMissingExchangeRates (__main__.TestMoney)
------------------------------------------------------------------
KeyError: 'USD->Kalganid'

During handling of the above exception, another exception occurred:

...
AssertionError:
```

```
"Missing exchange rate\(s\):\[USD\->Kalganid,EUR->Kalganid,KRW->Kalganid]"
    does not match "'USD->Kalganid'"
```

This reveals that our test *is* throwing an Exception; however, the message in the Exception does not match what our test demands. Notice that the message in the Exception that *is* thrown is 'USD->Kalganid'—which is at least one part of our desired error message. We have a head start!

The 'USD->Kalganid' message is in the KeyError Exception that's raised when we look for a missing key in the dictionary of exchangeRates. Could we capture all such messages in evaluate and raise an Exception with the manicured message?

We need to modify our evaluate method to respond to exceptions arising from its calls to __convert. Let's unroll the lambda expression into a loop and add a try ... except block to capture any failures. If there are no failures, we return a new Money object as before. If there *are* failures, we raise an Exception whose message is a comma-separated list of the stringified KeyError exceptions that are caught:

```
def evaluate(self, currency):
    total = 0.0
    failures = []
    for m in self.moneys:
        try:
            total += self.__convert(m, currency)
        except KeyError as ke:
            failures.append(ke)

    if len(failures) == 0:
        return Money(total, currency) ❶

    failureMessage = ",".join(str(f) for f in failures)
    raise Exception("Missing exchange rate(s):[" + failureMessage + "]") ❷
```

❶ If there are no failures, a new Money object with the correct amount and currency is returned.

❷ If there are conversion failures, an Exception listing all the failed conversions is returned.

When we run our test now, we get an AssertionError:

```
AssertionError:
  "Missing exchange rate\(s\):\[USD->Kalganid,EUR->Kalganid,KRW->Kalganid\]"
    does not match
  "Missing exchange rate(s):['USD->Kalganid','EUR->Kalganid','KRW->Kalganid']" ❶
```

❶ Actual and expected values differ by the presence/absence of the ' single-quote character.

Ah! The difference is that the stringified `KeyError` contains single quotes that are missing from our desired message.

So close and yet so far! We are tempted to change our test to add the single quotes around each missing exchange-rate key. Should we do that?

On occasion, there may be valid reasons to change our requirements to match our result—if the change isn't that overwhelming, or the feature isn't that critical. We *could* mount both those arguments against further changes to the `evaluate` method in this case.

However, there is something icky about moving the goalposts after the game has started. And we are so close! A quick examination of the documentation of `KeyError` reveals that, like all subclasses of `BaseException`, it has an `args` property that contains a list of string arguments provided when the exception object is created. The first message in this list—at index 0—is the message we seek. A simple change to the way we assemble our `failureMessage` can fix our problem:

```
failureMessage = ",".join(f.args[0] for f in failures) ❶
```

❶ Using `f.args[0]` instead of `str(f)` removes the single-quote characters.

All the tests are now green, and we've accomplished what we set out to do: the items in Table 10-1. However, that icky feeling that things aren't great—that we don't have the simplest code that works—is still with us. For one thing, we unrolled our compact lambda expression into a verbose loop.[3] For another, we reached into the depths of a built-in `Exception` class to craft our error message.

We'll add an item to our list to refactor the part of our code dealing with exchange rates.

---

3 There is no trivial way to catch exceptions within a Python lambda. There was an enhancement proposal to Python—PEP 463—that was about this very feature. However, that proposal was rejected in 2014 (*https://oreil.ly/6PYuS*).

Committing Our Changes

The error handling we added to our code merits a commit to our local Git repository. Let's do this:

```
git add .
git commit -m "feat: improved error handling for missing exchange rates"
```

---

4 As with many other software terms, Martin Fowler's website has a useful page on the topic of "CodeSmell" (*https://oreil.ly/c7imn*).

Where We Are

We have added error handling to the way we evaluate our `Portfolio`. The resilience this brings to our code is no mean feat.

In doing so, however, we've gradually become aware of the clumsy way in which we've modeled exchange rates thus far. By keeping the implementation not just within `Portfolio` but within the evaluation of a `Portfolio`, we've strayed away from the elegance of simplicity.

Let's add a feature to our list to improve our implementation of exchange rates:

~~5 USD × 2 = 10 USD~~

~~10 EUR × 2 = 20 EUR~~

~~4002 KRW / 4 = 1000.5 KRW~~

~~5 USD + 10 USD = 15 USD~~

~~Separate test code from production code~~

~~Remove redundant tests~~

~~5 USD + 10 EUR = 17 USD~~

~~1 USD + 1100 KRW = 2200 KRW#~~

~~Determine exchange rate based on the currencies involved (from → to)~~

~~Improve error handling when exchange rates are unspecified~~

Improve the implementation of exchange rates

Allow exchange rates to be modified

The code for this chapter is in a branch named "chap10" in the GitHub repository (*https://github.com/saleem/tdd-book-code/tree/chap10*).

CHAPTER 11

Banking on Redesign

On the whole it's worth evolving your design as your needs grow...[1]

> —Martin Fowler, *Patterns of Enterprise Application Architecture* (Addison-Wesley, 2002)

We introduced the `Portfolio` entity back in Chapter 3. It represents a key concept from our domain, so we're justified in giving it some responsibility. Now, our `Portfolio` does too much work and it shows. Its primary job is to be a repository of `Money` entities. However, it has taken on the added responsibility of converting between currencies. To do this, it has to hold on to an exchange rate table *and* the logic to do the conversion. This doesn't look like the responsibility of a `Portfolio`. Monetary conversion has as much business being in a portfolio as peanut butter has being on top of a pizza.

Our software program has grown along with our needs. It is worth improving our design and looking for a better abstraction than the shoved-in way conversion between currencies is currently implemented.

A principle of domain-driven design (DDD) is continuous learning. When we learn something new about our domain, we let our design reflect our acquired knowledge. The resulting design and software should reflect our improved understanding of our domain.

---

1 Stated in the context of object-relational metadata mapping. However, it's good advice in general.

Domain-driven design is a discipline that's ably supported by TDD. Eric Evans' book of the same title (*https://oreil.ly/RBXVv*) is the seminal work on the subject.

By implementing currency conversion over the last few chapters, we have gained fresh insight into our program. It's missing a key entity. What is the name of the real-world institution that helps us exchange money? A bank. Or a currency exchange. Often, a domain will have multiple similar entities that are indistinguishable from the perspective of our model. Learning which differences are salient and which are insignificant is vital to effective domain modeling.

We'll select the name `Bank` to represent this missing entity. What should be the responsibilities of the `Bank`? It should hold exchange rates, for one thing. And it should be able to convert money between currencies based on the exchange rate. The `Bank` should allow asymmetric exchange rates, because they exist in the real world. Finally, the `Bank` should clearly inform us when it cannot exchange money in one currency into another currency because of a missing exchange rate. (Refer to "Mixing Money" on page 95 in Chapter 8, which lists ground rules for currency conversions.)

By being the entity that holds exchange rates, `Bank` will also deodorize our code. An odious smell is that the creation of keys for storing exchange rates—e.g., `USD->EUR`— is peppered throughout the `Portfolio`. This smell is a reliable indicator that we have a leaky abstraction. By keeping the exchange rate representation—keys and values— inside the `Bank`, we'll simplify the way `Portfolio` performs evaluation.

When responsibilities spill over from one entity into another where they don't belong, it's called a *leaky abstraction*. In Joel Spolsky's words: "All non-trivial abstractions, to some degree, are leaky" (*https://oreil.ly/1T3jZ*). However, gaping holes should be plugged through redesign.

Dependency Injection

Having identified the need for this new entity, the next question is: how should the dependencies between `Bank` and the other two existing entities—`Money` and `Portfolio`—look?

Clearly, `Bank` needs `Money` to operate. `Portfolio` would need both `Money` and `Bank`. The former association is one of aggregation, and the latter is an interface dependency; `Portfolio` uses the `convert` method in `Bank`.

Figure 11-1 shows the three main entities in our program, their responsibilities, and their interdependencies.

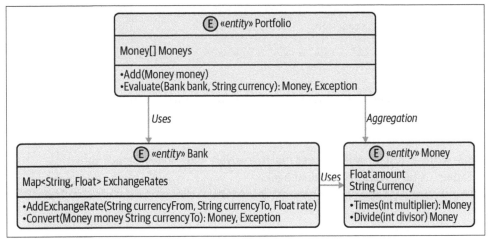

Figure 11-1. The three main entities in our program

The dependency of `Portfolio` on `Bank` is kept to a minimum: `Bank` is provided as a parameter to the `Evaluate` method. This type of dependency injection is called *method injection*, because we are "injecting" the dependency directly into the method that needs it.

 Dependency injection—the principle and practice of separating the *initialization* from the *usage* of a dependent entity—allows us to write loosely coupled code. There are several ways to inject a dependency (*https://oreil.ly/zMdFK*), such as constructor injection, property injection, and method injection.

Putting It All Together

We're about to do some major surgery to our code—how will we ensure the health and wellbeing of our patient?

One key benefit of test-driven development is that long after the original code has been written, the tests provide anesthetic safety during later refactoring and redesign.

The approach we'll take will be a combination of *writing new unit tests*—which is the heart of TDD and what we've done thus far—and *refactoring existing unit tests*. We know that the existing tests provide a valuable safeguard: they verify that the features we've built, all the crossed-out lines on our list, work as expected. We'll continue to run these tests, modifying their *implementation* as needed while keeping their *purpose* intact. This two-pronged approach of writing new tests and refactoring existing ones will give us the assurance we need as we heal our code of its ills.

Tests, especially unit tests, are a bulwark against regression failures during redesign.

With the theory and design out of the way, it's time to write some code.

Go

Let's write a test in `money_test.go` to convert one `Money` struct into another, using a yet-to-be-created Bank:

```go
func TestConversion(t *testing.T) {
    bank := s.NewBank()
    bank.AddExchangeRate("EUR", "USD", 1.2)
    tenEuros := s.NewMoney(10, "EUR")
    actualConvertedMoney, err := bank.Convert(tenEuros, "USD")
    assertNil(t, err) ❶
    assertEqual(t, s.NewMoney(12, "USD"), actualConvertedMoney)
}

func assertNil(t *testing.T, err error) { ❷
    if err != nil {
        t.Errorf("Expected error to be nil, found: [%s]", err)
    }
}
```

❶ Verifying that there is no error

❷ New helper function that does the verification

Inspired by how `NewMoney` works, we create a `Bank` struct (DNEY: does not exist yet) by calling a `NewBank` function (DNEY). We call an `AddExchangeRate` function (DNEY) to add a particular exchange rate to the `Bank`. We then create a `Money` struct and call the `Convert` method (DNEY) to obtain another `Money` struct in a different currency. Finally, we assert that there is no error during the conversion and that the converted `Money` matches our expectation based on the exchange rate. We wrote the assertion as a new `assertNil` helper function after the pattern established by the existing `assertEqual` function.

If there are too many concepts (structs and methods) that do not exist yet, it's because we're choosing to go faster. We *could* always slow down and write smaller tests as we did early on in our journey, if we wanted.

Using test-driven development, it is possible to write tests that introduce multiple new concepts—and thereby go faster—*if* we so desire.

We wrote our test with the assumption that the Convert method (DNEY) in Bank will have two return types: a Money and an error. Why did we change the signature of this Convert method from the convert method that already exists in Portfolio and returns a float64 and a bool? Because conceptually, the Bank converts Money in one currency to Money in another currency.

The first return value, therefore, is Money and not just a float64 expressing an amount. The second return value is an error so that we can use it to indicate the exchange rate for the failed conversion, which cannot be done with a mere bool.

We are doing just enough design based on what we know now. We're neither speculating (over-designing) nor dumbing things down (under-designing).

To make this test green, we need to craft all the things that are marked "DNEY." Let's create a new source file in the stocks package named bank.go:

```go
package stocks

import "errors"

type Bank struct {
    exchangeRates map[string]float64
}

func (b Bank) AddExchangeRate(currencyFrom string, currencyTo string,
        rate float64) {
    key := currencyFrom + "->" + currencyTo
    b.exchangeRates[key] = rate
}

func (b Bank) Convert(money Money, currencyTo string) (convertedMoney Money,
        err error) {
    if money.currency == currencyTo {
        return NewMoney(money.amount, money.currency), nil ❶
    }
    key := money.currency + "->" + currencyTo
    rate, ok := b.exchangeRates[key]
    if ok {
        return NewMoney(money.amount*rate, currencyTo), nil ❶
    }
    return NewMoney(0, ""), errors.New("Failed") ❷
}
```

```
func NewBank() Bank {
    return Bank{exchangeRates: make(map[string]float64)}
}
```

❶ When conversion is successful, a `Money` and a `nil` (no error) are returned.

❷ When conversion fails, a placeholder `Money` and an `error` are returned.

We introduce the missing concepts:

1. A `type` named `Bank`.

2. The `Bank struct` containing a `map` to store `exchangeRates`.

3. A function `NewBank` to create structs of `type Bank`.

4. A method named `AddExchangeRate` that stores exchange rates needed to convert `Money` structs.

5. A method named `Convert` that is largely similar to the existing `convert` method in `Portfolio`. The return values are a `Money` and an `error`. If the conversion is successful, a `Money` is returned and the `error` is `nil`. If the conversion fails due to a missing exchange rate, a placeholder `Money` object and an `error` are returned.

With these changes carefully done, our new test passes.

We know that the existing behavior of `Evaluate`—which we need to retain—returns an `error` with *all* the missing exchange rates. Where will these missing exchange rates emanate from? The `Convert` method, when we use it in `Evaluate` shortly. This means that the `error` returned from `Convert` must include the missing exchange rate. We have it readily available in the `Convert` method: it's in the variable named `key`. Even though replacing the hardcoded error message `"Failed"` with the variable `key` is a small change, let's test-drive it. Why? It would also allow us to address the snotty little smell of returning the placeholder `Money` struct when there *is* an error. It's better to have the two return values be symmetrical: `convertedMoney` should hold the result of conversion when `err` is `nil`, and when the latter describes a conversion error, the former is `nil`.

 Go's standard libraries have functions and methods (e.g., `os.Open()`, `http.PostForm()`, and `parse.Parse()`) that return a pointer for the first return value and an error for the second. While this is not a strictly enforced language rule, it is the style described in the Go blog (*https://oreil.ly/lElP1*).

Let's write a second test to drill the proper error message *and* this symmetry into our `Convert` method:

```
func TestConversionWithMissingExchangeRate(t *testing.T) {
    bank := s.NewBank()
    tenEuros := s.NewMoney(10, "EUR")
    actualConvertedMoney, err := bank.Convert(tenEuros, "Kalganid") ❶
    if actualConvertedMoney != nil { ❷
        t.Errorf("Expected money to be nil, found: [%+v]", actualConvertedMoney)
    }
    assertEqual(t, "EUR->Kalganid", err.Error()) ❸
}
```

❶ Converting Money in EUR to Kalganid

❷ Asserting that a nil Money pointer is returned

❸ Asserting that returned error contains the missing exchange rate

This test, TestConversionWithMissingExchangeRate, attempts to convert euros to Kalganid—a currency for which no exchange rate has been defined in the Bank. We expect the two return values from Convert to be a Money pointer that's nil and an error that contains the missing exchange rate.

This test fails to compile because of mismatched types:

```
... invalid operation: actualConvertedMoney != nil
        (mismatched types stocks.Money and nil)
```

This counts as a failing test. To allow nil values to be returned from Convert, we change the type of the first return value to be a pointer:

```
func (b Bank) Convert(money Money, currencyTo string) (convertedMoney *Money, ❶
        err error) {
    var result Money
    if money.currency == currencyTo {
        result = NewMoney(money.amount, money.currency)
        return &result, nil ❷
    }
    key := money.currency + "->" + currencyTo
    rate, ok := b.exchangeRates[key]
    if ok {
        result = NewMoney(money.amount*rate, currencyTo)
        return &result, nil ❷
    }
    return nil, errors.New("Failed") ❸
}
```

❶ First return type is now a Money pointer.

❷ When conversion is successful, a valid pointer to Money and a nil error are returned.

❸ When conversion fails, a nil Money pointer and an error with missing exchange rate are returned.

Running this test now gives us a failure message in an older test, TestConversion, reminding us about dereferencing pointers:

```
=== RUN    TestConversion
   ...    Expected {amount:12 currency:USD} Got &{amount:12 currency:USD} ❶
```

❶ Expected a Money, got a Money pointer

That little ampersand & makes a world of difference! The actualConvertedMoney variable in TestConversion is now a *pointer* to a Money and needs to be dereferenced:

```
assertEqual(t, stocks.NewMoney(12, "USD"), *actualConvertedMoney) ❶
```

❶ The * dereferences the actualConvertedMoney pointer back into the struct it points to.

With these changes, we get the assertion failure we are chasing:

```
=== RUN    TestConversionWithMissingExchangeRate
   ...    Expected EUR->Kalganid Got Failed
```

Replacing the string "Failed" with key in the Convert method gets the test to pass:

```
return nil, errors.New(key) ❶
```

❶ Last line of the Convert method

We're in the *refactor* phase. One thing we can improve is our assertNil method. It's only good for verifying if an error is nil; if it could take any type (like assertEqual already does), we could use it to assert that the Money pointer is nil, too.

Let's try an implementation for assertNil following the lead of assertEqual:

```
func TestConversionWithMissingExchangeRate(t *testing.T) {
...
    assertNil(t, actualConvertedMoney) ❶
...
}

func assertNil(t *testing.T, actual interface{}) { ❷
    if actual != nil {
        t.Errorf("Expected to be nil, found: [%+v]", actual) ❸
    }
}
```

❶ Using the modified assertNil to verify a nil pointer

❷ Using empty interface to represent (almost) anything

❸ Using the %+v verb to print non-nil values

With this implementation in use, we get a rather strange failure when we run our tests:

```
=== RUN   TestConversionWithMissingExchangeRate
    money_test.go:108: Expected to be nil, found: [<nil>]
```

That's puzzling! If nil was expected and <nil> was found, what's the problem?

Those little angle brackets give us a clue. In Go, interfaces are implemented as two elements: a type T and a value V. The way Go stores a nil *inside* an interface means that only V is nil whereas T is a pointer to whatever type the interface represents (a *Money in our case). Since the type T is *not* nil, the interface itself is also *not* nil.

To use an analogy, an interface is like the wrapping paper and box surrounding a gift. You have to rip it open to see what the gift is. It is possible that there is *nothing* inside the box—the ultimate gag gift—but you can't find that out until you unwrap and unbox the gift.

A Go interface will be non-nil (*https://oreil.ly/IyfG7*) even when the pointer value inside it is nil.

The way to unwrap an interface and examine the value inside is to use the reflect package. The ValueOf function in that package returns the value V, which can then be checked by calling the IsNil function, also defined in the reflect package. To avoid panic errors from inspecting nil interfaces, we must first check if the given interface{} is nil, too.

Here's what the corrected assertNil function looks like:

```
import (
    s "tdd/stocks"
    "testing"
    "reflect" ❶
)
...
func assertNil(t *testing.T,actual interface{}) {
    if actual != nil && !reflect.ValueOf(actual).IsNil() { ❷
        t.Errorf("Expected to be nil, found: [%+v]", actual)
    }
}
```

❶ We need the reflect package to examine the interface.

❷ The assertion error is raised if neither the interface{} itself nor the wrapped value is nil.

Excellent! Our tests all pass, and we have the symmetric Convert method we set out to write. We're ready to introduce Bank as a dependency of the Evaluate method in Portfolio.

Since we have a battery of tests for the Evaluate method, we'll sally forth and redesign that method now. Any test failures we get—and we do expect to get many—will keep us on the RGR track.

We change the signature of the Evaluate method in Portfolio to have a Bank as the first parameter. We also change the type of its first return value to be a Money pointer. As for the body of the method, the changes are few and specific. We call Bank's Convert method instead of the soon-to-be-retired local function convert. Whenever a call to Convert returns an error, we save the error message. Instead of returning a Money struct, we return a pointer to it. And when there are errors, we return a nil as the first value and the error as the second:

```
func (p Portfolio) Evaluate(bank Bank, currency string) (*Money, error) { ❶
    total := 0.0
    failedConversions := make([]string, 0)
    for _, m := range p {
        if convertedCurrency, err := bank.Convert(m, currency); err == nil {
            total = total + convertedCurrency.amount
        } else {
            failedConversions = append(failedConversions, err.Error())
        }
    }
    if len(failedConversions) == 0 {
        totalMoney := NewMoney(total, currency)
        return &totalMoney, nil ❷
    }
    failures := "["
    for _, f := range failedConversions {
        failures = failures + f + ","
    }
    failures = failures + "]"
    return nil, errors.New("Missing exchange rate(s):" + failures) ❸
}
```

❶ A Money pointer and an error are returned.

❷ When the Money pointer is not nil, a nil error is returned.

❸ When there is an error, the a nil Money pointer is returned.

With its signature changed, every call to Evaluate in our test fails to compile. We need to create a Bank and pass it to Evaluate. Could we do it once in money_test.go and not within each individual test method?

Absolutely! Let's declare a Bank variable outside all tests in money_test.go and use an init function to initialize this Bank with all necessary exchange rates:

```
var bank s.Bank ❶

func init() { ❷
    bank = s.NewBank()
    bank.AddExchangeRate("EUR", "USD", 1.2)
    bank.AddExchangeRate("USD", "KRW", 1100)
}
```

❶ In money_test.go, outside any test method

❷ New init function

There are multiple ways to set up shared state in Go. Each test file can have one or more init() functions (*https://oreil.ly/qWdAW*), which are executed in order. All init functions must have identical signatures. Alternatively, we can override the MainStart function (*https://oreil.ly/bPRAf*) in a test file and call one (or more) setup/teardown methods, which may have arbitrary signatures.

Now we can use this bank in each call to Evaluate in our tests, e.g., portfolio.Evalu ate(bank, "Kalganid").

Since Evaluate now returns a Money pointer and an error, we have to change how we assign these return values to variables and how we assert them.

Here's how our TestAddition looks after making the necessary changes:

```
func TestAddition(t *testing.T) {
    var portfolio s.Portfolio

    fiveDollars := s.NewMoney(5, "USD")
    tenDollars := s.NewMoney(10, "USD")
    fifteenDollars := s.NewMoney(15, "USD")

    portfolio = portfolio.Add(fiveDollars)
    portfolio = portfolio.Add(tenDollars)
    portfolioInDollars, err := portfolio.Evaluate(bank, "USD") ❶

    assertNil(t, err) ❷
    assertEqual(t, fifteenDollars, *portfolioInDollars) ❸
}
```

❶ Injecting the bank dependency into the Evaluate method

❷ Asserting that there is no error

❸ Dereferencing the pointer to Money before using it as the last parameter in the assertEqual function

After fixing the other tests similarly—using bank as the first parameter to Evaluate and dereferencing the pointer to get a reference to Money—we get all tests to pass. We're now ready to remove the unused convert function in Portfolio. Deleting unused code is so gratifying!

Since we have a general-purpose and robust assertNil function available to our tests, we replace all blank identifiers _ with actual variables and verify that they're nil. For example, in TestAdditionWithMultipleMissingExchangeRates, we can verify that the Money pointer is nil:

```
func TestAdditionWithMultipleMissingExchangeRates(t *testing.T) {
...
    expectedErrorMessage :=
        "Missing exchange rate(s):[USD->Kalganid,EUR->Kalganid,KRW->Kalganid,]"
    value, actualError := portfolio.Evaluate(bank, "Kalganid") ❶

    assertNil(t, value) ❷
    assertEqual(t, expectedErrorMessage, actualError.Error())
}
```

❶ Receive the first return value, a Money pointer, in a named parameter instead of a blank identifier.

❷ Verify that a nil Money pointer is returned.

We now have a much better code organization: Bank, Portfolio, and Money have specific responsibilities. We have robust tests that validate the behavior of all these types. A good indicator of our improved code is that each file in the stocks package is of comparable size: a few dozen lines of code. (If we write Godoc comments—which is a great thing—the files would be longer.)

JavaScript

Let's write a new test in test_money.js to convert one Money object into another, using the Bank class that we intend to create:

```
const Bank = require('./bank'); ❶
...
    testConversion() {
        let bank = new Bank(); ❷
```

```
        bank.addExchangeRate("EUR", "USD", 1.2); ❸
        let tenEuros = new Money(10, "EUR");
        assert.deepStrictEqual(
            bank.convert(tenEuros, "USD"), new Money(12, "USD")); ❹
    }
```

❶ Import statement for bank module (Does Not Exist Yet).

❷ Call to Bank constructor (DNEY).

❸ Call to addExchangeRate (DNEY).

❹ Call to convert (DNEY).

Notice that the module being imported, the class Bank, and its methods addExchange
Rate and convert do not exist yet (DNEY).

Anticipating (or observing) the test failures, let's create a new file named bank.js
containing the requisite behavior of the Bank class:

```
const Money = require("./money"); ❶

class Bank {
    constructor() {
        this.exchangeRates = new Map(); ❷
    }

    addExchangeRate(currencyFrom, currencyTo, rate) {
        let key = currencyFrom + "->" + currencyTo; ❸
        this.exchangeRates.set(key, rate);
    }

    convert(money, currency) { ❹
        if (money.currency === currency) {
            return new Money(money.amount, money.currency); ❺
        }
        let key = money.currency + "->" + currency;
        let rate = this.exchangeRates.get(key);
        if (rate === undefined) {
            throw new Error("Failed"); ❻
        }
        return new Money(money.amount * rate, currency);
    }
}

module.exports = Bank; ❼
```

❶ The Bank class requires the Money class.

❷ Create an empty Map in constructor for use later.

❸ Forming a key to store the exchange rate.

❹ This convert method resembles the convert method in Portfolio class.

❺ Creating a new Money object when currencies are the same.

❻ When exchange rate is undefined, throw an Error with the string "Failed".

❼ Exporting Bank class for use outside this module.

The addExchangeRate creates a key using the "from" and "to" currencies, and it stores the rate using this key.

Most of the behavior of the convert method is heavily influenced by the existing code in Portfolio class. The one difference is that Bank.convert returns a Money object when successful (instead of only the amount) and throws an Error upon failure (instead of returning undefined). Additionally, the Bank.convert method always creates a new Money object, even when the "from" and "to" currencies are identical. This prevents accidental side effects by always returning a new Money object, never the one that's the first parameter to the method.

  JavaScript objects (and arrays) are passed by reference (*https://oreil.ly/OFYJP*). If we need to simulate pass-by-value semantics—important to reduce side effects—we must create new objects explicitly.

The tests are all green.

We need to retain the existing behavior of evaluate, which returns an Error with *all* the missing exchange rates. The evaluate method will need this new convert method to provide all those missing exchange rates. Therefore, the Error thrown from convert must include the missing exchange rate. We have this value already available in the key variable of the Bank.convert method. Even though this is a small change, let's test-drive it.

We add a new test in test_money.js to verify the behavior we need:

```
testConversionWithMissingExchangeRate() {
  let bank = new Bank(); ❶
  let tenEuros = new Money(10, "EUR");
  let expectedError = new Error("EUR->Kalganid"); ❷
  assert.throws(function () { bank.convert(tenEuros, "Kalganid") },
    expectedError); ❸
}
```

❶ New Bank with no exchange rates defined

❷ Expected error including the missing exchange rate

❸ Using anonymous function with `assert.throws` to verify the error message

We use the same `assert.throws` idiom, using an anonymous function, that we did in Chapter 10 while writing `testAdditionWithMultipleMissingExchangeRates`.

This test fails with the expected assertion failure:

```
Running: testConversionWithMissingExchangeRate()
AssertionError [ERR_ASSERTION]: Expected values to be strictly deep-equal:
+ actual - expected

  Comparison {
+   message: 'Failed',
-   message: 'EUR->Kalganid',
    name: 'Error'
  }
```

Getting this test to pass is simple: we use key when throwing `Error` from `convert` :

```
    convert(money, currency) {
...
        if (rate === undefined) {
            throw new Error(key);   ❶
        }
...
    }
```

❶ Using key ensures the `Error` includes the missing exchange rate.

With these changes to the Bank class, all our tests pass. We're ready to change the `Portfolio` class. Because we have a suite of tests for `Portfolio`, we'll jump into the redesign. We trust our tests—and their anticipated failures—to ensure that we do the redesign correctly.

The `evaluate` function should accept a `Bank` object as a dependency. We'll put this as the first parameter to the `evaluate` method. The rest of the method is modified to work with the `Error` that `Bank.convert` throws. The error message wraps the missing exchange rate, so we can keep a record of any missing exchange rates and throw one `Error` with the aggregated error message from `evaluate`, when necessary:

```
    evaluate(bank, currency) {
        let failures = [];
        let total = this.moneys.reduce( (sum, money) => {
            try {
                let convertedMoney = bank.convert(money, currency);   ❶
                return sum + convertedMoney.amount;
```

```
        }
        catch (error) {
            failures.push(error.message);
            return sum;
        }
    }, 0);

    if (!failures.length) {
        return new Money(total, currency);
    }
    throw new Error("Missing exchange rate(s):[" + failures.join() + "]");
}
```

❶ Calling Bank's convert method

 JavaScript has the throw keyword to signal an exception and try ... catch and try ... catch ... finally constructs to respond to exceptions (*https://oreil.ly/GTr4Q*).

Since we have changed the signature of evaluate, we have no justifiable hope that any of our addition tests will pass. Just for giggles, we run the test suite as it is. When we run it, we get a strange-looking error:

```
Running: testAddition()
...
Error: Missing exchange rate(s):[bank.convert is not a function,
    bank.convert is not a function]
```

That looks odd: whatever shortcomings it may have, bank.convert is surely a function since we just wrote it! The reason for this error message is that our test calls evaluate with only one parameter, and JavaScript's rules allow this. The currency string is assigned to the first parameter, and the second parameter is set to undefined, as shown in Figure 11-2.

portfolio.evaluate("Kalganid"); [Undefined]

evaluate(bank, currency) {

...

}

Figure 11-2. In JavaScript, any missing parameters in a method call are left as undefined

JavaScript does not enforce any rules (*https://oreil.ly/xInaU*) on the number or types of parameters that are passed to a function, regardless of what the function definition states.

Even though it's assigned to the parameter named bank, the first parameter's value is a mere string. The Node.js runtime is justified in saying that it doesn't have a convert method.

Let's create a Bank object and pass it as the first parameter to the evaluate method. This is sufficient for testAddition, which uses the same currency throughout (i.e., no exchange rates required):

```
testAddition() {
  let fiveDollars = new Money(5, "USD");
  let tenDollars = new Money(10, "USD");
  let fifteenDollars = new Money(15, "USD");
  let portfolio = new Portfolio();
  portfolio.add(fiveDollars, tenDollars);
  assert.deepStrictEqual(portfolio.evaluate(new Bank(), "USD"),
    fifteenDollars); ❶
}
```

❶ No exchange rates are needed in this test, just a Bank object.

The testAddition passes. The failure message progresses to the next test in our test suite.

We need to fix the other tests similarly, albeit with exchange rates defined. Since we're going to need a Bank object and exchange rates in multiple tests, it'd be nice to only define the Bank once with all the exchange rates needed for our tests. We can define bank as a member variable and initialize it in a MoneyTest constructor:

```
constructor() {
    this.bank = new Bank();
    this.bank.addExchangeRate("EUR", "USD", 1.2);
    this.bank.addExchangeRate("USD", "KRW", 1100);
}
```

In *most* of the addition tests, we can use this.bank directly, without having to create a method-local bank. For example:

```
testAdditionOfDollarsAndEuros() {
...
    assert.deepStrictEqual(portfolio.evaluate(this.bank, "USD"),
      expectedValue); ❶
}
```

❶ The bank object created in the constructor is accessible as this.bank in the test.

The *one* exception to using `this.bank` is `testAdditionWithMultipleMissingEx changeRates`, where we deliberately seek to cause an error. Because the parameter to the assert statement in this test is an anonymous function object, the reference to `this.bank` will fail...because `this` has changed!

Let's untangle the previous paragraph. When we create an object, say ABC in JavaScript, any code within ABC can use `this` to refer to ABC. Any objects *outside* ABC cannot be accessed using `this`.

In JavaScript, `this` refers to the nearest enclosing object, including anonymous objects, and not any other objects surrounding it.

We *could* get a local reference to the bank and use it in the assertion inside `testAddi tionWithMultipleMissingExchangeRates`:

```
////////////////////////////////////
// We *could* do this; but let's not!
////////////////////////////////////
let bank = this.bank; ❶
assert.throws(function() {portfolio.evaluate(bank, "Kalganid")},
    expectedError); ❷
```

❶ Store the reference to `this.bank` in a local variable.

❷ Use local variable `bank` to avoid having to use `this.bank` inside the anonymous function.

The above code, although correct, is ungainly. There is an alternate syntax using arrow functions that's more succinct and does not require storing `this.bank` in a local variable.

```
assert.throws(() => portfolio.evaluate(this.bank, "Kalganid"), expectedError); ❶
```

❶ Using an arrow function to call `portfolio.evaluate()` using `this.bank` directly as an argument

Yay: green tests! We're now ready to remove the unused `convert` function in `Portfo lio`. Deleting unused code is pure exhilaration!

The arrow function declaration (*https://oreil.ly/396SH*) in JavaScript, introduced in ES6, allows us to write syntactically shorter functions.

We now have well-organized code: Bank, Portfolio, and Money have specific responsibilities. A good indicator is that each file is now of comparable size.

Python

Our first goal is to write a test to convert one Money object into another, using the as-yet-undefined Bank abstraction:

```python
from bank import Bank ❶
...
    def testConversion(self):
        bank = Bank() ❷
        bank.addExchangeRate("EUR", "USD", 1.2) ❸
        tenEuros = Money(10, "EUR")
        self.assertEqual(bank.convert(tenEuros, "USD"), Money(12, "USD")) ❹
```

❶ Import statement for the bank module (DNEY).

❷ Create a new Bank (DNEY).

❸ Call to addExchangeRate (DNEY).

❹ Call to convert (DNEY).

We are using several things that do not exist yet (DNEY): the bank module, the Bank class, and the addExchangeRate and convert methods in the Bank class.

Anticipating (or observing) the test errors we get—such as ModuleNotFoundError: No module named 'bank'—let's create a new file named bank.py that defines the Bank class with the minimal necessary behavior:

```python
from money import Money ❶

class Bank:
    def __init__(self):
        self.exchangeRates = {} ❷

    def addExchangeRate(self, currencyFrom, currencyTo, rate):
        key = currencyFrom + "->" + currencyTo ❸
        self.exchangeRates[key] = rate

    def convert(self, aMoney, aCurrency): ❹
        if aMoney.currency == aCurrency:
            return Money(aMoney.amount, aCurrency) ❺

        key = aMoney.currency + "->" + aCurrency
        if key in self.exchangeRates:
            return Money(aMoney.amount * self.exchangeRates[key], aCurrency)
```

```
    raise Exception("Failed") ❻
```

❶ The Bank requires Money as a dependency.

❷ Initializing empty dictionary in __init__ method.

❸ Forming a key to store the exchange rate.

❹ This convert method resembles the __convert method in the Portfolio class.

❺ Creating a new Money object when currencies are the same.

❻ Raising an Exception when conversion fails.

The Bank class—especially its convert method—borrows generously from the existing code in Portfolio. The two key differences are in the signature of Bank.convert. It returns a Money object when successful (instead of merely an amount) and raises a general Exception when the conversion fails (instead of a KeyError).

With this new Bank class, our test passes.

We need to keep the existing behavior of evaluate, which returns an Exception with *all* the missing exchange rates. The evaluate method will need the convert method to provide the missing exchange rates. The Exception raised from convert must include the missing exchange rate—the value is in the key variable in convert. Let's test-drive this change, small though it is.

We write a new test that expects an Exception with a specific message from the convert method:

```
def testConversionWithMissingExchangeRate(self):
    bank = Bank() ❶
    tenEuros = Money(10, "EUR")
    with self.assertRaisesRegex(Exception, "EUR->Kalganid"): ❷
        bank.convert(tenEuros, "Kalganid") ❸
```

❶ New Bank with no exchange rates defined

❷ Expected Exception with specific message

❸ Call to convert with "Kalganid" as the currency

This test fails as expected:

```
FAIL: testConversionWithMissingExchangeRate (__main__.TestMoney)
...
Exception: Failed
```

```
...
AssertionError: "EUR->Kalganid" does not match "Failed"
```

To fix this, we use key to create the Exception that's raised from convert:

```
    def convert(self, aMoney, aCurrency):
...
        raise Exception(key) ❶
```

❶   Using key ensures the Exception includes the missing exchange rate.

All tests are green. With the new Bank class in place, we're ready to change the evaluate method in Portfolio to accept a Bank object as a dependency. We have no fewer than four tests for the addition of Money objects that exercise the evaluate method. We fully expect these tests to fail, thereby keeping us firmly on the RGR track.

We'll place bank as the second method parameter to evaluate, after the obligatory self. The rest of the method is modified to work with the Exception that Bank.convert throws when there's a missing exchange rate:

```
    def evaluate(self, bank, currency):
        total = 0.0
        failures = []
        for m in self.moneys:
            try:
                total += bank.convert(m, currency).amount ❶
            except Exception as ex:
                failures.append(ex)

        if len(failures) == 0:
            return Money(total, currency)

        failureMessage = ",".join(f.args[0] for f in failures)
        raise Exception("Missing exchange rate(s):[" + failureMessage + "]")
```

❶   Delegate to bank.convert method

As soon as we we make these changes to evaluate, several of our tests fail with a rather strange error:

```
TypeError: evaluate() missing 1 required positional argument: 'currency'
```

That's strange: the only "positional argument" we're passing in *is* the currency; what's missing is the bank! The reason for this rather phantasmagoric error message is that Python is a dynamically typed language. It assumes that the first (and only) argument we're passing corresponds to the first positional argument in the evaluate method declaration. Since it doesn't find a *second* argument matching currency—it complains about it.

Figure 11-3 shows how actual parameters are associated with the formal parameters in a Python method call.

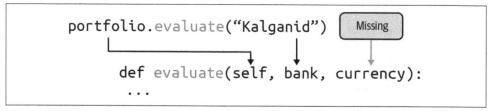

```
portfolio.evaluate("Kalganid")    [ Missing ]

        def evaluate(self, bank, currency):
            ...
```

Figure 11-3. In Python, parameters are assigned left to right based on position, regardless of their type

We need a Bank with a couple of exchange rates to satisfy the needs of all our addition-related tests.

It'd be nice if we could declare this initialization code *once*, rather than in each test. There is a way to do this. Our test class, by virtue of subclassing from unittest.Test Case, inherits its behavior. One aspect of this inherited behavior is that if there is a setUp method in the class, it'll be called before each test. We can define our Bank object in this setUp method:

```
def setUp(self): ❶
    self.bank = Bank() ❷
    self.bank.addExchangeRate("EUR", "USD", 1.2)  ❸
    self.bank.addExchangeRate("USD", "KRW", 1100) ❸
```

❶ Overridden setUp method from TestCase superclass

❷ New Bank object needed by tests

❸ Exchange rates needed by tests

In the test methods, we can simply use self.bank as the first argument to each call to evaluate, as in this example:

```
    def testAddition(self):
...
        self.assertEqual(fifteenDollars, portfolio.evaluate(self.bank, "USD")) ❶
```

❶ Using self.bank declared in the setUp method

After fixing all calls to evaluate in this way, the tests are pristine green. The scene is set for us to ceremoniously delete the old __convert method in Portfolio. Deleting code is a sweet feeling: savor it!

Committing Our Changes

This has been a sizable modification to our code: the introduction of `Bank` and the resultant refactoring. Let's commit our code to our local Git repository, with a message that reflects what we did:

```
git add .
git commit -m "feat: added Bank; refactored Portfolio to use Bank"
```

Where We Are

We changed the internal organization of our code in a significant way, extracting the `Bank` entity from the obscurity of being embedded in `Portfolio` into a first-class citizen of our domain. And we used a combination of new tests and our existing suite of tests to ensure that no features were harmed during this writing of the new and improved code. We also cleaned up our tests by declaring a `Bank` variable, once before the tests run and then using this instance in the relevant tests.

We have one more item on our list: the ability to modify existing exchange rates. Before we get to that, let's add the satisfaction of crossing one more item off our list to the sumptuous pleasure that redesigning and deleting code has provided us:

~~5 USD × 2 = 10 USD~~

~~10 EUR × 2 = 20 EUR~~

~~4002 KRW / 4 = 1000.5 KRW~~

~~5 USD + 10 USD = 15 USD~~

~~Separate test code from production code~~

~~Remove redundant tests~~

~~5 USD + 10 EUR = 17 USD~~

~~1 USD + 1100 KRW = 2200 KRW#~~

~~Determine exchange rate based on the currencies involved (from → to)~~

~~Improve error handling when exchange rates are unspecified~~

~~Improve the implementation of exchange rates~~

Allow exchange rates to be modified

The code for this chapter is in a branch named "chap11" in the GitHub repository (*https://github.com/saleem/tdd-book-code/tree/chap11*).

PART IV

Finishing Up

CHAPTER 12

Test Order

My journey has always been the balance between chaos and order.

—Philippe Petit

In Chapter 11, we undertook a relatively significant design change by introducing the Bank entity. Both the new test we wrote and the existing tests helped us accomplish this goal.

One feature of the new Bank entity is its ability to accept and store an exchange rate between any pair of currencies. The way we designed (and tested) it—the exchange rates are stored in a hashmap and in the keys formed from the two currencies—gives us reason to believe that we *already* have the next feature on our list. That feature is to *allow exchange rates to be modified.*

One way to gain confidence that this feature works is (no prizes for guessing) to write a test to prove it. Why should we write a test when the feature is likely already there? In other words, what could a new test possibly drive, if the development has already been done?

Three answers can be provided to this question:

1. To repeat: a new test would *increase our confidence* in this feature, even if no new production code is necessary.
2. The new test would serve as *executable documentation* of this feature.
3. The test may expose *inadvertent interactions* between existing tests, thereby prompting us to address them.

Tests are an effective way to document our code. Because we can (and should) use meaningful names for our tests, and because they lay out in detail *what* a feature does (as opposed to *how* it works), tests are an excellent way for newcomers to learn about our code. They can even help us reorient ourselves to *our own* code when we forget subtle yet significant details about its behavior. And as we shall see, writing new tests can expose problems with existing tests.

Enlightened by this justification to write tests, let's turn our focus to this possibly implemented-but-not-tested feature on our list:

~~5 USD × 2 = 10 USD~~

~~10 EUR × 2 = 20 EUR~~

~~4002 KRW / 4 = 1000.5 KRW~~

~~5 USD + 10 USD = 15 USD~~

~~Separate test code from production code~~

~~Remove redundant tests~~

~~5 USD + 10 EUR = 17 USD~~

~~1 USD + 1100 KRW = 2200 KRW#~~

~~Determine exchange rate based on the currencies involved (from → to)~~

~~Improve error handling when exchange rates are unspecified~~

~~Improve the implementation of exchange rates~~

Allow exchange rates to be modified

Changing Exchange Rates

We'll start by modifying our existing test for conversion. We already know that conversion with a rate between two currencies (e.g., EUR→USD) works. We'll add to the test by adding a *different* rate for the *same* pair of currencies. We'll verify that subsequent conversions utilize this new exchange rate.

If our test works out of the box, we'd have blitzed through the *green* phase. We'll address any necessary refactoring in the last phase.

Go

Let's add a few more lines to the end of `TestConversion`. We'll modify the exchange rate to 1.3 and validate that it takes effect. We'll also rename the test to reflect its intent. Here is the entire test:

```
func TestConversion(t *testing.T) {
    tenEuros := s.NewMoney(10, "EUR")
    actualConvertedMoney, err := bank.Convert(tenEuros, "USD")
    assertNil(t, err)
    assertEqual(t, s.NewMoney(12, "USD"), *actualConvertedMoney) ❶
```

```
    bank.AddExchangeRate("EUR", "USD", 1.3) ❷
    actualConvertedMoney, err = bank.Convert(tenEuros, "USD") ❸
    assertNil(t, err)
    assertEqual(t, s.NewMoney(13, "USD"), *actualConvertedMoney) ❹
}
```

❶ This was previously the last line in the test.

❷ Updated exchange rate between the same two currencies.

❸ Reusing the same variables with = instead of := operator.

❹ Verifying that the conversion takes the updated rate into account.

Voilà! The test passes at first attempt.

By way of refactoring, we change the name of the test to better reflect its new intent:
TestConversionWithDifferentRatesBetweenTwoCurrencies.

Out of curiosity: does the exchange rate between EUR and USD stay at 1.3 for tests
that run *after* this test? That's easy to verify. Let's write a new test *beneath* TestConver
sionWithDifferentRatesBetweenTwoCurrencies in the money_test.go file. (Tests
are run in the order they're specified in the source file.)

```
func TestWhatIsTheConversionRateFromEURToUSD(t *testing.T) { ❶
    tenEuros := s.NewMoney(10, "EUR")
    actualConvertedMoney, err := bank.Convert(tenEuros, "USD")
    assertNil(t, err)
    assertEqual(t, s.NewMoney(12, "USD"), *actualConvertedMoney) ❷
}
```

❶ Test name reflects its exploratory nature

❷ Body of test is borrowed from the first half of the TestConversionWithDiffe
   rentRatesBetweenTwoCurrencies test

And the test fails with the unlucky number 13!

```
=== RUN    TestWhatIsTheConversionRateFromEURToUSD
    ... Expected {amount:12 currency:USD} Got {amount:13 currency:USD}
```

We needn't be superstitious: it turns out that the init() function runs *once* during
the test run, *not* before each test method. Any shared state modified by one test is
visible to tests that run later. That is how we get $13.

Each init() function in a Go file runs once, in the order in which it's specified (*https://oreil.ly/vnMDR*).

It would be nice to keep our tests independent of each other: the behavior of one test leaching into another as a side effect isn't a good thing.

The problem is grounded in the interplay of these two facts:

1. The bank is shared among several tests.
2. There is no initialization of this shared state before each test.

We could solve the problem by altering *either* of these two facts. We could remove the shared bank *or* we could ensure any shared state is properly initialized before each test.

Keeping the shared bank is useful: we can reference bank directly from any test that needs it. Let's move the initialization of the bank to happen before each test.

The simplest way to do this is to rename init to, say, initExchangeRates and explicitly call it from each test that needs bank with prepopulated exchange rates:

```
func initExchangeRates() { ❶
        bank = s.NewBank()
        bank.AddExchangeRate("EUR", "USD", 1.2)
        bank.AddExchangeRate("USD", "KRW", 1100)
}
...
func TestAdditionOfDollarsAndWons(t *testing.T) {
        initExchangeRates() ❷
... ❸
}
```

❶ This is the old init method, now renamed.

❷ Explicit call to initExchangeRates in a test needs the bank struct.

❸ The rest of the test is the same.

With these changes, all tests pass.

Should we keep the exploratory test we wrote: TestWhatIsTheConversionRateFrom EURToUSD? It doesn't test any new feature. What it did do is expose a certain brittleness in our tests—a brittleness borne of unwarranted and unwanted dependency between tests.

What we *really* need is a mechanism to randomize the order in which tests are run so that we ferret out any such false interdependencies between tests, now and in the future.

Randomizing the Run Order of Our Go Tests

Go 1.17 introduced the `-shuffle` flag, which allows us to randomize the order in which tests are executed. Here's how this flag can be used:

```
go test -v -shuffle on ./... ❶
```

❶ Command to shuffle tests in a random order; the ... has to be typed literally

Try it a few times and see the test run-order change right before your eyes. The tests should all pass, regardless of order.

 The `-shuffle` flag (*https://oreil.ly/Mj7C6*), added to the `go test` command in version 1.17 of Go, allows us to randomize the order in which tests are run. This helps unearth any accidental dependencies between tests.

With our curiosity sated, and knowing now there is a better way to discover accidental coupling between tests, we can delete the `TestWhatIsTheConversionRateFromEUR ToUSD` test. It has served its purpose.

Go's `testing` package provides other mechanisms for setting up and tearing down the common state between tests. In particular, TableDrivenTests (*https://oreil.ly/ Wae0X*) allows sophisticated strategies to organize your tests. A detailed discussion of such strategies, while interesting, is outside the scope of this book.

JavaScript

We'll add a few more lines to the end of `testConversion`. We'll modify the exchange rate between EUR and USD to 1.3 and verify that this change takes effect. Here's the updated test method:

```
testConversion() {
  let tenEuros = new Money(10, "EUR");
  assert.deepStrictEqual(this.bank.convert(tenEuros, "USD"),
    new Money(12, "USD")); ❶

  this.bank.addExchangeRate("EUR", "USD", 1.3); ❷
  assert.deepStrictEqual(this.bank.convert(tenEuros, "USD"),
    new Money(13, "USD")); ❸
}
```

❶ This is the test we had before.

❷ Updated exchange rate between the same two currencies.

❸ Verifying that the conversion takes the updated rate into account.

And lo! The test passes as written.

We refactor the name of the test to better indicate its purpose: `testConversionWith` `DifferentRatesBetweenTwoCurrencies`.

There is a subtle side effect of our test, though. Because `bank` is a shared object among all the tests, the fact that we have changed the exchange rate is visible to all tests that run subsequently. We can verify this by writing a test *after* `testConversionWith` `DifferentRatesBetweenTwoCurrencies`. (Our tests are discovered, and therefore run, in the order they're declared in the source file.)

```
testWhatIsTheConversionRateFromEURToUSD() { ❶
  let tenEuros = new Money(10, "EUR");
  assert.deepStrictEqual(this.bank.convert(tenEuros, "USD"),
    new Money(12, "USD")); ❷
}
```

❶ Test name reflects its exploratory nature

❷ Body of test is borrowed from the first half of the `testConversionWithDiffe` `rentRatesBetweenTwoCurrencies` test

And the test duly fails with an assertion error:

```
Running: testWhatIsTheConversionRateFromEURToUSD()
AssertionError [ERR_ASSERTION]: Expected values to be strictly deep-equal:
+ actual - expected

  Money {
+   amount: 13,
-   amount: 12,
    currency: 'USD'
  }
```

There are several ways to eliminate this undesirable side effect of one test on another. We could do any of the following:

1. Restore the EUR→USD exchange rate to the value set in the `constructor` at the end of the `testConversionWithDifferentRatesBetweenTwoCurrencies`.

2. Test-drive a new feature in the `Bank` class (namely, `removeExchangeRate`), and then use it at the end of `testConversionWithDifferentRatesBetweenTwo` `Currencies`.

3. Use a new `Bank()` object local to `testConversionWithDifferentRatesBetweenTwoCurrencies` so there are no side effects.

4. Test-drive a "setUp / tearDown" feature in our test harness that allows us to create a new `Bank()` object before each test.

5. Use a different exchange rate in `testConversionWithDifferentRatesBetweenTwoCurrencies` that is not used by any other test.

We'll go with the penultimate option and create a `setUp` method.

We have a failing test, so we can write code to make it green. What's the shortest path to green? We can rename the `constructor` to `setUp` and call it manually before each test in our `runAllTests` method:

```
setUp() { ❶
  this.bank = new Bank();
  this.bank.addExchangeRate("EUR", "USD", 1.2);
  this.bank.addExchangeRate("USD", "KRW", 1100);
}
...
runAllTests() { ❷
  let testMethods = this.getAllTestMethods();
  testMethods.forEach(m => {
    console.log("Running: %s()", m);
    let method = Reflect.get(this, m);
    try {
      this.setUp(); ❸
      Reflect.apply(method, this, []);
    } catch (e) {
      if (e instanceof assert.AssertionError) {
        console.log(e);
      } else {
        throw e;
      }
    }
  });
}
```

❶ The `constructor` has been renamed as the `setUp` method.

❷ The existing `runAllTests` method.

❸ Call to the `setUp` method before each test method invocation.

That's all it takes: the test suite passes. We have enhanced our test harness to have a `setUp` method that's called before each test method. If needed, we can add a `tearDown` method in much the same way—although we'd drive it via a failing test, of course!

We can now delete the exploratory testWhatIsTheConversionRateFromEURToUSD—it has served its exploratory purpose.

Randomizing the Run Order of Our JavaScript Tests

Interdependency between tests can come from multiple root causes. In our JavaScript tests, the shared Bank was one such cause. We have solved that problem through the setUp method. But how can we be sure there aren't other undesirable side effects from one test to another?

One technique that's often used to discover such side effects is to randomize the order of tests. How would we do that? We could use the Math.random() function to shuffle the test methods in our test harness. Here's a method that'd do that:[1]

```
randomizeTestOrder(testMethods) {
  for (let i = testMethods.length - 1; i > 0; i--) {
    const j = Math.floor(Math.random() * (i + 1));
    [testMethods[i], testMethods[j]] = [testMethods[j], testMethods[i]];
  }
  return testMethods;
}
```

How would you use Table 6-2 in Chapter 6 to test drive the above method?

Refer to the code for this chapter (*https://github.com/saleem/tdd-book-code/tree/ chap12*) in the GitHub repository to see the results.

Python

We start by adding a few lines to the end of testConversion. We'll vary the exchange rate between EUR and USD to 1.3 and assert that this new rate is used for a second conversion between the two currencies. Here's the test method in its entirety:

```
def testConversion(self):
    tenEuros = Money(10, "EUR")
    self.assertEqual(self.bank.convert(tenEuros, "USD"), Money(12, "USD"))  ❶

    self.bank.addExchangeRate("EUR", "USD", 1.3)  ❷
    self.assertEqual(self.bank.convert(tenEuros, "USD"), Money(13, "USD"))  ❸
```

❶ This is the test we had before.

❷ Updated exchange rate between the same two currencies.

---

1 Inspired by the code at w3docs (*https://oreil.ly/y13Uw*).

❸ Verifying that the conversion takes the updated rate into account.

Success! The test passes at first attempt.

We rename the test to `testConversionWithDifferentRatesBetweenTwoCurrencies`. This captures the new intent of the test more fully.

Out of curiosity, is the updated EUR→USD exchange rate in `testConversionWith DifferentRatesBetweenTwoCurrencies` visible to other tests? To verify this, we can write a test whose name causes it to run after all other tests.

> By default, tests in Python are run in the order (*https://oreil.ly/ Auwug*) of their alphabetically sorted test method names.

```
def testWhatIsTheConversionRateFromEURToUSD(self):  ❶
    tenEuros = Money(10, "EUR")
    self.assertEqual(self.bank.convert(tenEuros, "USD"), Money(12, "USD"))  ❷
```

❶ Test name reflects its exploratory nature

❷ Body of this test is borrowed from the first half of `testConversionWithDiffe rentRatesBetweenTwoCurrencies` test

And this test also passes. Excellent! Python's test framework ensures that there are no side effects from one test to another, because the `setUp` method is run before each test.

> Using Python's `unittest` package, subclassing the `TestCase` class, and overriding the `setUp` method promotes test isolation. The `setUp` method runs before *each* test, ensuring common objects are created afresh.

With our curiosity about test independence quelled, we delete `testWhatIsTheConver sionRateFromEURToUSD`—it has served its short-lived purpose.

With this fast lap around the RGR cycle, we're done with this feature.

> ### Randomizing the Run Order of Our Python Tests
>
> When we run our Python tests with `python3 test_money.py`, the tests run in alphabetical order by name. Could we randomize the order in which these tests are run, to expose any other nefarious interdependencies lurking between the tests?
>
> The pytest-random-order plugin (*https://oreil.ly/heHzg*) for the pytest-testing framework (*https://docs.pytest.org*) allows us to do just that. We haven't used any testing frameworks thus far in this book. Appendix B does introduce PyTest, which is compatible with the Python tests we've written.
>
> Using Pytest with the pytest-random-order plugin, we could easily randomize our tests by running this command:
>
> ```
> pytest -v --random-order  ❶
> ```
>
> ❶ Running our Python tests using pytest-random-order plugin
>
> This would run the tests in—you guessed it—a random order. The precise order will vary from one run to the next—thereby increasing the likelihood that any side effects between tests are laid bare through failures.

Committing Our Changes

We added tests to showcase an existing feature. Let's highlight this in our Git commit message:

```
git add .
git commit -m "test: verified behavior when modifying an existing exchange rate"
```

Where We Are

In this chapter, we added tests to document an existing feature and learned about test independence. We looked at ways to randomize the order in which tests are run, to expose any unintentional side effects. This makes our entire test suite more robust.

Tests—especially unit tests—should be independent of each other. One test should not rely on the success, failure, or even side effects caused by another test.

We're done with all the features on our list.

There remains one significant aspect that our code would benefit from. It's not a feature that would be present in production code, such as we've added in several preceding chapters. It's not even a test that would give us more confidence, like the one we carried out in this chapter. It's something that would add value by *continuously* validating our code.

 The code for this chapter is in a branch named "chap12" in the GitHub repository (*https://github.com/saleem/tdd-book-code/tree/chap12*).

CHAPTER 13

Continuous Integration

> The principle of continuous integration applies as well to testing, which should also be a continuous activity during the development process.
>
> —Grady Booch et al., *Object-Oriented Analysis and Design with Applications* (Addison-Wesley, 2007)

> With continuous integration, your software is proven to work (assuming a sufficiently comprehensive set of automated tests) with every new change—and you know the moment it breaks and can fix it immediately.
>
> —Jez Humble and David Farley, *Continuous Delivery* (Addison-Wesley, 2010)

Software entropy, like its counterpart in thermodynamics, is the principle that the degree of disorder in a system tends to increase over time. There may be no way out of entropy in physics—the second law of thermodynamics forbids it. Is there a way to stem entropy in software?

Our best current defense against the ruinous effects of code chaos is *continuous delivery (CD)*. The term comes from the first principle behind the Agile Manifesto (*https://agilemanifesto.org/principles.html*), which places customer satisfaction through the "early and continuous delivery of valuable software" as the highest priority.

A related term that precedes the Agile Manifesto by about a decade is *continuous integration (CI)*, coined by Grady Booch and refined by Kent Beck, Martin Fowler, Jez Humble, David Farley, and others. In a team with more than one developer, the reliable integration of code is even more vital, and thus should be done frequently.[1]

---

1 Martin Fowler defines continuous integration (*https://oreil.ly/vS6k1*) as "a software development practice where members of a team integrate their work frequently, usually each person integrates at least daily—leading to multiple integrations per day."

For continuous integration to exist, there must be automated tests. How else would we know that new changes have been "integrated" with existing code, for no amount of manual effort can "continuously" test software as it grows. This point is vital enough to be emphatically restated.

 There is no continuous integration without automated tests.

To get even more value out of the unit tests we've written thus far, we can run them as part of a continuous integration build process. This can be done using a wide variety of tools. In this penultimate chapter, we'll set up a continuous integration server using GitHub Actions.

Core Concepts

Continuous integration is the first phase in a software maturity continuum which evolves to continuous deployment and culminates in continuous delivery. Thus, CI is the first evolutionary step toward continuous delivery.

Figure 13-1 shows the general overview of continuous integration, deployment, and delivery (CI/CD).

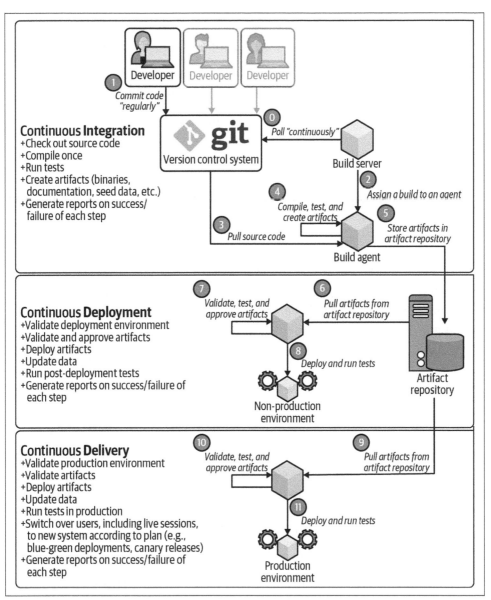

Continuous Integration
+Check out source code
+Compile once
+Run tests
+Create artifacts (binaries, documentation, seed data, etc.)
+Generate reports on success/ failure of each step

Continuous Deployment
+Validate deployment environment
+Validate and approve artifacts
+Deploy artifacts
+Update data
+Run post-deployment tests
+Generate reports on success/failure of each step

Continuous Delivery
+Validate production environment
+Validate artifacts
+Deploy artifacts
+Update data
+Run tests in production
+Switch over users, including live sessions, to new system according to plan (e.g., blue-green deployments, canary releases)
+Generate reports on success/failure of each step

Figure 13-1. Continuous integration and continuous deployment are evolutionary precursors to continuous delivery

Version Control

Continuous integration requires that all code that's needed to build the software be stored in a *version control* system.

A version control system must provide, at minimum, the following features:

1. Storing current (latest) revisions of files and folders in any arbitrary structure and depth.

2. Storing these files and folders under a unified "repository" and not merely as disparate elements.

3. Storing old (historic) revisions of files and folders—including those that have been subsequently deleted, renamed, moved, or otherwise modified.

4. Discrete and chronological versioning of all revisions—up to and including the current revision—of all these files and folders so that it's easy and unambiguous to track the history of any one file over time.

5. Ability to push (commit) changes to the code repository in a deterministic manner. (That is, a push should be accepted or rejected based on clear rules.)

6. Ability to query the code repository to detect any fresh changes.

7. Providing a CLI for the "push code," "pull code," and "query changes" features.

In addition, these features are highly desirable:

8. Storing multiple independent branches in the code repository, where branches can be created (forked), deleted, and rejoined (merged) with other branches.

9. Ability to resolve conflicts (which happen when two or more incompatible changes are made to the same file/folder).

10. Providing all these features in the CLI, without the need to resort to a GUI. This facilitates automation.

11. Supporting or providing a GUI for users who need/prefer it. This facilitates widespread adoption.

In common practice, each member of a development team regularly commits their code to one (or more) shared code repositories. Each person may commit code several times during a typical workday, leading to dozens (or even scores) of CI builds running daily.

A version control system like Git (*https://git-scm.com*) provides all the features listed above and many others. Git can be used as a distributed version control system with no centralized repository—individual developers share code with each other in a peer-to-peer fashion. Git's "patch" feature can be used to share changes with other team members using any existing, out-of-band mechanism, e.g., shared network folders or even email.

For the purpose of enabling CI, it's much more common to have a *centralized* Git server to which all developers connect. This centralized Git server contains the definitive and canonical code repositories. All other team members are expected to push code to, and pull code from, this centralized Git server.

With a centralized Git server, it's fairly common (bordering on universal) to use a platform as a service (PAAS) provider[2] instead of installing and maintaining a Git server of one's own. The ready availability of PAAS Git providers, including several that offer a generous "zero-price" tier—such as GitHub (*https://github.com*), GitLab (*https://gitlab.com*), and Bitbucket (*https://bitbucket.org*)—makes this an irresistible option.

Build Server and Agent

Automatically running the build takes multiple processes:

1. A *build server* process to regularly monitor the version control system and detect any changes
2. A *build agent* process to run a build whenever there are changes
   - There may be multiple build agent processes to run builds concurrently, run them on different operating systems, or build them with different sets of dependencies.

Typically, the build server conscripts one build agent for each build that needs to run. The build agents are independent of (and therefore, unaware of the existence of) other build agents.

In this book, we'll use the build server and build agents provided by GitHub Actions. We will use declarative programming to indicate which build agents we need and what should be installed on them. This declarative style is common in CI/CD systems—like GitHub Actions—which provide cloud-based build agents.

If the build agents are independent of each other, how do they share artifacts? This is where an artifact repository comes in.

Artifact Repository

To share build artifacts between build agents, an *artifact repository* is used. In principle, an artifact repository is a shared filesystem that each build agent can access.

---

2 This is a good primer for PAAS (*https://oreil.ly/NVq9x*).

Advanced features provided by an artifact repository may include versioning of each build artifact, seamless backup of artifacts for recoverability, and fine-grained read/write privileges (i.e., allowing specific build agents or other processes read-only or read-write access, as needed).

The artifact repository is similar to the version control system inasmuch as both are used to store and version files and folders. The two could even share the same underlying implementation. The key difference is in *what* they are used to store. The version control system is used to store source files that are authored and managed directly by the developers crafting the software. The artifact repository, in contrast, stores files generated by the act of building the software. Many of these files are binaries—executable programs, libraries, and data files. However, other generated files are not binary: API and code documentation, test results, and even source files generated during the build process. Regardless of whether the files are binary (i.e., not meant for human eyes) or human readable, storing them in the artifact repository ensures they are kept separate from the source files—the fountainhead of the software system.

 A *transpiler* (*https://oreil.ly/5isdB*) is a program that generates new source files, often in a different language, from given source files. The generated source code may be stylized for readability (e.g., JavaScript generated from CoffeeScript) or minimized for size or other considerations (e.g., minification of CSS or JavaScript files before loading in a web browser).

We do not need an artifact repository in this chapter, because we do not have any artifacts to share between different builds. However, GitHub does provide a mechanism to store build artifacts (*https://oreil.ly/1ux43*) using the same code repository that stores the source code.

Deployment Environment

After a successful CI build has run in a build agent, the build artifacts thus generated need to be deployed into a *deployment environment*. This allows these artifacts to be tested (mostly by automated tests but also by people) and released to end users (mostly people but also automated systems).

The deployment of build artifacts to one or more deployment environments is a key step in achieving continuous deployment and continuous delivery.

In this chapter, we'll focus on the first phase: continuous integration. Continuous deployment and continuous delivery—deploying the packaged software in an environment and ensuring that it is delivered to the end users—are out of the scope of this book.

Putting It All Together

We'll use GitHub Actions to add continuous integration to our project. This requires us to set up and verify a GitHub account, and possibly change some configuration information (e.g., two-factor authentication and/or SSH keys). These steps aren't directly relevant to the act of setting up a CI pipeline, and more properly belong in a book on GitHub. The remainder of this chapter focuses on the steps to get our code working in a continuous integration pipeline.

Here are the steps to build a CI pipeline for our code:

1. Create and/or verify our GitHub account.
2. Create a new project in GitHub.
3. Push our code repository to GitHub.
4. Prepare the source code for CI build scripts.
5. Create a CI build script for each language (Go, JavaScript, and Python).
6. Push the build scripts to GitHub.

Create Your GitHub Account

To create a CI pipeline using GitHub Actions, we need a GitHub account. If you already have a GitHub account, great! You may skip this section.

If you don't have a GitHub account, create one by visiting *https://github.com*. You do not need to pay anything for a free account, which is enough for our needs. (A free GitHub account is sufficient for many individual developers, as it allows unlimited public and private repositories and 2000 GitHub Actions minutes per month.

> Every minute (or fraction thereof) of activity using GitHub Actions counts toward your monthly quota, which is 2,000 minutes for the free GitHub plan.

All you need to create a GitHub account is a valid email address. It's strongly recommended that you set up two-factor authentication, which can be done in a variety of ways. See GitHub's documentation (*https://oreil.ly/MPEZc*) for more details.

Verify Your GitHub Account

Make sure you can log in to your GitHub account. If you decide to use the SSH protocol to interact with GitHub, you'll need to generate and add an SSH key. If you have other projects on GitHub and you regularly push and pull code to them, you probably don't need to do much by way of verifying your GitHub account.

> Using SSH allows you to designate specific devices—such as your development computer—as trusted by GitHub (*https://oreil.ly/ydY6K*). This means you can forgo specifying your username and personal access token at each visit.

If you haven't used your GitHub account in a while, you may want to fork a repo to verify your account is in pristine working condition. Go to *https://github.com/saleem/tdd-book-code* and use the "Fork" option to fork the repo. See Figure 13-2.

Figure 13-2. Fork a repository, like the one containing the code for this book, to verify that your GitHub account is working as expected

Of course, you'll use *your* handwritten (and highly cherished) code for the rest of this chapter—not the prefabricated and intellectually unsatisfying code you forked from this book's GitHub site! The purpose of forking is to verify that your GitHub account is working correctly.

Push Code Repository to GitHub

Up until the end of the preceding chapter, we regularly committed our code to our local Git repository. Now is the time to push our code repository to GitHub. The conceptual difference between these two actions is shown in Figure 13-3.

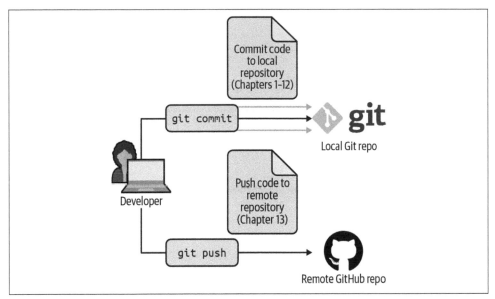

Figure 13-3. The difference between committing code to a local repository and pushing code to a remote repository

We first create a project in GitHub that will house all the code in our local code repo. To do this, we click the "New Repo" button. This starts a short (two-screen) workflow to create a new repository.

Figure 13-4 shows the first screen. This is where we enter the repository name. We use `tdd-project` for the name, which is the same name as our TDD Project Root folder. This makes things easier for us to remember. We also have the choice to make the repository private so no one else can see it, or leave it public so we can collaborate on it with others. Do *not* select any of the options under the "Initialize this repository with" heading. We already have a repository with several files in it.

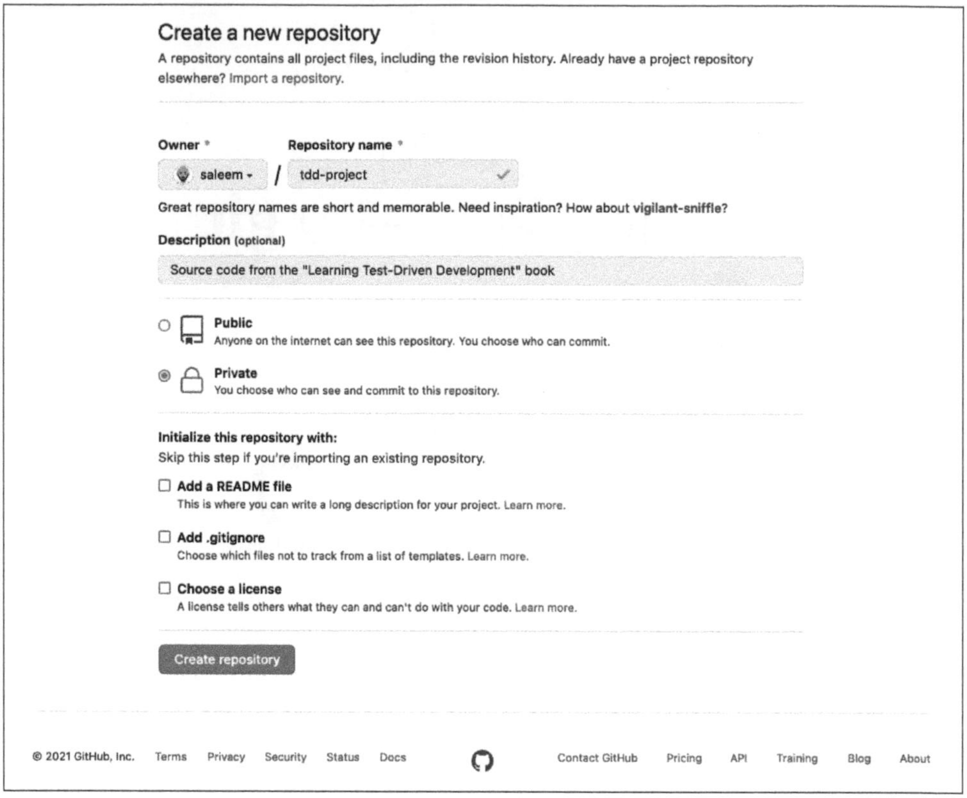

Figure 13-4. First step of creating a new repository on GitHub

The second screen shows the quick setup guide. We will use the instructions under the section "…or push an existing repository from the command line," as shown in Figure 13-5.

The command-line instructions in this section are already configured for *your* GitHub account name—you can simply copy and paste the three lines of code verbatim. Leave the browser screen as it's shown in Figure 13-5 and use the commands in a shell window to push your code to GitHub.

Figure 13-5. Second step of creating a new repository on GitHub

Figure 13-6 shows the results of the three commands for my GitHub repo. Notice that the first two commands silently succeed. The third command—`git push -u origin main`—produces some output on the screen.

```
tdd-project> git remote add origin git@github.com:saleem/tdd-project.git
tdd-project> git branch -M main
tdd-project> git push -u origin main
Enumerating objects: 109, done.
Counting objects: 100% (109/109), done.
Delta compression using up to 12 threads
Compressing objects: 100% (100/100), done.
Writing objects: 100% (109/109), 15.71 KiB | 2.62 MiB/s, done.
Total 109 (delta 36), reused 0 (delta 0), pack-reused 0
remote: Resolving deltas: 100% (36/36), done.
To github.com:saleem/tdd-project.git
 * [new branch]      main -> main
Branch 'main' set up to track remote branch 'main' from 'origin'.
tdd-project> _
```

Figure 13-6. Pushing code from our local Git repository to the GitHub repository

After you've successfully pushed your code to GitHub, simply refresh the browser window that previously showed the commands (shown in Figure 13-5). The contents of that browser page should change, showing you the code you just pushed, as seen in Figure 13-7.

Figure 13-7. Code after it's been pushed to the GitHub repository

Our code is ready to be spruced up with the awesomeness that is continuous integration!

Prepare for CI Build Scripts

Our code has different folders with source code for the three languages. Here's the complete folder structure under the TDD_PROJECT_ROOT folder:

```
tdd-book-code
├── go
│   ├── go.mod
│   ├── money_test.go
│   └── stocks
│       ├── bank.go
│       ├── money.go
│       └── portfolio.go
├── js
│   ├── bank.js
│   ├── money.js
│   ├── portfolio.js
│   └── test_money.js
└── py
    ├── bank.py
```

```
├── money.py
├── portfolio.py
└── test_money.py
```

Our CI build scripts will be in a new folder, actually, a new subfolder in a new folder. It needs to be named .github/workflows. Pay attention to the . in the front! It's imperative that this folder be created exactly as named.

 The continuous integration scripts using GitHub workflows must be in a folder named .github/workflows under the TDD_PROJECT_ROOT.

To create this folder, type the following command in the shell, from the TDD_PROJECT_ROOT:

```
mkdir -p .github/workflows
```

This will create both the .github folder and the workflows folder underneath it, all at once.

Our CI scripts will be in YAML format. Our YAML scripts for Go, JavaScript, and Python will follow a similar structure, which is shown in the following code fragment:

```
name: Name of script ❶
on:
  push:
    branches: [ main ] ❷
jobs:
  build:
    name: Build ❸
    strategy:
      matrix: ❹
...
        platform: [ubuntu-latest, macos-latest, windows-latest] ❺
    runs-on: ${{ matrix.platform }} ❻
    steps: ❼
    - name: Set up language-specific environment ❽
...
    - name: Check out code
      uses: actions/checkout@v2 ❾
    - name: Test ❿
      run:...
      shell: bash ⓫
```

❶ A meaningful name for the entire script.

❷ The script runs on each push to the main branch.

❸ There is only one `job` in each script, named `Build`.

❹ We use a `matrix` build `strategy`, allowing us to build on multiple operating systems and language versions.

❺ We signal our intent to use the "latest" versions of Ubuntu, macOS, and Windows operating systems in the `matrix.platform` variable.

❻ The previously defined `matrix.platform` variable is used here to run the build.

❼ There will be exactly three steps in our build job for each CI script.

❽ First step: language-specific environment configuration will be done here.

❾ Second step: this is how we'll check out code, regardless of language.

❿ Third step: language-specific commands will `run` the tests here.

⓫ We specify that the Bash shell should be used for the preceding commands in the third step.

 YAML—a recursive and defiant acronym for "YAML Ain't Markup Language"—is a data serialization standard widely used for configuration files like our continuous integration scripts. Its official website is *https://yaml.org*.

The script structure is dense but packs a lot of punch! Let's analyze its various components.

The first line is the name of the script. The property `name` is used in many places in this script. Names can be anything we want; therefore, it's best to name it something that will describe the purpose of the script well. We'll name each script after the language for which it is intended.

Next we describe when the script should run. The `on: {push: {branches: [ main ]}}` section dictates that the script should run on every `push` to the `main` branch.[3]

---

3 The single-line representation of a YAML dictionary requires curly braces. Alternately, we can use multiple lines with indentation, as we'll do in the actual YAML files. Here is a basic tutorial on YAML (*https://oreil.ly/SjYru*).

Next we define our `jobs` section. There is exactly one job in each script: `build`. We chose "Build" as the `name` of this job. We choose a "matrix strategy" for our builds. A matrix strategy is a powerful feature provided by GitHub Actions: it allows us to run the same build on multiple operating systems, language compilers, etc. This is immensely helpful to ensure that our code builds and runs on a variety of environments, not just the one we are currently using. If you have ever heard any rendition of the "it works on my machine" joke, you know how important this feature is!

Our `matrix` comprises two dimensions: operating systems and language compilers. We'll choose the three popular families of operating systems for each language: Ubuntu, macOS, and Windows. The compiler dimension will vary for each language. The `runs-on` property ensures that our build will run on each of these three operating systems.

Figure 13-8 shows the general formulation of the matrix.

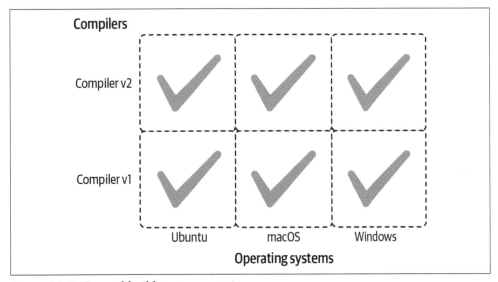

Figure 13-8. General build strategy matrix

The last section lists the `steps` in our build process. Each CI script will have three steps, the first and last of which are language specific:

1. The first step will set up the build environment needed by that language.

2. The second step, checking out the code from the GitHub repository, is identical for all three build scripts. This step uses the `checkout` action provided by GitHub Actions.

3. The last step runs the tests for the specific language. This step will look familiar to us: it will include commands to run the tests for each language that we have used throughout this book.

 There are many readily available GitHub Actions written by an active community of developers. We'll use several of these actions in our CI build scripts. See *https://github.com/actions* for details.

With this overview of the structure of CI build script and YAML behind us, let's get to the business of writing the specific build scripts for each of our three languages.

Go

For Go, we will choose to support versions 1.16 and 1.17 of the language. Even though we have consistently used Go 1.17 to build the code in this book, it's valuable to support two versions of the language. Go's release history states that the two most recent major releases are supported (*https://oreil.ly/S8QNR*).

For the first build step, we'll use the `setup-go` action published by GitHub Actions to set up our Go environment.

For the third build step, we'll do four different tasks:

1. Set the `GO111MODULE` environment variable to on.
2. Set the `GOPATH` environment variable to an empty string.
3. Switch to the go directory under `TDD_PROJECT_ROOT`.
4. Run our tests with the tried and tested `go test -v ./...` command.[4]

All these tasks are familiar to us. We encountered the first two back in Chapter 0. The other two we've used throughout our work.

With these special considerations for Go understood, we create a file named `go.yml` in the `.github/workflows` folder. Here are the full contents of that file:

```
name: Go CI ❶
on:
  push:
    branches: [ main ]
```

---

4 Recall that the three dots in `go test -v ./...` are to be typed in literally; they do not represent any omitted code!

```
jobs:
  build:
    name: Build
    strategy:
      matrix:
        go-version: [1.16.x, 1.17.x] ❷
        platform: [ubuntu-latest, macos-latest, windows-latest]
    runs-on: ${{ matrix.platform }}
    steps:
    - name: Set up Go ${{matrix.go-version}}
      uses: actions/setup-go@v2 ❸
      with:
        go-version: ${{matrix.go-version}} ❹
    - name: Check out code
      uses: actions/checkout@v2
    - name: Test
      run: | ❺
        export GO111MODULE="on" ❻
        export GOPATH="" ❼
        cd go ❽
        go test -v ./...❾
      shell: bash
```

❶ Name of the Go CI script.

❷ The two versions of Go we support.

❸ We use version v2 of the prefabricated setup-go action.

❹ This refers to the go-version property defined above.

❺ The run tasks are run in succession using the pipe | operator.

❻ Setting GO111MODULE to "on".

❼ Clearing out GOPATH by setting it to an empty string.

❽ Switching to the go folder.

❾ Running all our Go tests.

That's it: our CI build script for Go is ready.

JavaScript

We have targeted our JavaScript code for Node.js versions 14 and 16. We'll use the latest minor releases of these versions in our matrix.

For the first build step, we'll use the `setup-node` action published by GitHub Actions to set up our Node.js environment.

For the third build step, we'll use our familiar node `js/test_money.js` command to run all the JavaScript tests.

We create a file named `js.yml` in the `.github/workflows` folder incorporating the aforementioned configuration details. Here are the full contents of that file:

```
name: JavaScript CI ❶
on:
  push:
    branches: [ main ]
jobs:
  build:
    name: Build
    strategy:
      matrix:
        node-version: [14.x, 16.x] ❷
        platform: [ubuntu-latest, macos-latest, windows-latest]
    runs-on: ${{ matrix.platform }}
    steps:
    - name: Set up Node.js ${{ matrix.node-version }}
      uses: actions/setup-node@v2 ❸
      with:
        node-version: ${{ matrix.node-version }} ❹
    - name: Check out code
      uses: actions/checkout@v2
    - name: Test
      run: node js/test_money.js ❺
      shell: bash
```

❶ Name of the JavaScript CI script.

❷ The two versions of Node.js we support.

❸ We use version v2 of the prefabricated `setup-node` action.

❹ This refers to the `node-version` property defined above.

❺ Running all our JavaScript tests.

With these configuration changes saved, our CI build script for JavaScript using Node.js is ready to be used.

Python

The two most recent releases of Python as of late 2021 (*https://oreil.ly/PM13F*) are 3.9 and 3.10. We'll target the latest minor release number for both of these, i.e., 3.9.x and 3.10.x.

For the first build step, we'll use the `setup-python` action published by GitHub Actions to set up our Python environment.

For the third build step, we'll use the by now familiar `python py/test_money.py -v` command to run all the Python tests.

Let's create a file named `py.yml` in the `.github/workflows` folder with these configuration details. Here's how that file looks in its entirety:

```yaml
name: Python CI ❶
on:
  push:
    branches: [ main ]
jobs:
  build:
    name: Build
    strategy:
      matrix:
        python-version: [3.9.x, 3.10.x] ❷
        platform: [ubuntu-latest, macos-latest, windows-latest]
    runs-on: ${{matrix.platform}}
    steps:
    - name: Set up Python ${{ matrix.node-version }}
      uses: actions/setup-python@v2 ❸
      with:
        python-version: ${{ matrix.python-version }} ❹
    - name: Checkout code
      uses: actions/checkout@v2
    - name: Test
      run: python py/test_money.py -v ❺
      shell: bash
```

❶   Name of the Python CI script.

❷   The two versions of Python we support.

❸   We use version v2 of the prefabricated `setup-python` action.

❹   This refers to the `python-version` property defined in ❷.

❺   Running all our Python tests.

Our CI script for Python is now ready to be put to use.

Committing Our Changes

With the continuous integration scripts written and saved in the .github/workflows folder, we can now commit them en masse to GitHub and watch them run:

```
git add . ❶
git commit -m "feature: continuous integration scripts using GitHub Actions" ❷
git push -u origin main ❸
```

❶ Adding all the new files in the .github/actions folder

❷ Committing our changes

❸ Pushing our changes to GitHub

This is where the magic happens!

Open up a web browser and go to your project on GitHub. Navigate to the "Actions" tab of your project.

 You can bookmark the "Actions" tab of your project, if you like: it ends in "/actions". For the GitHub repository accompanying this book, the Actions tab is directly accessible at *https://github.com/ saleem/tdd-book-code/actions*.

You should see something similar to what's shown in Figure 13-9.

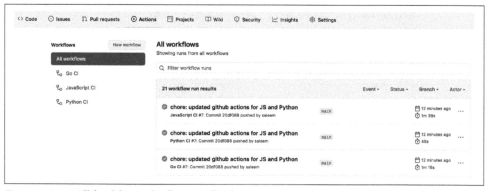

Figure 13-9. All builds on the "Actions" tab in our GitHub project

Voilà! Through GitHub Actions, we have run the CI scripts for each language, and unless we made any typos in our YAML files, things should be all green. We can navigate to different builds and examine the details—the layout is self-explanatory. For example, Figure 13-10 shows what we see when we click on "Go CI" on the left and then click on one entry in the list of commits.

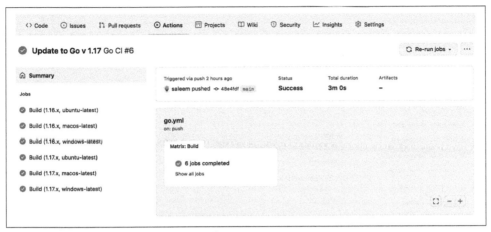

Figure 13-10. Go builds for our GitHub project

Notice that there are six jobs that ran from this one commit. This is because of our strategy matrix. We have tested our Go code for each version of Go (1.16 and 1.17) on each operating system (Ubuntu, Windows, and macOS).

The JavaScript builds are shown in Figure 13-11. Again, we have six different jobs, corresponding to the two versions of Node.js (14 and 16) and the three operating systems.

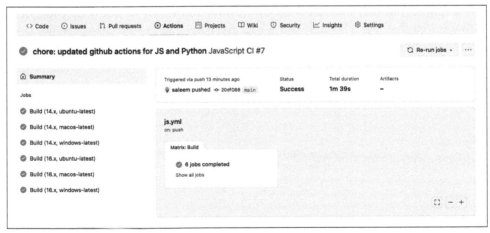

Figure 13-11. JavaScript builds for our GitHub project

The Python builds are similar, as shown in Figure 13-12. Yet again, we have six different jobs, corresponding to the two versions of Python (3.9 and 3.10) and the three operating systems.

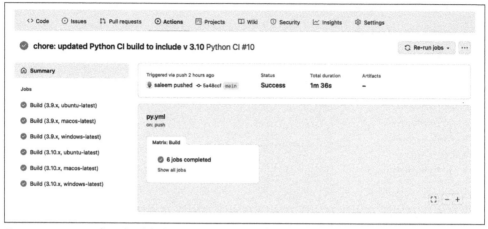

Figure 13-12. Python builds for our GitHub project

Pretty comprehensive, isn't it!

We can also drill down into the details of any of these 18 builds to see exactly what happened at each step of any one build. That's a lot of information. To illustrate, Figure 13-13 shows some details emitted by the build that ran our Go tests using Go version 1.17 on the Windows operating system.

What's more, not only have we successfully built and tested all our code *once*, we've also ensured that it will be built and tested *every time* we push a change to the main branch of our GitHub repository. That's continuous integration in a nutshell, and our code is better for it.

Figure 13-13. Details of the Go v1.17 build on the Windows operating system

Running GitHub Actions Locally

GitHub Actions, as described in this chapter, provide a glorious array of features: multiple operating systems, multiple compiler versions, and a wide range of actions in its marketplace (*https://oreil.ly/CyCnu*) to choose from. However, you do have to commit code to GitHub first to get all these benefits. You may want to run GitHub Actions locally on your computer before you commit changes to GitHub. It could be because of a slow or unreliable network connection. Or perhaps you want to conserve the number of GitHub Actions minutes you use per month. Regardless of the reasons, it is a legitimate question. Is there a way to have the best of both worlds: the power of GitHub Actions running locally on your computer?

The act (*https://oreil.ly/reAh3*) tool offers a fairly good solution. You can install it on your development computer and then simply type act in the shell to run it from the TDD_PROJECT_ROOT folder. The act tool downloads Docker (*https://www.docker.com*) images on your computer and uses them to run the GitHub Actions builds.[5] Even though windows-latest and macos-latest—two of the three operating systems we have used in this chapter—are unsupported as of late 2021, support for ubuntu-latest is there. If you like quick feedback (and who doesn't?), act may be an answer.

Figure 13-14 shows the first several lines of output after using act in our TDD_PROJECT_ROOT folder. Notice that only 6 out of the 18 builds are supported: 2 each for Go, JavaScript, and Python on the Ubuntu operating system.

---

5 Docker is a suite of software tools that provides containers. It allows differences in operating systems, compilers, libraries, etc. to be neatly and reliably abstracted. It is a popular and strongly recommended mechanism to package and deploy applications.

```
tdd-project>act
[Python CI/Build-3      ] ⚏  Skipping unsupported platform 'windows-latest'
[Go CI/Build-3          ] ⚏  Skipping unsupported platform 'windows-latest'
[JavaScript CI/Build-6] ⚏  Skipping unsupported platform 'windows-latest'
[Python CI/Build-2      ] ⚏  Skipping unsupported platform 'macos-latest'
[JavaScript CI/Build-1] ✏  Matrix: map[node-version:14.x platform:ubuntu-latest]
[Go CI/Build-1          ] ✏  Matrix: map[go-version:1.16.x platform:ubuntu-latest]
[Python CI/Build-1      ] ✏  Matrix: map[platform:ubuntu-latest python-version:3.9.x]
[JavaScript CI/Build-1] 🚀  Start image=catthehacker/ubuntu:act-latest
[JavaScript CI/Build-3] ⚏  Skipping unsupported platform 'windows-latest'
[Go CI/Build-1          ] 🚀  Start image=catthehacker/ubuntu:act-latest
[Python CI/Build-5      ] ⚏  Skipping unsupported platform 'macos-latest'
[Python CI/Build-6      ] ⚏  Skipping unsupported platform 'windows-latest'
[Go CI/Build-5          ] ⚏  Skipping unsupported platform 'macos-latest'
[Python CI/Build-1      ] 🚀  Start image=catthehacker/ubuntu:act-latest
[JavaScript CI/Build-5] ⚏  Skipping unsupported platform 'macos-latest'
[Go CI/Build-6          ] ⚏  Skipping unsupported platform 'windows-latest'
[Go CI/Build-4          ] ✏  Matrix: map[go-version:1.17.x platform:ubuntu-latest]
[Go CI/Build-4          ] 🚀  Start image=catthehacker/ubuntu:act-latest
[Python CI/Build-4      ] ✏  Matrix: map[platform:ubuntu-latest python-version:3.10.x]
[Python CI/Build-4      ] 🚀  Start image=catthehacker/ubuntu:act-latest
[JavaScript CI/Build-2] ⚏  Skipping unsupported platform 'macos-latest'
[JavaScript CI/Build-4] ✏  Matrix: map[node-version:16.x platform:ubuntu-latest]
[JavaScript CI/Build-4] 🚀  Start image=catthehacker/ubuntu:act-latest
[Go CI/Build-2          ] ⚏  Skipping unsupported platform 'macos-latest'
```

Figure 13-14. The act *tool run on our project, showing supported and unsupported platforms*

Where We Are

We're at end of our journey of writing code to solve the "Money" problem. *Chairete, nikomen!*[6]

We have covered a lot of ground. We have written code, written tests, deleted and refined both, and added continuous integration. We deserve a collective pat on the back!

There's something more that we deserve and need: a review of our journey. That's what we'll do in Chapter 14, the final chapter.

---

6 "Rejoice, we win!"—words made famous by Philippides after the battle of Marathon.

Retrospective

Retrospectives can be a powerful catalyst for change. A major transformation can start from a single retrospective.

—Esther Derby and Diana Larsen, *Agile Retrospectives—Making Good Teams Great* (Pragmatic Bookshelf, 2006)

We have finished all the features on our list. Here's the cumulative list, lightly edited for clarity:

~~5 USD × 2 = 10 USD~~

~~10 EUR × 2 = 20 EUR~~

~~4002 KRW / 4 = 1000.5 KRW~~

~~5 USD + 10 USD = 15 USD~~

~~5 USD + 10 EUR = 17 USD~~

~~1 USD + 1100 KRW = 2200 KRW~~

~~Remove redundant tests~~

~~Separate test code from production code~~

~~Improve the organization of our tests~~

~~Determine exchange rate based on the currencies involved~~

~~Improve error handling when exchange rates are unspecified~~

~~Improve the implementation of exchange rates~~

~~Allow exchange rates to be modified~~

~~Continuously integrate our code~~

Does the act of crossing out every line in the list mean we're done? Decidedly not! For one thing, change is the only constant in software. Even if we decide to not touch anything in our code because it is fit for our purposes, the things surrounding our code are bound to change over time. During the time it took to write this book, the following things changed in the ecosystem:

1. Go v1.17 was released (*https://oreil.ly/zKGK4*).
2. Node.js v16 was released (*https://oreil.ly/jteMp*).
3. Python versions 3.9 and 3.10 were released (*https://oreil.ly/xNLPa*).
4. New versions of the GitHub Actions `setup-node` (*https://oreil.ly/0Strt*) and `setup-python` (*https://oreil.ly/sGZDj*) were released.
5. And significantly, vaccines for COVID-19 were released and approved (*https://oreil.ly/IGEb5*), changing yet again how we structure our lives, do our work, and conduct our social interactions—of which writing software is one aspect.

It is almost certain that by the time you read these words, other significant changes will have happened in the myriad things that exist in the ecosystem in which our code lives.

Beyond the great unknown of the future, are there things about our code in the here-and-now that we could potentially improve?

Let's take some time to recap what we did and reflect upon how we did it. We'll frame our retrospective along these dimensions:

Profile
　　This refers to the shape of the code.

Purpose
　　This includes what the code does and—more importantly—does not do.

Process
　　How we got to where we are, what other ways might have been possible, and the implications of taking a specific path.

Profile

I use the term *profile* to include both subjective aspects, such as readability and obviousness, and their objective manifestations, namely complexity, coupling, and succinctness. In other disciplines, the word *form* is also used to describe analogous aspects.

In the Preface, we identified *simplicity* as a key term in the definition of test-driven development. We can measure the simplicity of our code now using some metrics.

Cyclomatic Complexity

Cyclomatic complexity is a measure of the degree of branching and looping in code, which contributes to the difficulty in understanding it. This measure was defined by Thomas McCabe in a paper published in 1976 (*https://oreil.ly/isAAw*). Later, McCabe and Arthur Watson developed this concept specifically in the context of a testing methodology (*https://oreil.ly/yTVWR*). McCabe's definition of cyclomatic complexity —independent of the syntactical differences between languages and rooted in the organization of source code as a control-flow graph—is relevant to us as we analyze things from the vantage point of TDD.

In the simplest terms, the cyclomatic complexity of a block of code is the number of loops and branches in the code plus one.

> The cyclomatic complexity of a block of code with p binary decision predicates is $p + 1$. A *binary decision predicate* is any point in code where one of two paths can be taken, i.e., a branch or a loop on one Boolean condition.

A block of code with no branches or loops—that is, one where control flows linearly from one statement to the next—has a cyclomatic complexity of 1.

McCabe's original paper recommended that developers "limit their software modules by cyclomatic complexity instead of physical size." McCabe provided an upper limit of 10 and pragmatically called this "a reasonable, but not magical, upper limit."

Coupling

Coupling is a measure of the interdependency of a block of code (e.g., a class or method) on other blocks of code. The two kinds of coupling are *afferent* and *efferent* *coupling*.

Afferent coupling
    This is the number of other components that depend on a given component.

Efferent coupling
    This is the number of other components that a given component depends on.

Figure 14-1 shows a class diagram with various dependencies. For `ClassUnderDiscus sion`, the afferent coupling is 1 and the efferent coupling is 2.

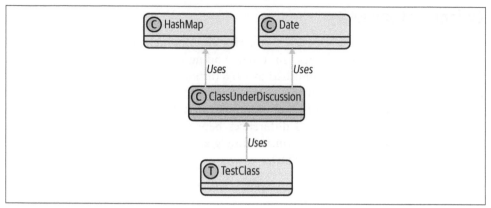

Figure 14-1. Afferent and efferent coupling

 Useful mnemonic: *afferent* coupling is indicated by the number of dependency arrows that *arrive* at a given component; *efferent* coupling reflects the number of arrows that *exit* from a given component.

A measure of the stability of the code is the balance between afferent and efferent coupling. The *instability* of a component can be defined by the following formula:

Instability = (efferent)/(efferent + afferent)

That is, the instability of a component is a fraction between 0 and 1. Zero indicates a completely stable component that does not depend on anything else. This is virtually impossible for any component written in a general-purpose language, since any such component would, at minimum, depend on components provided by the language (i.e., primitives or system classes). A value of 1 indicates maximum instability: such a component depends on other components and nothing depends on it.

For the ClassUnderDiscussion in Figure 14-1, the instability is 2/3.

Succinctness

Lines of code is a dangerous metric—especially across different languages. The expressive power of languages varies widely. An obvious reason for this is the presence or absence of certain linguistic features—keywords, idioms, libraries, and patterns—in a particular language. Even something as trivial as formatting conventions can artificially increase or decrease the line count across languages. Consider the following two behaviorally identical "Hello World" programs, one in C# and the other in Go:

```
namespace HelloWorld ❶
{
    class Hello ❷
    {
        static void Main(string[] args) ❸
        {
            System.Console.WriteLine("Hello World!"); ❹
        }
    }
}
```

❶ Declare namespace for program.

❷ Define a class to contain the method.

❸ Define the method that does the work.

❹ The line of code that prints "Hello World," with a dependency on `System
.Console.WriteLine` method.

```
package main ❶

import "fmt" ❷

func main() { ❸
    fmt.Println("Hello World!") ❹
}
```

❶ Declare package for program.

❷ Include `fmt` package as a dependency.

❸ Define the method that does the work.

❹ The line of code that prints "Hello World" using the `Println` method from the
`fmt` package.

It's clear that it takes 10 lines of C# code to do the same work as 7 lines of Go code. Is this a fair or even meaningful comparison? No! Despite the structural similarities between the two languages—both require the declaration of dependencies, the definition of a namespace, a "main" method that does the work, and a single line of code to print "Hello World"—there are sufficient differences to make a comparison of lines of code (LOC) silly. For another thing, C# requires a class within which the Main method must be defined, there is no such need for the Go main function. Yet another difference is that Go requires opening braces be put at the end of the lines where the method (or any other block, like an if or for statement) is defined. Contrastingly,

C#'s conventions require that the opening brace be put by itself on a new line. This latter difference itself contributes to three extra lines of code in the C# program.[1]

A better metric is to compare the lines of test code to the lines of production code in the same language. This normalizes for any language-specific quirks and conventions —especially as the code size increases and the line count takes on a statistical (as opposed to anecdotal) significance.

Purpose

Aesthetics are important. However, all code is written to meet some need. The extent to which it meets that need, and the manner in which it does so, are what I call *purpose*. In other disciplines, the word *function*—especially in contrast to *form*—is used. I've avoided using this term because of the risk of confusing an aspect of code with the software meaning of the word *function*.

The extent to which a piece of code meets its purpose can be looked at from two perspectives: does it do everything it's intended to do? And does it do only what it should do? The latter is termed *cohesion*, and the former *completeness*.

Cohesion

Cohesion is a measure of the *relatedness* of the code in a module. High cohesion reflects that the code in a module—method, class, or package—represents a single, unified concept.

Cohesion is a subjective measure. However, cohesion is of different types, some of which are preferable to others. The most desirable form of cohesion is *functional cohesion*, which is when all parts of a module contribute to a single, well-defined task. At the other end of the spectrum is *coincidental cohesion*, which is when the parts of a module are grouped arbitrarily with no discernible singularity of purpose.

Completeness

Does our code do everything it should? Functionally, we finished all the items on our checklist—we crossed everything off. That's one indicator of completeness.

How complete are our tests, though? Could we gain more confidence by writing additional tests? Consider these cases:

---

1 The reason Go requires that the open brace be on the same line is more than merely aesthetics; it's rooted in how the language's compiler figures out where one statement ends and another begins (*https://oreil.ly/foav0*).

Overflow

This is the condition that results from storing a number that's too large to be stored in a particular data type. Adding `Money` entities or multiplying a `Money` with another number can cause overflow.

Underflow

This is the condition that results from storing a number that's too small (i.e., very close to zero). There aren't enough significant digits to represent the number correctly. Dividing `Money` by a large number can cause underflow, as can the presence of a very small exchange rate.

Division by zero

The result of dividing a nonzero number by zero is infinity. The result of dividing zero by zero is undefined.

None of these scenarios are currently tested, and therefore the code is unable to deal with them. It's compelling evidence that the code is incomplete. However, we know how to build these features: by driving them via tests.

Process

Both *profile* and *purpose* measure the code on various attributes of quality. They judge the destination of the journey. In contrast, it is equally important to assess the process of how we got to the final version of our code, including the various intermediate incarnations that may not have survived till the end. This is a judgment of the path we took along our journey.

What if we had started building our features in a different order than what was on our checklist? It's quite possible, perhaps likely, that we would end up with a different implementation. For example, our `Money` entity has methods for multiplication and division, but not for addition. If we had implemented the feature "5 USD + 10 USD = 15 USD" in Chapter 1 instead of Chapter 3, we may have had an addition method in the `Money` entity.

There was a logical progression in the way we arranged our features: simple ones first. However, had we started by, say, building the addition feature with different currencies (e.g., "5 USD + 10 EUR = 17 USD"), we would have had to introduce exchange rates quite early. Where would we have put them? Probably in `Money`, since that's still a reasonable first abstraction. Would we have recognized and extracted the `Portfolio` and `Bank` entities? It's difficult to speculate, but I'm tempted to say it would have required more effort to identify multiple abstract concepts while building one feature.

Putting It All Together

We have seen the three dimensions—profile, purpose, and process—that we can use to analyze our code. Let's project our code onto the three dimensions and see what reflections we see.

Go

Profile

We can measure the cyclomatic complexity of our code by using a tool like gocyclo (*https://github.com/fzipp/gocyclo*). This tool, itself written in Go, can be installed as an executable and then used to analyze the cyclomatic complexity of any Go code. If we run `gocyclo .` in our go folder, here are the most complex methods. Every other method has the minimal possible cyclomatic complexity of 1:

```
5 stocks (Portfolio).Evaluate stocks/portfolio.go:12:1
3 main assertNil money_test.go:129:1
3 stocks (Bank).Convert stocks/bank.go:14:1
2 main assertEqual money_test.go:135:1
```

We see that the most complicated method—`Portfolio.Evaluate`—has a cyclomatic complexity of 5. Even though this is well below the heuristic threshold of 10, it's illustrative to see that this complexity could be reduced by using the extract method refactoring one or more times. For example, the creation of a failure message could be extracted into a new method, which is then called from within `Portfolio.Evaluate`:

```
func (p Portfolio) Evaluate(bank Bank, currency string) (*Money, error) {
  ... ❶
  failures := createFailureMessage(failedConversions) ❷
  return nil, errors.New("Missing exchange rate(s):" + failures)
}

func createFailureMessage(failedConversions []string) string { ❸
  failures := "["
  for _, f := range failedConversions {
    failures = failures + f + ","
  }
  failures = failures + "]"
  return failures
}
```

❶ Unchanged code in `Evaluate`, omitted for brevity.

❷ Call a private function to create failure message.

❸ Function `createFailureMessage` extracted from within the `Evaluate` method.

Is this better? It depends on your perspective. The cyclomatic complexity of `Evaluate` is lower (4), but the combined cyclomatic complexity of the two methods is now higher (6).

The coupling within our code is low. `Portfolio` depends on `Money` and `Bank`. `Bank` depends on `Money`. The Test class—unavoidably—depends on all three. The only reasonable reduction in coupling we can do is to separate the tests into classes: `Test Money`, `TestPortfolio`, and `TestBank`.

In terms of succinctness, Go provides a tool to check for suspicious code. It is the vet command (*https://oreil.ly/Fo5QC*), and it's instructive to run the `go vet ./...` (the ellipses are to be typed literally) and notice the output. For our program, there are no warnings, which is how we should endeavor to keep all our programs. The vet command not only looks for superfluous code—useless assignments and unreachable code, for example—but it also warns against common errors in Go constructs.

Purpose

Our Go code has good cohesion: three named types with well-defined responsibilities. The one criticism that can be laid at our doorstep is that, because there is no `Add` method in `Money`, the addition of amounts happens within `Portfolio.Evaluate` and not in `Money`.

What if we had a `Money.Add` method? We could simplify our `Portfolio.Evaluate` a bit, as shown here:

```
func (p Portfolio) Evaluate(bank Bank, currency string) (*Money, error) {
  totalMoney := NewMoney(0, currency) ❶
  failedConversions := make([]string, 0)
  for _, m := range p {
    if convertedMoney, err := bank.Convert(m, currency); err == nil {
      totalMoney = *totalMoney.Add(convertedMoney) ❷
    } else {
      failedConversions = append(failedConversions, err.Error())
    }
  }
  if len(failedConversions) == 0 {
    return &totalMoney, nil ❸
  }
  ... ❹
}
```

❶ Sum is accumulated in `totalMoney` whose type is `Money`, not `float64`

❷ Using the new `Money.Add` method, assuming it has only one return value

❸ Returning a `Money` pointer, as before

❹ Rest of the method is identical, omitted for brevity

How would we test-drive the Money.Add method? We may find it propitious to adhere to this design:

1. The method should accept a single other *Money argument.

2. Its return value should be *Money type, representing the sum of this Money and other Money.

3. It should add the other Money only if the currencies of other and this Money match.

4. When the currencies of the two Moneys differ, it should indicate the failure to add them, either by returning a nil or by panicing—mildly justifiable in this case because it's only ever called from Portfolio.Evaluate when currencies match after conversion.

Process

We started by putting the Money and Portfolio code in a single source file and then separating them into two files in the stocks package. We then created Bank in this package later. Could we have identified this separation earlier, perhaps right at the beginning? Or conversely, could we have coded all of it in one giant file and separated them at the end? What if we didn't separate code into discrete files at all?

The process we followed minutely affected the shape of our Go code. As a general rule, a process should be judged by the results it produces. In TDD, we have a significant lever to control the process: the pace at which we proceed. Our single-file production code had acquired two distinct abstractions—Money and Portfolio—by the end of Chapter 3. That's why we modularized at that juncture. Now that you've finished the features, what do you think? Would you make a similar choice if you redid the code, perhaps to teach someone else?

JavaScript

Profile

To gather complexity metrics for our JavaScript code, we can use a tool like JSHint (*https://jshint.com*). JSHint comes in many guises, the home page provides an online editor in which you can paste JavaScript code and measure its complexity. For our purposes, the NodeJS package is more appropriate. JSHint can be installed globally by running npm install -g jshint at a command line.

To use `jshint`, we need to specify a couple of configuration parameters. The simplest way to do this is to create a file named `.jshintrc` in the `js` folder:

```
{
    "esversion"     : 6, ❶
    "maxcomplexity" : 1  ❷
}
```

❶   Specifying the version of ECMAScript to use

❷   Setting the maximum cyclomatic complexity to the lowest possible value

Note that we have set the `maxcomplexity` to 1—the lowest possible cyclomatic complexity for any method. The goal isn't to meet this threshold. As mentioned earlier, 10 is a more typical value for `maxcomplexity`. The reason we set it to 1 here is to force `jshint` to print every method with a higher cyclomatic complexity as an error.

With this short `.jshintrc` file in place, we can simply run `jshint *.js` from the command line in the `js` folder to examine which methods have a cyclomatic complexity that exceeds 1:

```
bank.js: line 13, col 12,
  This function's cyclomatic complexity is too high. (3)

portfolio.js: line 14, col 41,
  This function's cyclomatic complexity is too high. (2)
portfolio.js: line 12, col 13,
  This function's cyclomatic complexity is too high. (2)

test_money.js: line 80, col 21,
  This function's cyclomatic complexity is too high. (2)
test_money.js: line 91, col 44,
  This function's cyclomatic complexity is too high. (2)
test_money.js: line 99, col 30,
  This function's cyclomatic complexity is too high. (3)

6 errors
```

We see that there are a couple of methods with a cyclomatic complexity of 3, and a few more with a complexity metric of 2.

This validates a key claim of test-driven development. The incremental and evolutionary style of coding that TDD encourages results in code with a more uniform complexity profile. Instead of one or two "superman" methods or classes, we get a better distribution of responsibility across our modules.

The coupling in our code is low. Both `Portfolio` and `Bank` depend on `Money`, which is a natural consequence of our domain. There is also a more subtle dependency from `Bank` to `Portfolio`. It's subtle, because unlike `Money`, the `Portfolio` does not require an object of type Bank. The evaluate method in Portfolio requires a "bank-like object"—that is, an object that implements a convert method. This is a dependency on an interface and not a specific implementation. This is different from how Portfolio depends on Money: there is an explicit call to new Money() in the evaluate method.

 When class A *creates* a new instance of class B, it is difficult to use dependency injection. However, if A only *uses* methods defined by B—i.e., A has an interface dependency on B—it is easier to use dependency injection.

We encountered dependency injection in Chapters 4 and 11. We can inject *any* object that implements a convert method to test Portfolio.evaluate—it doesn't have to be an actual Bank object. Consider this strangely written but valid—and passing—test:

```
testAdditionWithTestDouble() {
  const moneyCount = 10; ❶
  let moneys = []
  for (let i = 0; i < moneyCount; i++) {
    moneys.push(
      new Money(Math.random(Number.MAX_SAFE_INTEGER), "Does Not Matter") ❷
    );
  }
  let bank = { ❸
    convert: function() { ❹
      return new Money(Math.PI, "Kalganid"); ❺
    }
  };
  let arbitraryResult = new Money(moneyCount * Math.PI, "Kalganid"); ❻

  let portfolio = new Portfolio();
  portfolio.add(...moneys);
  assert.deepStrictEqual(
    portfolio.evaluate(bank, "Kalganid"), arbitraryResult ❼
  );
}
```

❶ Number of Money objects in our test.

❷ Each Money object has a random amount, and its currency is also made up.

❸ A Bank test double.

❹ Overridden convert method.

❺ Always return "π Kalganid".

❻ The result is expected to be "π times moneyCount" Kalganid.

❼ Assertion, which passes.

We have created a silly implementation of a Bank in our test: silly from a business standpoint, yet completely valid from an interface perspective. This Bank always returns "π Kalganid" from its convert method, regardless of any arguments it is given.[2] This means that for each call to this convert method from Portfolio.evaluate, the Portfolio accumulates "π Kalganid." Thus the final result is π times the number of Money objects, in Kalganid.

Even though the test is peculiar, it illustrates the key concepts of "test doubles" (*https://oreil.ly/PR7fq*) and interface dependency.

 A "test double" is a replacement for "real world" (i.e., production) code—method, class, or module—that's substituted in a test so that the system under test uses this replacement code instead of the real code as a dependency.

It's obvious that we could follow the pattern shown in the preceding test and rewrite all our tests for Portfolio.convert to use test doubles instead of the "real" Bank. The real question is, should we?

The answer is not obvious. As a general rule, use the path of least resistance. If the effort to introduce a test double is greater than using the real code, then use the real code. Otherwise, use a test double.

There is also a risk in using a test double: if there are non-obvious side effects caused by calling a method or function of the system under test, a test double may inadvertently mask these side effects. Or the test double may *introduce* new side effects that are not present in the real code. Either way, there is a risk that testing with the test double may not faithfully replicate testing with the "real" dependency in place.

Is there a way out of this? Using stateless code with a well-defined interface is a start. A method that is stateless—that is, one whose behavior depends completely on its

---

2 Notice that the convert method here doesn't even define any arguments, since it's going to ignore them anyway. Recall from Chapter 6 that JavaScript does not enforce any rules on the number or types of parameters that are passed to a function, regardless of the function definition.

parameters—is much easier to replace with a test double than a method that relies heavily on mutable state of surrounding objects that are not passed as parameters.[3]

Purpose

The three classes in our JavaScript display singularity of purpose: a class for each key concept.

Is there something worth improving? There is a bit of a leaky abstraction in the `try` block in the `Portfolio.evaluate` method:

```
try {
    let convertedMoney = bank.convert(money, currency);
    return sum + convertedMoney.amount;
}
```

Did you spot it? The conversion of `money` into a new `currency` yields a compact, self-contained object: `convertedMoney`. We then pry open this object to look at its `amount` and add it to a `total`...only for us to later put Humpty Dumpty back together again when we `return new Money(total, currency)` at the end of the method!

How would our code look if the `Money` class had an `add` method? Specifically, how might we drive it through tests, and what would the refactored `Portfolio.evaluate` look like?

We can think of a few tests we may use to drive out the behavior of `Money.add`. Adding two `Money` objects in the same currency should work in a straightforward way, obeying the commutative law of addition of numbers. Adding two `Money` objects with different currencies should fail with an appropriate exception. We can justify this exceptional behavior on the grounds that adding multiple currencies requires us to maintain a `Portfolio`—which already carries the responsibility of conversion:

```
testAddTwoMoneysInSameCurrency() { ❶
  let fiveKalganid = new Money(5, "Kalganid");
  let tenKalganid = new Money(10, "Kalganid");
  let fifteenKalganid = new Money(15, "Kalganid");
  assert.deepStrictEqual(fiveKalganid.add(tenKalganid), fifteenKalganid);
  assert.deepStrictEqual(tenKalganid.add(fiveKalganid), fifteenKalganid);
}

testAddTwoMoneysInDifferentCurrencies() { ❷
  let euro = new Money(1, "EUR");
  let dollar = new Money(1, "USD");
  assert.throws(function() {euro.add(dollar);},
    new Error("Cannot add USD to EUR"));
```

---

3 The methods most difficult to replace with test doubles are those that rely on global state—another reason why globals are to be avoided like zombies during the apocalypse!

```
        assert.throws(function() {dollar.add(euro);},
          new Error("Cannot add EUR to USD"));
    }
```

❶ Test to verify directly adding two Money objects in same currency

❷ Test to verify exception when attempting to add two Money objects with different currencies

After we write a Money.add method that fulfills the above tests,[4] we can use it to reduce the leaky abstraction in Portfolio.evaluate.

```
    evaluate(bank, currency) {
        let failures = [];
        let total = this.moneys.reduce( (sum, money) => {
            try {
                let convertedMoney = bank.convert(money, currency);
                return sum.add(convertedMoney); ❶
            }
            catch (error) {
                failures.push(error.message);
                return sum;
            }
        }, new Money(0, currency)); ❷
        if (!failures.length) {
            return total; ❸
        }
        throw new Error("Missing exchange rate(s):[" + failures.join() + "]");
    }
```

❶ Using the Money.add method.

❷ The initial value is a Money object, not a number.

❸ The total can be returned directly: it's a Money object.

Is the cost of removing the leaky abstraction worth the extra method in Money class and the tests for it?

There isn't a cut-and-dried answer for it. We could reason that the add method is a worthy companion to the times and divide methods already in Money and that preventing the Portfolio.evaluate method from prying into Money is a good thing. On the other hand, we could reason that Bank.convert already pries into both the currency and amount of the Money object it's given and that there's no obvious way to

---

4 The Money.add method is "left as an exercise for the reader"—a phrase no workbook should be without. There is an implementation in the GitHub repository, for the curious (or irritated) subset!

remove *that* leaky abstraction without adding substantially more behavior to Money—at the expense of Bank, probably.

The contrasting answers are reflective of the element of subjectivity inherent in the notion of "fit for purpose." It's reasonable to have different opinions on the question of "what is the purpose of this class?" The code that results from the different opinions will also be different—invariably and unavoidably.

Process

In the beginning, all our source code was in one file. We introduced separation of concerns in Chapter 4 and used it to partition our code into modules in Chapter 6. The Bank class was introduced in Chapter 11. It's likely that our code would have turned out differently had we followed another path. Could it have been better?

If we were to solve the problem again, we might separate the tests from the production code earlier—perhaps as soon as we have one green test. Early separation of concerns can have benefits: it forces us to make our dependencies explicit and think critically about what each module exports. This can lead to better encapsulation (i.e., information hiding).

Can you think of shortcomings in our JavaScript code? Which steps during the incremental growth of our code caused them? And were there any stages where we could have corrected them?

Python

Profile

The Python ecosystem provides a choice of tools and libraries to measure the complexity of code. Flake8 (*https://oreil.ly/LCvRG*) is one such tool. Flake8 combines the static analysis capabilities of several other tools. That's why it provides *a lot* of features, including testing for cyclomatic complexity using the mccabe (*https://oreil.ly/Z2SW3*) module.

Flake8 can be installed using the Python package manager. The command python3 -m pip install flake8 is all that's needed. Once installed, running flake8 in a folder with Python source files, such as the py folder in our TDD_PROJECT_ROOT, will scan the code for all violations and warnings. To limit the output to warnings of a specific kind, we can use the well-defined Flake8 error codes (*https://oreil.ly/gSrf0*). For example, the command flake8 --select=C will display only cyclomatic complexity violations as detected by the mccabe module. Since the default complexity threshold is 10, we will not see any warnings if we run the above command. To get any output, we have to set a lower complexity threshold.

Let's try `flake8 --max-complexity=1 --select=C` on our Python code and see what comes up:

```
./bank.py:12:5: C901 'Bank.convert' is too complex (3)
./portfolio.py:12:5: C901 'Portfolio.evaluate' is too complex (5)
./test_money.py:75:1: C901 'If 75' is too complex (2)
```

We see that `Portfolio.evaluate` and `Bank.convert` are the two methods with the highest complexity. However, both are well within the heuristic limit of 10 recommended by McCabe. This is a vindication of one of the claims of test-driven development: that it yields code with lower complexity.

Could we improve the readability of the code in some tangible way? Consider the `Portfolio.evaluate` method and how we test for the presence of `failures`:

```
def evaluate(self, bank, currency):
    ...
        if len(failures) == 0: ❶
            return Money(total, currency)
    ...
```

❶ Checking if `failures` is empty to determine whether a `Money` object should be returned

We're checking for the absence of errors by seeing if the length of `failures` is zero. Is there a simpler way?

It turns out that there is. In Python, empty strings evaluate to `false`, so we can simplify the two checks.

```
    ...
        if not failures: ❶
            return Money(total, currency)
    ...
```

❶ An empty string evaluates to `false`, allowing us to use `not failures` in both lines of code.

 In Python, any object can be tested for its truth value (*https://oreil.ly/POxOL*), and empty sequences or collections are treated as `false`.

Using language idioms is another way to simplify code, even if it doesn't reduce the cyclomatic complexity metric. Keeping things consistent with linguistic norms ensures that our code subscribes to the principle of least surprise.

Principle of Least Surprise

Described by Jerome H. Saltzer and M. Frans Kaashoek in their book *Principles of Computer System Design—An Introduction* (Morgan Kaufmann, 2009), the principle of least surprise (or astonishment) aims to create software systems that align with the user's anticipations. To quote the authors:

> People are part of the system. The design should match the user's experience, expectations, and mental models.

This dictum is meant not just for the people typically thought of as end users of the system. It's equally applicable when the "users" are other developers who maintain our code. A "user" could even be a future version of ourselves who has to read our own code months down the road. We should strive to be empathic to our future selves.

Purpose

Our Python code shows fidelity to its purpose: each of the three main classes does one thing and does it reasonably well.

There is a leaky abstraction in `Portfolio.evaluate` that sticks out like a sore thumb. This method is too nosey about the internals of the `Money` class. Specifically, it probes into each `Money` object returned by `Bank.convert` and keeps track of the `amount` attribute. Then, at the end of the method, it creates a new `Money` object with this cumulative `total`.

The law of Demeter, often expressed in the pithy saying "don't talk to strangers," advocates looser coupling and higher cohesion in code. Writing code with the law of Demeter in mind creates modules that are shy: that is, they don't chatter with other modules that aren't related to them!

Could we make `Money` a shier object that doesn't need to be examined so intimately by the `Portfolio.evaluate` method? We could, if we could add `Money` objects directly and not just their `amount` fields.

We can do that by overriding a hidden method whose signature is __add__(self, other).

In Python, to override the + operator for a particular class, we must implement the __add__(self, other) method for that class.

We can test-drive the behavior of the __add__ method through this test:

```python
def testAddMoneysDirectly(self):
    self.assertEqual(Money(15, "USD"), Money(5, "USD") + Money(10, "USD"))
    self.assertEqual(Money(15, "USD"), Money(10, "USD") + Money(5, "USD"))
    self.assertEqual(None, Money(5, "USD") + Money(10, "EUR"))
    self.assertEqual(None, Money(5, "USD") + None)
```

We want to be able to add two Money objects as long as they have the same currency. Otherwise, we want to return None. To ensure that the commutative property of addition holds, we verify that adding two Money objects in either order yields the same result.

The following implementation of Money.__add__ fits the bill:

```python
def __add__(self, a):
    if a is not None and self.currency == a.currency:
        return Money(self.amount + a.amount, self.currency)
    else:
        return None
```

To further streamline our code, we can redesign Bank.convert so that there are two values: a Money and a key for any missing exchange rate.

1. If the exchange rate is found, a valid Money object is returned. The second return value is None.

2. If the exchange rate is undefined, the first return value is None. The second return value is the missing exchange rate key.

Here are the refactored tests that we can use for this redesign:

```python
def testConversionWithDifferentRatesBetweenTwoCurrencies(self):
    tenEuros = Money(10, "EUR")
    result, missingKey = self.bank.convert(tenEuros, "USD")
    self.assertEqual(result, Money(12, "USD"))
    self.assertIsNone(missingKey)
    self.bank.addExchangeRate("EUR", "USD", 1.3)
    result, missingKey = self.bank.convert(tenEuros, "USD")
    self.assertEqual(result, Money(13, "USD"))  ❶
    self.assertIsNone(missingKey)  ❷

def testConversionWithMissingExchangeRate(self):
    bank = Bank()
    tenEuros = Money(10, "EUR")
    result, missingKey = self.bank.convert(tenEuros, "Kalganid")
    self.assertIsNone(result)  ❸
    self.assertEqual(missingKey, "EUR->Kalganid")  ❹
```

❶ When conversion works, the first return value is a valid Money object,

❷ and None is the second return value.

❸ When the exchange rate is undefined, None is the first return value,

❹ and the second return value is the missing exchange rate key.

The modified Bank.convert method—not shown here—no longer throws any exception.[5]

With this implementation in place, we can refactor the Portfolio.evaluate method:

```
def evaluate(self, bank, currency):
    total = Money(0, currency)
    failures = ""
    for m in self.moneys:
        c, k = bank.convert(m, currency)
        if k is None:
            total += c
        else:
            failures += k if not failures else "," + k
    if not failures:
        return total
    raise Exception("Missing exchange rate(s):[" + failures + "]")
```

Not only is the resultant Portfolio.evaluate method shorter and more elegant, it also has a lower cyclomatic complexity. Run flake8 --max-complexity=1 --select=C and verify for yourself!

Process

We wrote our first tests and the first bits of production code all in one file. By the time we got to separating code in modules in Chapter 7, we had three classes: two corresponding to the domain concepts of Money and Portfolio, and one class for our tests. Later, we introduced the third domain class of Bank in Chapter 11. How did the order in which we developed the features influence the resultant code?

One significant effect of the direction we took was the introduction (in Chapter 3) and subsequent removal (in Chapter 10) of the lambda expression in the Portfolio.evaluate method. Could we reintroduce the brevity and refinement of the lambda expression? It would require reimagining our code, but it could be done. Recall the structure of the lambda function from Chapter 8, slightly changed here to use Bank.convert method (instead of the self.__convert that existed in Chapter 8):

---

5 The source code for the modified Bank.convert method, along with all other changes, is available in the online repository.

```
total = functools.reduce(operator.add,
        map(lambda m: bank.convert(m, currency), self.moneys), 0)
```

The limitation of lambdas is that we cannot write conditional code given how they're applied. However, what if we we accumulated, through the add operator, both the converted Money objects *and* any missing exchange rates returned by the multiple calls to the Bank.convert method?

It is doable—it requires changes to the signature of Bank.convert and an overridden __add__ method that can add a (Money, string) tuple. Is it advisable to do so?

There isn't a right or a wrong answer to this question. Software is meant to be read much more often than it's written. Would the resultant code be easier to read? We can and should write it first before forming too strong an opinion. However, even *after* writing it, we shouldn't expect a definitive answer on which style—with or without the lambda—is "better." The element of subjectivity remains even after we sift our code through the measurable metrics of complexity, cohesion, and coupling.

Isn't TDD Dead?

It isn't uncommon to find articles pronouncing the demise of test-driven development. Speakers at tech conferences can occasionally be heard declaiming the hazards of TDD, not just as a ritual but also as a practice, and wishing it a speedy snuffing. There is even a recorded and transcribed series of conversations (*https://oreil.ly/iI1zd*) among leading industry stalwarts on this subject.

So what's the verdict? Is TDD indeed a cadaver that may, at best, be dissected to learn about the anatomy of a dead idea? Or is there any life in it yet?

It's exceedingly difficult to give a definitive answer to this question without making oneself vulnerable to excoriation! Despite this risk, it's my opinion that reports of TDD's demise are both premature and exaggerated.

To restate something from the Preface, TDD is a technique for designing and structuring code whose goal is to promote simplicity and increase one's confidence in the code. The unit tests we write during TDD are a means to this end—they are not an end unto themselves. This is obvious enough when we attend to the needs of end users: only the production code is packaged and deployed, not the tests.

It's an imperfect analogy, but unit tests are to production code what scaffolding is to a building that's being built. The structure that has value, which will be used and admired, is the edifice itself. The scaffolding only exists so that the building can be erected and supported during construction. Unit tests are similar in many ways, except one: we remove the scaffolding after the building is finished because we do not foresee any changes to the external architecture. We can seldom make such assurances about code: any piece of software that's in active use is also in constant flux.

Therefore, the practice of keeping the unit tests around, executing them regularly via the CI/CD server, and refining them as the production code evolves, is indispensible. In a sense, software is a building that's always undergoing renovation even as its inhabitants actively use it; therefore, the scaffolding has to be maintained along with the habitable construction.

However, one should never lose sight of the fact that the purpose of TDD, and indeed all testing, is to craft better production code. If we could somehow conjure perfect production code into existence without exercising TDD, we'd do it without hesitation. We do not yet know how to do so. We favor TDD only because it offers a traversable path toward writing simple, robust, and high-quality production code.

Kent Beck clarified this point in a direct and stark manner in a response to a question on Stack Overflow (*https://oreil.ly/1meWo*). His statement makes for such powerful reading that it's worth quoting in its entirety:

> I get paid for code that works, not for tests, so my philosophy is to test as little as possible to reach a given level of confidence (I suspect this level of confidence is high compared to industry standards, but that could just be hubris). If I don't typically make a kind of mistake (like setting the wrong variables in a constructor), I don't test for it. I do tend to make sense of test errors, so I'm extra careful when I have logic with complicated conditionals. When coding on a team, I modify my strategy to carefully test code that we, collectively, tend to get wrong.
>
> Different people will have different testing strategies based on this philosophy, but that seems reasonable to me given the immature state of understanding of how tests can best fit into the inner loop of coding. Ten or twenty years from now we'll likely have a more universal theory of which tests to write, which tests not to write, and how to tell the difference. In the meantime, experimentation seems in order.

It has been more than a dozen years since Kent Beck wrote these lines, so we're near the middle of the range of his estimate. I do not have the power of clairvoyance: I have no clue if we'll have anything approaching a universal theory of tests in the next seven or eight years.[6] In the absence of such a theory, we should continue to rely on the empirical and theoretical evidence in favor of test-driven development—and we should continue to experiment and innovate.

---

6 A first step toward a universal theory of testing is the *test pyramid*—a term devised by Mike Cohn and described in detail by Ham Vocke in this article (*https://oreil.ly/O4zrm*).

Where We Are

We are at the end of our TDD journey in this book. However, this isn't the end.

You're encouraged to look at the source code in the accompanying repository for updates and things not covered in depth in this text.

You also have the opportunity to engage with other readers on alternate ways to solve the problem and on how to extend it.

As for your longer journey toward forming a habit of test-driving *most* if not *all* your code, this is just a beginning.

Development Environment Setup

Setting up your development environment is a prerequisite to writing any code. Fortunately, setting up a reliable "dev env" is easier today than it used to be. And it keeps getting easier.

By the time you read this book, there are possibly (perhaps likely) better alternatives to what I suggest below. If there is an easier mechanism to set up your dev env, use it. Also, share it with other readers of this book. (You may send an email to *bookquestions@oreilly.com*.)

This appendix is not an exhaustive list of all the ways you can set up a dev env. Nor does it offer step-by-step instructions on how to install each language, integrated development environment, plugin, or extension (or to manage multiple versions of any of these). Such details would be both tediously verbose and hopelessly susceptible to obsolescence: almost all of these tools are updated regularly (every few months or even weeks). Instead of providing detailed instructions that will become stale faster than a loaf of bread, I've opted to provide a general overview of *how* to set up your dev env. There are references with hyperlinks that should guide you to more details, when you need them.

Online REPLs

REPL stands for "Read-Eval-Print Loop." It is an interactive top-level shell that allows you to write short programs directly and easily. Any code you write in a REPL is *read*, then *evaluated* (i.e., parsed, then compiled and/or interpreted, depending on the language, and then executed). Finally, its results are *printed*. The whole thing runs in a *loop* so you can keep editing your program and running it for as long as you wish. The interactive nature of a REPL, coupled with its quick and detailed feedback, makes it an ideal environment in which to learn a new programming language.

As if that wasn't good enough, there are now several online REPLs for a variety of languages, and many of these REPLs are free to use. All you need is a computer with a web browser and a steady (not necessarily blazing fast) internet connection.

With all these benefits, there are caveats to using an online REPL to write substantial amounts of code, including the code examples in this book. In particular, here are some challenges you may face if you write a lot of code in an online REPL:

Difficulty in organizing your code as you want
You may find it difficult (or impossible) to organize your source files in folders (e.g., LeetCode free edition). You may find it difficult to name your files as you want (e.g., when writing Go in Repl.it, you can neither delete nor rename the file called *main.go*).

Difficulty in importing external packages
LeetCode, for example, allows you to import Go packages in the standard library, but it is non-trivial (perhaps impossible) to import external packages.

Limitation on the amount of code you can write
Online REPLs—especially in their free versions—often limit the amount of code you can write and store online. If you write *a lot* of code—which I encourage you to do!—it's likely you'll soon run into these limits.

Limitation on keeping your code private
Remember that any code you write using an online REPL is stored somewhere on their web servers ("in the cloud"). Oftentimes, you are compelled to make these code repositories public, especially in the free versions of online REPLs. Privacy of code is possibly unimportant to you if you're learning to write code, and perhaps even undesirable if you are actively looking to collaborate with others. However, as your programs grow in size—and especially if you start writing proprietary code—you may want or need to control access to your code repositories. Online REPLs may make this more difficult to achieve.

Risk of losing code because of browser crashes, etc.
Have you ever typed a bunch of text in a browser text field and then witnessed—in mild horror—your browser crash and lose all the text you typed? It's bad enough when you're typing a wall of text in a natural language (e.g., responding to a post on a social media website). It's downright distressing if the "text" you just lost was code that you had painstakingly written, tested, and refactored. With online REPLs, code loss is always possible. (Of course, you could always spill coffee on your computer and lose code that way; however, I'm assuming that like most developers, you experience browser crashes more frequently than coffee spills!)

In summary, it's OK to *start* writing the code in this book in an online REPL. However, I would not recommend that you write *all* of it in this manner. Sooner rather than later, you'll feel the need to set up a proper dev env on your computer.

Here are some online REPLs that can help you get started with minimal prerequisites.

Repl.it

Repl.it (*https://repl.it*) is the online REPL that I use most frequently, especially when I am trying out a new language or feature and don't want to spend time and effort in setting up my local dev environment. It supports dozens of languages—including all three used in this book (*https://repl.it/languages*). The free version is feature rich, so you can try things out before you decide if you need a paid subscription.

To run Go code in Repl.it, you need to know a few tricks:

1. You cannot delete the file named `main.go`. Leave this file empty—simply ignore it.

2. Create your test files following the Go naming convention, e.g., `money_test.go`.

3. If you want to run tests, do *not* click on the Run button with the green arrow. Instead, switch to the Shell tab on the right side, type `go test -v <name_of_test_file>.go`, and hit Enter.

Figure A-1 shows a Repl.it window with Go code from Chapter 1.

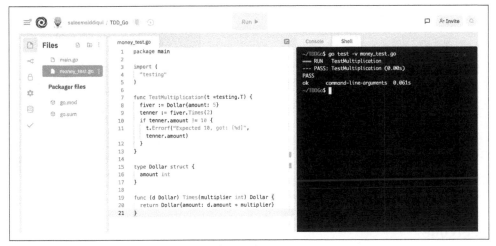

Figure A-1. Repl.it with with Go code from Chapter 1

Figure A-2 shows a Repl.it window with the JavaScript code we wrote in Chapter 1. Recall that there is no output on successful tests in the code we wrote at that point; that's why the code in Figure A-2 is modified with a deliberately failing test to illustrate how failures show up in Repl.it. To run the file, we switch to the Shell tab on the right and type node *<name_of_test_file>*.js and hit Enter.

Figure A-2. Repl.it with with JavaScript code from Chapter 1

Figure A-3 shows Python code from Chapter 1 in a Repl.it window. To run the file, we switch to the Shell tab on the right and type python *<name_of_test_file>*.py and hit Enter.

Figure A-3. Repl.it with with Python code from Chapter 1

LeetCode

LeetCode (*https://leetcode.com*) encourages social interaction with other developers through coding contests, challenges, and discussions. The "Playground" feature allows you to write code in several languages, including Go, JavaScript, and Python. However, there are some limitations. With Go, it is not trivial to import packages outside the standard library (*https://golang.org/pkg/#stdlib*) or to run tests via go test. With Python, it's not obvious how to run tests using the unittest package.

The free version restricts the number of Playgrounds (currently 10); the paid subscription removes this restriction and offers a host of other features, such as debugging and autocompletion.

Figure A-4 shows a LeetCode window with JavaScript code from Chapter 1. The test in the code has been deliberately broken to illustrate how test failures appear in LeetCode.

Figure A-4. LeetCode with JavaScript code from Chapter 1

CoderPad

CoderPad (*https://coderpad.io*) is good for real-time collaboration on code—such as pair or mob programming. This can be particularly useful if you are learning a new language as part of a group or cohort. For this reason, CoderPad is often used during technical interviews—so becoming familiar with it may also be good for your career!

CoderPad supports a variety of languages, including the three used in this book. However, like LeetCode, it is not trivial to import Go packages outside the standard library (*https://golang.org/pkg/#stdlib*).

Figure A-5 shows CoderPad with the JavaScript code from Chapter 1. Again, the code is purposefully shown with a broken test to illustrate how assertion failures appear in CoderPad.

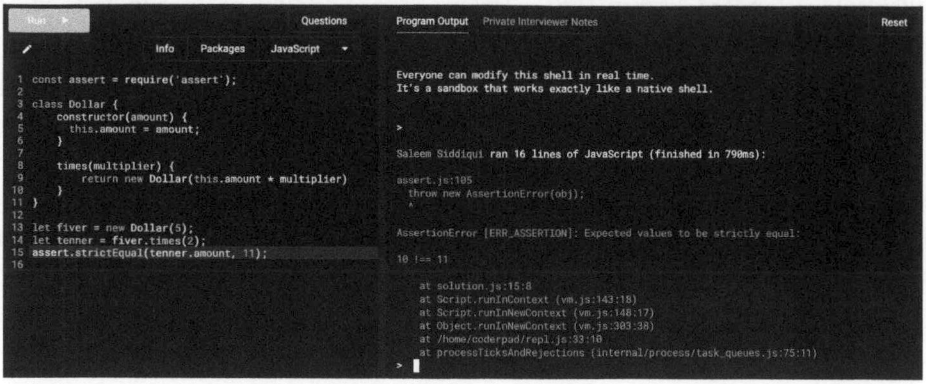

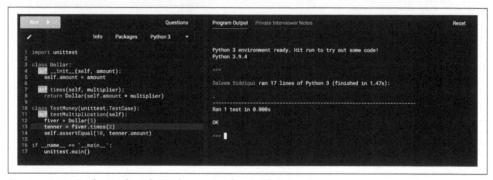

Figure A-5. CoderPad with JavaScript code from Chapter 1

Figure A-6 shows CoderPad with the Python code from Chapter 1.

Figure A-6. CoderPad with Python code from Chapter 1

The Go Playground

The Go Playground (*https://play.golang.org*) provides a REPL tailored for the Go programming language. This is particularly useful given the limitations of some other online REPLs for Go, as described in the previous sections.

Under Go Playground's minimalist user interface lies a powerful REPL engine. One useful feature is the ability to create a permalink for any code snippet you write. This makes sharing code easy. Best of all, the Go Playground is completely free.

You can write unit tests and production code and run tests directly from the Go Playground. You can even organize your code in multiple files. This can help you get started quickly in Go, if you so decide.

With Go Playground, you can import packages from publicly available repositories (e.g., GitHub.com) in the same way you'd do in an IDE. Figure A-7 shows code from Chapter 2 with an external package imported from this GitHub repository (*https://oreil.ly/yNlyD*).

```
The Go Playground   Run  Format  ☑ Imports  Share  Tests          About

 1 package main
 2
 3 import (
 4         "testing"
 5         "github.com/stretchr/testify/assert"
 6 )
 7
 8 func TestMultiplicationInDollars(t *testing.T) {
 9         fiver := Money{amount: 5, currency: "USD"}
10         actualResult := fiver.Times(2)
11         expectedResult := Money{amount: 10, currency: "USD"}
12         assert.Equal(t, expectedResult, actualResult)
13 }
14
15 func TestMultiplicationInEuros(t *testing.T) {
16         tenEuros := Money{amount: 10, currency: "EUR"}
17         actualResult := tenEuros.Times(2)
18         expectedResult := Money{amount: 20, currency: "EUR"}
19         assert.Equal(t, expectedResult, actualResult)
20 }
21
22 func TestDivision(t *testing.T) {
23         originalMoney := Money{amount: 4002, currency: "KRW"}
24         actualResult := originalMoney.Divide(4)
25         expectedResult := Money{amount: 1000.5, currency: "KRW"}
26         assert.Equal(t, expectedResult, actualResult)
27 }
28
29 type Money struct {
30         amount   float64
31         currency string
32 }
33
34 func (m Money) Times(multiplier int) Money {
35         return Money{amount: m.amount * float64(multiplier), currency: m.currency}
36 }
37
38 func (m Money) Divide(divisor int) Money {
39         return Money{amount: m.amount / float64(divisor), currency: m.currency}
40 }
41
42
43

=== RUN   TestMultiplicationInDollars
--- PASS: TestMultiplicationInDollars (0.00s)
=== RUN   TestMultiplicationInEuros
--- PASS: TestMultiplicationInEuros (0.00s)
=== RUN   TestDivision
--- PASS: TestDivision (0.00s)
PASS

All tests passed.
```

Figure A-7. Go Playground with code similar to what we developed in Chapter 2, with an external assertion library

The Comprehensive List of Online REPLs

Joël Franusic maintains a list of online REPLs (*https://oreil.ly/1rT0l*). I haven't tried all of them—there are just too many! However, if you find something you like, use it and share your experience with others.

Integrated Development Environments (IDEs)

Online REPLs are good to get started. However, you'll find that to do any amount of serious coding, you need a proper development environment on your computer.

IDEs are a reliable way to set up a dev env. Here are a few choices. While you may want to set up more than one, I'd recommend starting with one and getting familiar with it before you try another one. Being adept at using one IDE—including its keyboard shortcuts so you can minimize the use of a mouse or pointing device—is better than superficially knowing several IDEs.

Note that even if you use an IDE, you'll still have to install the runtime environment (RTE) for each language you use. You can then configure your IDE so that you can easily use each of these languages.

Visual Studio Code

Visual Studio Code (*https://oreil.ly/Cm8TK*) is the IDE that I used to develop the examples in this book. It has plugins that allow you to configure multiple languages simultaneously (including all three used in this book). It is available on Windows, macOS, and Unix operating systems. Microsoft has released Visual Studio Code as an open source product under the MIT License. This has proliferated the number of extensions (*https://oreil.ly/BsLLn*) that developers like you have written and shared publicly. These reasons make a compelling case to choose Visual Studio Code as your "go to" IDE.

According to some surveys, Visual Studio Code is the most popular IDE among developers (*https://oreil.ly/xVdnm*). As they say, there's wisdom in crowds!

IntelliJ IDEA

IntelliJ IDEA (*https://oreil.ly/TcnWz*) is one among a family of IDEs developed by the Czech software company JetBrains. The Ultimate Edition—for which you must purchase a license—supports Go, JavaScript, and Python (either natively or through plugins that you can install). The free Community Edition supports several languages (*https://oreil.ly/uUESk*), too. However, it does not support Go or JavaScript out of the box.

JetBrains offer a Community Edition of another product that supports Python: PyCharm (*https://www.jetbrains.com/pycharm*) for Python. However, for Go development, there is only a commercial edition of the IDE at the time this writing (mid-2021): GoLand (*https://oreil.ly/kaDFP*).

Eclipse

Eclipse (*https://oreil.ly/TOuLT*) is a free and open source IDE from the Eclipse Foundation. Eclipse runs on a Java Development Kit (JDK) and supports many languages. There are plugins for the languages used in this book: GoClipse for Go (*https://oreil.ly/g8lk4*), Enide for JavaScript (*https://oreil.ly/oy0zy*), and PyDev for Python (*https://oreil.ly/o9ffP*).

Installing Language Tools

If you're using one of the IDEs described earlier in this chapter, you will need to install the language compile and runtime tools. The IDEs cannot function without these tools. After you install the language tools, you can configure the IDE to use these tools (to compile, run, test, and debug your code, for example).

Go

Go (*https://golang.org*) is an open source programming language from Google. Binary distributions for it are available for Windows, macOS, and Unix operating systems. This book uses version 1.17 of Go.

You'll need to install Go if you want to use an IDE like Visual Studio Code or GoLand.

JavaScript / ES6

Of the three languages used in this book, JavaScript (*https://nodejs.org*) is unique in that you don't need to install a specific compiler, interpreter, or runtime environment for it. If you're interested in the minutiae of why this is the case, see the next sidebar.

The JavaScript Engine Within your Browser

The reason you don't have to install JavaScript tools to write simple JavaScript programs is that JavaScript is supported by all modern web browsers. So a browser is, in effect, a runtime environment for JavaScript. That is, you can write JavaScript code directly in a web browser and run it locally. This is different from running it using an online REPL, as described earlier, because the "JavaScript engine" runs within your browser.

However, you do need a runtime "JavaScript engine" for this to work. Popular JS engines include V8 (*https://v8.dev*) (used by the Chrome browser and Node.js), WebKit (*https://webkit.org*) (used by the Safari browser), and Gecko (*https://oreil.ly/2KFqZ*) (used by the Firefox browser). Early on in its history, different JS engines had significant variations in their support for JavaScript. If you had the good fortune of

---

building JavaScript-enhanced web applications in the early part of this millennium, you probably remember how you had to write browser-specific code. (Or perhaps you've chosen to forget that stage of your career—I do not blame you at all!) Fortunately, with the standardization of JavaScript as ECMAScript, the different JS engines are much more aligned (and demonstrably so) in their support of named ECMAScript versions. The most recent version of ECMAScript is ES 2020. The V8 JS engine, included in Node.js, has an excellent track record of supporting the latest ECMAScript specification by issuing an almost constant stream of updates. Any information I provide in print here is guaranteed to become obsolete before the book reaches your hands! I recommend you check the online documentation (*https://oreil.ly/48kbR*) for an up-to-date reference.

The simplest way to install a JavaScript engine—the thing that compiles and runs JS code—is to install Node.js. When you install Node (including Node Package Manager, or NPM) and add its location to the PATH variable, your IDE (such as VS Code or IntelliJ IDEA) should be able to find and use it.

For more advanced configuration options for JavaScript, consult your IDE's documentation (e.g., for VS Code (*https://oreil.ly/R8LTU*) and IntelliJ IDEA (*https://oreil.ly/H3aiM*)).

Python

Python (*https://www.python.org*) is an interpreted programming language created by Guido van Rossum. It is distributed under its own (i.e., Python Software Foundation's) open source license. It is available for Windows, macOS, Unix and other operating systems. Look at the Python website for instructions on how to install the language and its tools for your particular OS.

The code in this book requires Python 3. The older version, Python 2, was sunsetted on New Year's Day, 2020 (*https://oreil.ly/gmXVg*). You can probably still find software the uses Python 2.[1] The differences between Python 2 and Python 3 are several and significant.[2]

---

1 On several versions of macOS, including Big Sur, the python command is aliased to a Python 2 installation. You must explicitly type python3 on the shell if you want to use Python 3.

2 This article by Sebastian Raschka (*https://oreil.ly/tAZsG*) enumerates several differences between Python 2 and 3, with examples.

A Brief History of the Three Languages

Go

The Go language was designed at Google and officially released in 2009 (*https://blog.golang.org/11years*). It was created to improve upon the shortcomings of C/C++. Its guiding principles (*https://oreil.ly/xbpTl*) include simplicity, safety, readability, and minimalism. Of the three languages in this book, it's the youngest.

Go's design principle of simplicity means that many features present in other languages (including languages that inspired it) are absent in it (*https://golang.org/doc/faq*), namely:

1. Generics[1]
2. Different ways to write a loop
3. Classes (in the C++/Java sense)
4. Inheritance
5. Implicit conversion between types
6. Pointer arithmetic

However, Go includes many useful features that aren't in other languages, such as:

1. Concurrency
2. Package management
3. Formatting (`go fmt`)

---

1 Support for Generics in Go is a fast-evolving feature: *https://blog.golang.org/generics-next-step*.

4. Static code analysis (`go vet`)

5. Most significantly for *this* book: unit testing!

A major source of confusion (and some rancor) is *what is the proper name of the language?*[2] The official name of the language is simply "Go," although—probably because this is, ironically, a difficult thing to Google *and* because the official website of the language is *https://golang.org*—it's also referred to as "Golang." I have gone with the official name and called this language *Go* in this book, with the *G* always capitalized. I hope this doesn't irk you too much. Look at it this way, if this is the *biggest* source of our disagreement, we've much to be grateful for!

This book uses version 1.17 of Go (*https://golang.org/dl*).

JavaScript

This book uses the flavor of JavaScript that's provided by Node.js (*https://nodejs.org/en*), specifically version 14 or 16 (*https://oreil.ly/nEZ3E*) of Node.js. This flavor of JavaScript is *mostly* compliant with ECMAScript. ECMAScript is a language standard published by Ecma International (formerly ECMA—European Computer Manufacturers Association). The ECMAScript standard evolves relatively fast (compared to say, Java). In fact, the latest version of the standard is officially referred to as "ES.Next." You have to applaud the energy, enthusiasm, commitment, and focus of a technical committee that incorporates a *variable* in its standard's name![3]

Node.js Versions

Node.js version numbering follows a particular convention. Even-numbered releases like 14 and 16 are targeted for long-term support, typically 30 months. Odd-numbered releases like 15 and 17 are supported for only six months. This gives rise to interesting scenarios. Node.js version 12 will be supported for almost as long as version 17. And version 14 will outlast both versions 15 and 17!

It's important to note that ECMAScript is a standard as well as a language. This is no different from many other languages, such as C++ (*https://isocpp.org*), Java (*https://oreil.ly/v5Pck*), or Fortran (*https://oreil.ly/2aqHW*). As of this writing, the most recent

---

2 "@secretgeek" tweeted this updated version of the late Phil Karlton quote (*https://oreil.ly/Ori0n*), which does double duty as dev humor: "there are two hard problems in computer science: cache invalidation, naming things, and off-by-one errors!"

3 You could say C++ has a variable in its name too—and one whose value is literally being modified as you read it!

updates to the ECMAScript standard are part of what's called ECMA-262 (*https://oreil.ly/DgZzQ*)—"the twelfth edition of the ECMAScript Language Specification."

JavaScript can be thought of as a dialect of the ECMAScript standard. There are other dialects, too, such as Adobe's ActionScript (*https://oreil.ly/B4ywH*) and Microsoft's JScript (*https://oreil.ly/kR4ML*). However, it's no exaggeration to say that JavaScript is *the* most popular and oft-used implementation of ECMAScript, perhaps bordering on a monopoly. Part of this popularity is historical: JavaScript was created in the mid-1990s by Netscape to provide a way to create dynamic web content by allowing code to run right inside Netscape's Communicator web browser. JavaScript was the first scripting language to make it to users' desktop browsers—the first one to go live. (Its original name—LiveScript—pays homage to that bit of history.) In a sense, JavaScript jostled onto the field and got adopted before there was any standard for a web-scripting language. If you will excuse a labored sports analogy: JavaScript scored the first goal and got the first applause from spectators before the referee blew the whistle to officially start the game!

By late 1996, when Ecma got to standardizing "a cross-platform scripting technology for creating applications on the Internet and Intranets" (*https://oreil.ly/MXRZT*), JavaScript was already running inside hundreds of thousands of users' browsers. In fact, the meeting happened in part *because* Netscape submitted JavaScript to Ecma for consideration as an industry standard.

In other words: ECMAScript evolved as a standard out of the reality of JavaScript. There is no chicken-and-egg conundrum here: the history is clear on which came first.

History may be boring, but naming things conveniently so we can talk about them is important. Strictly speaking, I should have used "Node.js implementation of ECMAScript" in this book instead of "JavaScript." However, that would be confusing and way too pedantic. The facts are that:

- Modern JavaScript supports the ECMAScript standard.
- The name "JavaScript" retains a clear meaning in the minds of many (perhaps most) developers—they know what language is being spoken of when they hear it.
- The Node.js implementation has a very high degree of compliance to the ECMAScript standard.[4]

---

4 Node's latest versions have a 98% support score for the ECMAScript standard (*https://oreil.ly/yQgAc*).

For these reasons, I've chosen to use "JavaScript" to refer to the thing that in reality is "the Node.js implementation of the ECMAScript 262 standard." I hope you appreciate and approve of the brevity!

A few features used in this book are particular to Node.js.

The assert Module

There are many good testing libraries and frameworks for JavaScript. AVA (*https://oreil.ly/nB44m*), Jasmine (*https://oreil.ly/Re8ac*), Jest (*https://oreil.ly/CPIXd*), Mocha (*https://oreil.ly/36nmI*), tape (*https://oreil.ly/aT8LN*), teenytest (*https://oreil.ly/UobFo*), and Unit.js (*https://oreil.ly/cYkt6*) are a few testing frameworks that could have been used to demonstrate TDD in this book. Many of them are very popular—indeed, it may be asked: why wasn't one or the other of them chosen?

Here are my reasons for not choosing any of them.

Syntactical differences

The frameworks, while all capable of providing the necessary support, have quite different syntaxes (stemming from varying design philosophies). Compare the following two tests, for example, each of which compares two strings. Notice the different flavors of the syntactical sugar:

```
// filename: tape_test.js
// to run test: node tape tape_test.js
let test = require('tape'); ❶

test('hello world', function (t) { ❷
    t.plan(1); ❸
    t.equal('hello', 'world'); ❹
});
```

❶ The `tape` library exports a function named `Test`, which is assigned to a variable named `test` here.

❷ Each test is implemented as a call to `test` with two parameters, a human-readable name and an anonymous function with one parameter.

❸ Number of assertions to run, in this case one.

❹ The thing to assert, a failing comparison in this case.

```
// filename: __test__/jest_test.js ❶
// to run test: jest
test('hello world', () => { ❷
  expect('hello').toBe('world'); ❸
});
```

❶ Default location where Jest looks for test files.

❷ Each test is implemented as a call to `test` with two parameters, a human-readable name and an anonymous function with no parameters.

❸ The thing to assert, a failing expectation in this case.

Simplicity

The Node.js system already includes an assert module (*https://oreil.ly/CYMqD*) that, even though it's not a full-fledged testing framework, is sufficient to demonstrate the principle of unit testing.

As we saw in several chapters, particularly Chapter 6, using our own test harness kept us close to the code and allowed us to build parts of the test harness using test-driven development.[5]

Openness

By adopting none of the testing frameworks, the JavaScript code in this book leaves the option open to you: you are free to refactor to *any* of the frameworks, now that you know the tests inside out.

By keeping the syntax of the tests simple, by staying away from the intricacies of individual frameworks, and by building the (small) test harness ourselves, we know exactly what we need from any testing framework. Therefore, the adoption of any of the aforementioned frameworks (or even others not mentioned here) becomes conceptually easier.

The Module Mechanism

The JavaScript module mechanism is discussed in Chapter 6. For historical reasons, support for modules came late to the ECMAScript standard. By the time the ESModules feature was standardized in ES5, there were already many competing standards in existence that defined modules. As is the case for using the `assert` that's part of

---

5 This practice—of using the very thing you're making—is often called "eating your own dog food" (*https://oreil.ly/Wwg8E*). It's a healthy habit, even though it may not sound palatable!

Node.js, this book uses the CommonJS module standard that is also the default in Node.js.

Chapter 6 describes the other module mechanisms in some detail, including source code for UMD and ESModules.

Python

Python was created by Guido van Rossum at the research institute he was working at, Centrum Wiskunde en Informatica (CWI) in Amsterdam. It evolved from an earlier language named ABC. Like many other languages, *simplicity* was the fulcrum around which the language's design evolved.[6] In the case of Python, simplicity meant incorporating these features:

Scripting language
> The need for automating tasks necessitated a language geared toward writing scripts.

Indentation
> In marked contrast with many other languages, Python uses whitespace instead of visible symbols (such as braces {}) to group blocks of code.

"Duck" typing
> Variable types aren't explicitly declared; they're inferred from the values the variables hold.

Obvious operators
> Operators like *, +, -, and / work naturally across data types. Some data types don't support some operators—e.g., strings do not support -.

Extensibility
> Programmers can write their own modules and extend the behavior of the language.

Interoperability
> Python can `import` and use modules written in other languages like C.

The "duck" typing and obvious operators allow us to do nifty tricks in Python, as shown in the following code snippet. You may run this using the Python REPL directly in your shell: type `python3` and hit enter to get the interactive REPL.

```
>>> arr = ["hello", True, 2.56, 100, 2.5+3.6j, ('Tuple', True)] ❶
>>> for v in arr: ❷
```

---

6 This 2003 interview of Guido van Rossum (*https://oreil.ly/NZ625*) mentions his motivation to seek simplicity in Python's design.

```
...    print(v * 2)
...
hellohello ❸
2 ❹
5.12 ❺
200 ❺
(5+7.2j) ❺
('Tuple', True, 'Tuple', True) ❻
```

❶ An array of elements with different types: string, Boolean, floating-point number, integer, complex number, and tuple.

❷ Iterating over each element of the array and multiplying it by 2.

❸ String multiplication yields a repeated string.

❹ Boolean True is treated like the number 1 when being multiplied.

❺ Numeric types, including complex numbers, are multiplied according to rules of arithmetic.

❻ A tuple is also multiplied according to arithmetic rules: repeating its elements in order.

The traditional implementation of Python, available at its website, is called CPython. There are other active implementations as well, namely:

Jython (https://www.jython.org)
A Java implementation of Python, intended to run on a JVM.

IronPython (https://ironpython.net)
An implementation that runs on the .NET platform.

PyPy (https://www.pypy.org)
A fast, compliant implementation of Python using a just-in-time (JIT) compiler.

These implementations build on the interoperability feature of Python, allowing Python code to be used alongside code in another language.

One of the biggest changes in Python's history came about in 2008 with the release of Python 3, which is incompatible in significant ways with the preceding Python 2. Python 2 has reached its end of life; no more updates or patches are planned for Python 2.

This book uses the most recent stable version of Python, 3.10 (*https://oreil.ly/crCeX*).

Acknowledgments

Writing a book is a strange endeavor. The wordsmith, ancient or modern, toils alone—whether quill in hand or keyboard at hand. The gossamer-like ideas often resist being ensnared in coherent sentences, and the turns of phrase seldom come perfectly formed. When the prose works, the code doesn't; and when the prose doesn't yield…well, the code still doesn't!

However, the strangest aspect of the endeavor is not this lonesome toil. It's that behind every hermitic author is a veritable legion of supporters without whose tireless efforts, the ideas would never find a reified life in a published book.

Firstly, my fervor for writing software and for *driving* it from *tests* could not have been kindled without the impassioned and dedicated people who pioneered programming. Foremost among them are the "ENIAC Women" (*https://oreil.ly/qKhhm*) who *invented* programming—Kathleen Antonelli, Jean Bartik, Betty Holberton, Marlyn Meltzer, Frances Spence, and Ruth Teitelbaum. Kent Beck rediscovered test-driven development and wrote the endearing and enduring book on the subject. I am indebted to all of them for paving the way.

I'm grateful to the people at O'Reilly for making me a better author. The world of publishing has changed drastically since my first book almost two decades ago. Eleanor Abraham, Kristen Brown, Michele Cronin, Melissa Duffield, Suzanne Huston, and others ensured that my second foray into publishing was seamless despite the long hiatus.

Dr. Konstantin Läufer, my comp-sci teacher at Loyola University Chicago, instilled in me both curiosity and wonderment—traits that have had a lasting influence on me.

Neal Ford has been a friend and a mentor to me throughout my career. Without his encouragement and feedback, I would not have finished this book.

Hermann Vocke reviewed the book's text and code in detail and provided many suggestions, most of which are incorporated herein. Edward Wong also provided feedback that made the book better. Any remaining flaws are entirely my own.

I have benefited from the wise counsel and support of many people in my professional life. Karen Davis, Hany Elemary, Marilyn Lloyd, Jennifer Mounce, Paula Paul, Bill Schofield, and Jen Stille have spurred me on with their words and actions—often in ways that I suspect they undervalued yet I could not have done without.

And lastly, to my dear family: my gratitude to you is inexpressible only because of my poverty as a writer, not because of any lack of sincerity nor emotion. Dr. Janelle Scharon is a thought partner par excellence. Dr. Salma Siddiqui, Dr. Shakeel Siddiqui, Dr. Nadeem Siddiqui, and Dr. Rashid Qayyum—my familial panel of doctoral wisdom—enrich and refine my thoughts. Safa Siddiqui and Sumbul Siddiqui are my pillars of strength. You have paid for this book by excusing my absences. The evenings and weekends where you did without my company (such as it is!) were far too frequent. Thank you for all you have given me.

Index

Symbols

+ operator, overriding for a class in Python, 210
== and != (equality) operators in Go, 69
=== (strict equality) operator in JavaScript, 37
=>, arrow functions in JavaScript, 146

A

abstraction
    leaky, 130, 207
    missing, in code, 22
Actions tab of GitHub project, 186
__add__ method, 210
afferent coupling, 195
aliases, package names in Go, 67
AMD (asynchronous module definition), 76
arithmetical reciprocals, exchange rates and, 96, 106
arrays
    mapping and reducing in Python, 50
    reducing in JavaScript, 48
arrow functions in JavaScript, 146
artifact repository, 171
    version control system versus, 172
assert module (JavaScript), 230
assert package, 15, 79
AssertionError, handling, 86
assertions
    assertRaisesRegex method in Python, 124
    deepStrictEqual, 36, 39
    failing, running all tests after, 86
    failure in Python, error message for, 100
    producing output only upon failure, 20
assertNil helper function, 132, 136
    verifying nils for actual variables, 140

B

asynchronous module definition (AMS), 76
authentication, two-factor, for GitHub account, 173
automatically discovering and running tests, 83

Bank entity, 130
    committing code changes for, 151
    convert method in Python, cyclomatic complexity, 209
    dependencies between Money, Portfolio, and, 130
    exchange rates, accepting and storing, 155
    performing currency conversions in Go, code refactor for, 132-140
    performing currency conversions in Java-Script, code refactor for, 140-150
    performing currency conversions in Python, 147-150
    shared among several tests in Go, 158
    shared among several tests in JavaScript, 160
Bash-like shell, 3
Beck, Kent, 127, 214, 235
binary decision predicates, 195
binary files, 172
Bitbucket, 171
Bower (package management system), 76
branching and looping in code (cyclomatic complexity), 195
breaking tests deliberately, 81
browsers, JavaScript engine within, 225
build scripts (CI), preparing for, 178-182
    general build strategy matrix, 181
    steps in build process, 181

Y

YAML, CI scripts in, 179

Z

zero, division by, 199

About the Author

Saleem Siddiqui is a software developer, trainer, speaker, and author. Through a career spanning a few tech boom-and-bust cycles, he's delivered software for healthcare, retail, government, finance, and pharmaceutical sectors as a part of teams large and small. He has made several unorthodox, unrepeated, and mostly unrepentant mistakes in software and is eager to share the lessons thus learned with others.

Saleem enjoys that his work takes him the world over. He often writes about his experiences (*http://thesaleem.com/blog*), occasionally in third person.

Colophon

The animal on the cover of *Learning Test-Driven Development* is the desert finch *(Rhodopechys obsoleta)*. This sandy-brown bird can be identified by its unique wings, which have flashes of bright pink and silver. It has an average wingspan of ten inches, a stout black bill, and black-and-white flight feathers. The male is slightly brighter than the female, but otherwise all adults are similar in color pattern.

Usually found in the Canary Islands, across North Africa, the Middle East, and into Central Asia, the desert finch is largely residential with only some populations migrating elsewhere for the winter. As a desert resident, the desert finch can be found in areas of the desert where water is more readily available. It has also been spotted congregating near rural and remote human settlements and feeding on seeds and small insects, while in large flocks of its own species or mixed finch flocks. Typically found nesting in trees, the female lays about 4–6 pale green, lightly speckled eggs every breeding season.

The desert finch was thought to be an evolutionarily modern species. However, in the early part of this century, studies of its mitochondrial DNA revealed that the desert finch is a relatively ancient breed: about six million years old. It's the ancestor of other finch species. This fact makes the desert finch a particularly suitable animal to feature on the cover of this book. Test-driven development is also a historically old practice, even though it is often thought of as something newfangled and gimmicky!

Currently, the conservation status of the desert finch is of least concern but these unique birds still face the danger of population decline due to loss of habitat, use of pesticides, and window collisions. Many of the animals on O'Reilly covers are endangered; all of them are important to the world.

The cover illustration is by Susan Thompson, based on a black-and-white engraving from Lydekker's *Royal Natural History*. The cover fonts are Gilroy Semibold and Guardian Sans. The text font is Adobe Minion Pro; the heading font is Adobe Myriad Condensed; and the code font is Dalton Maag's Ubuntu Mono.